Contents   Block 2   Units 5-8

The Open University

Social sciences: a third level course
Historical data and the social sciences
Units 5-8

Historical demography: problems and projects

Hatfield Polytechnic

Wall Hall Campus
Aldenham, Watford
Herts WD2 8AT

This book must be returned or renewed
on or before the last date stamped below.
The library retains the right to recall
books at any time.

The Open University Press

Front cover: Detail from 'Voice of the people' by Marianne McElroy, relief sculpture. Private collection.

Back cover: Extract from Iver (Bucks) parish register of births and baptisms, 1780. Bucks County Record Office.

The Open University Press
Walton Hall Milton Keynes

First Published 1974

Designed by the Media Development Group of the Open University.

Printed in Great Britain by
Coes the Printers Limited
Rustington Sussex

ISBN 0 335 04811 0

This text forms part of an Open University course. The complete list of units in the course appears at the end of this text.

For general availability of supporting material referred to in this text, please write to the Director of Marketing, The Open University, P.O. Box 81, Walton Hall, Milton Keynes, MK7 6AT.

Further information on Open University courses may be obtained from the Admissions Office, The Open University, P.O. Box 48, Walton Hall, Milton Keynes, MK7 6AB.

Historical demography: problems and projects

Introduction to Units 5–8

'When you have said that [a human being] is born, lives for a certain time during which he reproduces himself, travels about and finally dies, you have defined essentially what demography is about. Everything in demography can be reduced to these essential happenings' (Bourgeois–Pichat 1973 p 7). Given such an all-embracing definition it is hardly surprising that population analysis enters all social science disciplines and that demographic variables occupy such an important place in the study of so many social problems.

One such problem, or problem area, is the so-called 'modernization' process: the term embraces all the social, economic, technological, political and psychological processes involved in the creation, over the last three hundred years, of what, loosely, we call the western societies of today. Here, in these four units, we shall be focusing mainly on one aspect of this process, namely the Industrial Revolution. This is not, of course, the short and cataclysmic process that the analogy with a political revolution might suggest. Nevertheless, the life style of a country's population at the 'end' of the process is very different from that at the 'beginning', though only a couple of centuries may have elapsed. People live in towns and conurbations rather than villages or isolated homesteads; drive, or are driven, to work, rather than walk; are engaged in industrial occupations and service industries rather than agriculture, their fortunes determined by the trade cycle rather than the harvest. Few institutions remain unchanged – the family, the school, the organs of government, the Church, all take on new roles, or adapt their old ones. Within this period, or process, we shall be examining the relationship between population change and economic growth. This has been one of the central interests of historical demographers over the past twenty-five years and it is one which still remains a promising field for applied historical studies.

The reasons for that promise are not far to seek. The continuing rapid growth in the population of the world, particularly in those parts with the least industrialized economies, is a problem of considerable concern to social scientists both as citizens and in their professional capacity. However, the study of this phenomenon is hampered considerably by the lack of reasonably reliable statistical data, a consequence of the low level of literacy and the short histories of effective administration in many of the underdeveloped countries. Not surprisingly, therefore, some attention has been directed at the pre-industrial and early industrial periods of the now industrialized countries of the west. Attempts have been made to seek out the points of similarity and of difference between the current demographic situation in the underdeveloped world and that in the supposedly analogous stage of the development of the west. The article by Krause in the course reader (Drake 1973 pp 155–93) is one such attempt.

This concern with using historical information to supplement or complement that which is available on contemporary societies places historical demography firmly within the field of applied historical studies. The study of population behaviour in the past is, of course, far more extensive than this; just as the study of history embraces far more than applied historical studies. But for these wider studies the term *demographic history* is more appropriate. The distinction between *historical demography* and *demographic history* is not widely accepted or recognized by many practitioners of either. And it would be pedantic to mention it here, were it not for the fact that the distinction is important for applied historical studies. It is so because whereas the demographic historian may study any demographic phenomena occurring in the past largely for their own sake and using any array of tools, the historical demographer studies only those phenomena which illustrate the present concerns of the social

5

sciences, in so far as they involve population data, and then only with the use of those particular techniques accepted by demographers today. In many cases the links may be tenuous and, because of the inadequacies of the historical data, the techniques may be rudimentary. Nevertheless for the purposes of the next four units we shall attempt to maintain the distinction.

285

Buckinghamshire (to wit)

Borough OF Buckingham

A Register of the Names and Occupations of all persons residing within the said Borough (not engaged in any Military Capacity) between the Ages of Fifteen and Sixty Years returned by the petty Constables within the said Borough in pursuance of a precet from John Penn Esq. High Sheriff of the said County bearing date the 16 day of February 1798 For the better ascertaining the Civil power of the said County

Buckingham

Names of persons returned	Occupations	Remarks
Philip Box Esq.	Banker	
Thomas Hearn	Attorney	
John Turvey	Attorneys Clerk	
Revd Mr Pearson	} Ministers	
Revd Mr Eyres		
Revd Mr Hutton		
Geo Scragg	Dissenting Minister	
Jnᵒ Southam	} Surgeons	Quaker
Orwell Foster		Quaker
Meads		

Part cover: Page from the *Posse Comitatus* 1797. Source: Bucks County Record Office.

Contents Unit 5

Objectives

After studying this unit you should be able to:

1 Give a brief summary of Malthusian population theory and of the theory of the demographic transition, together with the main criticisms of them.

2 Given appropriate data, calculate a crude birth rate, a general fertility rate, a total fertility rate, a gross and a net reproduction rate.

3 Describe the main advantages and disadvantages of each of the rates mentioned in Objective 2.

4 Using the information presented by Krause in the course reader (Drake 1973 pp 155–83) and in Section 7 of this unit, list the suggested differences between the demographic experience of the pre-industrial west and the currently under-developed world.

Population and economy

1 Introduction

With this unit we turn to the second intellectual component of applied historical studies: theory. We shall be setting this within the context of historical demography, which means that the historical data we draw upon will be of a demographic nature and the quantitative measures we refer to will be those developed by demographers. A rudimentary examination of those measures appears in an appendix to this unit. Former students of the Social Sciences Foundation Course *Understanding Society* may recognize this as being part of what I wrote in Unit 32 of that course.

In looking for a theoretical framework for Units 5–8 I was anxious to find one which was as all embracing, as 'grand' as possible. This was because I want, in this unit, to provide you with an explanation of the relationship between population growth and economic growth which you may corroborate or refute as you go through subsequent units or in the light of your project work. You may remember from Unit 1 that we gave a social scientific definition of theory as 'an explanation of data phrased with such care that we can test the validity of the explanation itself with another set of data'. In the event I chose two theories. One is that associated with the name of the Reverend T. R. Malthus. The other is the so-called theory of the demographic transition.

Any course involving demographic analysis must pay its respects to Malthus, born over 200 years ago in 1766. Despite the passage of two centuries, the apparent refutation of his theory by events and by a legion of critics, he remains a key figure. Before him there was no coherent population theory of note. In a very real sense he is the first major population theorist: the daddy of them all. For students of applied historical studies, Malthus provides useful lessons in the relationship between deductive and inductive theory and in how *not* to use historical data to test such theory. It is also of interest to examine the context in which Malthus's theory emerged and the reasons for its widespread acceptance by contemporaries, for this may alert us to the role of historical circumstances in the determination of theory.

2 The core of the Malthusian population theory

An Essay on the Principle of Population, as it Affects the Future Improvement of Society, with Remarks on the Speculations of Mr. Godwin, M. Condorçet and other writers by the Rev. T. R. Malthus first appeared in 1798. This edition was the first of six to be published in Malthus' lifetime and is by far the most readable. Compared to the ponderous later editions it is almost racy in style. Here are some key quotations from it:

> I think I may fairly make two *postulata*. First, that food is necessary to the existence of man. Secondly, that the passion between the sexes is necessary and will remain nearly in its present state.
>
> Towards the extinction of the passion between the sexes, no progress whatever has hitherto been made. Assuming then my *postulata* as granted, I say, that the power of population is infinitely greater than the power in the earth to produce subsistence for man ... population when unchecked increases in a geometrical ratio. Subsistence increases only in an arithmetical ratio. A slight acquaintance with numbers will show the immensity of the first power in comparison with the second.
>
> By that law of our nature which makes food necessary to the life of man, the effects of these two unequal powers must be kept equal. (Boulding (ed) 1959 pp 4–5.)

These two unequal powers were kept equal by what Malthus called 'positive' and 'preventive' checks. By the 'positive' check, Malthus meant 'the check that represses an increase which has already begun', ie war, epidemics, famine. On the other hand

Malthus seems to be assuming here that productivity increases in food production are impossible, and that consequently output can only be increased by additional land being worked.

'a foresight of the difficulties attending the rearing of a family acts as a preventive check'.

Furthermore, Malthus argued 'it is difficult to conceive any check to population which does not come under the description of some species of misery or vice'. For he believed that even 'the slightest check to marriage, from a prospect of the difficulty of maintaining a family, may be fairly classed under the same head', namely 'a species of misery'. Malthus repeated the basis of his theory several times in the first essay always in slightly different words and it is by this repetition that we grasp the core of his meaning. In another place he remarked:

> That population cannot increase without the means of subsistence is a proposition so evident that it needs no illustration. That a population does invariably increase where there are the means of subsistence, the history of every people that have ever existed will abundantly prove, and that the superior power of population cannot be checked without producing misery or vice, the ample portions of these two bitter ingredients in the cup of human life and the continuance of the physical causes that seem to have produced them bear too convincing a testimony.

To sum up the main points then of the first edition:

(a) Man needs food to survive.
(b) Man has a sex drive so strong that – unchecked – it will lead to a geometrical rate of population increase, eg 1, 2, 4, 8, 16, 32.
(c) Man can only increase his output of food at an arithmetical rate of growth, ie 1, 2, 3, 4, 5, 6.
(d) These two forces – the force to procreate and the force to provide subsistence for the human output – must be kept in equilibrium.
(e) They are kept in equilibrium by a variety of checks – positive and preventive – all of which involve either misery or vice.

The prospect is not a pretty one. However, in the second and subsequent editions of the *Essay*, Malthus changed his tune somewhat. The reason for this change was as follows. In the first edition the argument had been almost entirely deductive, that is to say his explanation as to the state of a population in any particular place at any particular time was drawn from assumed, or as he believed in his case, self-evident principles. He called these principles – '*postulata*'. Yet even in the first edition Malthus confessed that 'The *Essay* might, undoubtedly, have been rendered much more complete by a collection of a greater number of facts in illustration of the general argument'. In other words the theory could have had an *inductive* character, that is to say he could have collected 'facts' and drawn his theory from them, ie gone from the particular to the general rather than the general to the particular. But he admitted he was too eager to get the *Essay* published, to have time to collect such facts. In 1799, however, he did manage a tour of parts of Scandinavia and Russia, writing down, as he travelled, anything relevant to his population theory. In later years he travelled to other parts of Europe and he also read widely.

As a result of his travelling and reading, Malthus discovered that his theory had been foreshadowed by other writers. Marx was to call him 'the great plagiarist'. He also came to believe that the 'preventive check' was much more powerful than he had first supposed and that in many countries it was the more powerful of the two checks. Furthermore this check operated still, through restraints on entry into marriage, more for 'the preservation of comfort than the contemplation of misery' (Boulding 1959 p 4).

Summing up the final version of his theory Malthus wrote in the sixth edition:

(a) Population is necessarily limited by the means of subsistence.
(b) Population invariably increases where the means of subsistence increases unless prevented by some very powerful and very obvious checks.

(c) These checks, and the checks which repress the superior power of population and keep its effects on a level with the means of subsistence are all resolvable into *moral restraint*, vice, and misery [my italics].

In essence there appears to be very little change from the first edition except to praise 'moral restraint'. This phrase does however undermine not only the Malthusian thesis but also the entire *raison d'être* of the *Essay*. To see just why this is so we must look at the context in which the *Essay* came to be written.

3 The context of the *Essay*

Malthus wrote the first edition of his essay because he was, like many young men, before and since, fed-up with his father; or to put it more accurately fed-up with his father's views on the nature of man and the prospects for human society. Essentially Malthus' father had accepted the views of French writers, particularly Condorçet, on the perfectibility of man, and those of an Englishman, Godwin, who argued that man was miserable only because the institutions under which he lived were unsuited to his needs. Condorçet and Godwin together argued that all men could live happily and would do so once they reorganized their institutions.

Malthus argued all this was nonsense because those who believed in the perfectibility of man failed to recognize the 'superior power of population'. Man was engaged in a constant battle between his power to produce new mouths and his power to fill them adequately. First one, then the other, would forge ahead: only to be brought back to an equilibrium. Thus the superior power of population would exert itself and population would rise faster than the supply of food. As a result the price of food would rise; the price of labour fall. Distress would ensue. Man would feel the positive and preventive checks more strongly. That is to say the death rate would rise as the poorer and weaker succumbed to the distress. The marriage rate – and as a consequence the birth rate – would fall as men were brought to realise the misery into which marriage would lead them. However, 'the cheapness of labour, the plenty of labourers and the necessity of an increased industry amongst them' would encourage farmers to turn up more land, cultivate what they had more intensively, and in doing so employ more labour and produce more food, 'till ultimately the means of subsistence become in the same proportion to the population as at the period from which we set out. The situation of the labourer being again then tolerably comfortable the restraints to population are in some degree loosened, and the same retrograde and progressive movements with respect to happiness are repeated'.

Malthus, then, wrote his essay to refute the Utopian notions of his father and to discredit those who like his father had supported the ideas that had helped to bring about the violence of the French Revolution. But there was another context in which Malthus wrote and refined his essay: that of an England battling abroad with a revolutionary France and at home with the consequences of perhaps the most widespread upheaval in her history; the Industrial Revolution. We know this revolution was associated with – I want to be no more specific than that for the moment – a rapid and continuous growth of population. Frequently large sections of this growing population were unable to provide themselves with enough to live on and were forced to seek relief from the local authorities, which at the time meant those at the parish level. Whether the proportion of paupers in the population was increasing does not concern us (Malthus certainly thought it was). What is certain is that the amount spent on the poor was rising sharply. And it was here among the poor that Malthus saw the finest demonstration of his law of population. For, he argued, the English Poor Laws actually encouraged early marriage by guaranteeing to support a man, his wife and his family if, for any reason, he should be unable to do so. Thus the population grew faster than the food supply; the price of food rose; the price of labour fell and more members of the labouring classes had to come to the parish for relief.

Thus the laws:

> contributed to impoverish that class of people whose only possession is their labour. . . . The whole business of settlements, even in its present amended state, is utterly contradictory to all ideas of freedom. The parish persecution of men whose families are likely to become chargeable; and of poor women who are near lying-in, is a most disgraceful and disgusting tyranny. And the obstructions continually occasioned in the market of labour by these laws have a constant tendency to add to the difficulties of those who are struggling to support themselves without assistance.

Malthus went on to say:

> It is also difficult to suppose that they [ie the Poor Laws] had not powerfully contributed to generate that carelessness and want of frugality observable among the poor, so contrary to the disposition frequently to be remarked among petty tradesmen and small farmers. The labouring poor to use a vulgar expression seem always to live from hand to mouth.

It is not surprising that many members of the English ruling class should willingly embrace Malthus and his theory at this time. At one go he had struck a blow for English pride in undermining the ideology of the French Revolution; and shown that by cutting the main form of direct taxation – namely the poor rate – the happiness of the poor would actually be increased! Malthus in fact said this in so many words:

> I feel little doubt in my own mind that if the poor laws had never existed, though there might have been a few more instances of very severe distress, yet the aggregate mass of happiness among the common people would have been much greater than it is at present.

To be cynical one might say that in playing on both the Englishman's pride and his pocket, Malthus ensured the success of his *Essay*. It was certainly a magnificent occasion piece. His theory was simple yet comprehensive. Time and again it has formed the framework for research. Even the objections to it – to which we will now turn – have been a stimulus to demographic enquiry.

4 Objections to the Malthusian population theory

It is obviously true that if *all* men produced as many offspring as *some* men and if all these survived and produced as many again, then the world would soon reach a position of standing room only. Take for instance the case of John Eli Miller who died about 1960 on his farm in Ohio, just short of his 95th birthday. It was alleged that Miller left behind him 'five of his seven children, sixty-one grandchildren, three hundred and thirty-eight great-grandchildren and six great-great-grandchildren, a grand total of 410 descendants' (Glen D. Everett in Hardin 1964 p 47). There are other such cases, but they are rare. And they are rare because although Malthus may be right in his assumption that 'towards the extinction of the passion between the sexes, no progress whatever has hitherto been made' it is also true that man has done a great deal to curb the effects of this passion and had done so long before Malthus wrote. Malthus, as one might expect, abhorred contraception partly on moral grounds. He was after all a minister of the Church of England, an institution which continued to condemn birth control for 150 years after the first edition of the *Essay* appeared. (The decisive shift on this issue did not come until 1948 in the Church of England – a point to be remembered by its adherents who belabour the Catholic Church for its stand on the question.) It should be noted however that Malthus did not only disapprove of birth control on moral grounds. He was also against it because he thought it would tend to remove 'a necessary stimulus to industry'.

Quite apart from the birth control issue, Malthus weakened his original position by qualifying the meaning originally given to what he called the 'preventive check'. Initially he said the preventive check, operating through the mechanism of delayed marriage, was a form of misery, resorted to in order to avoid the greater misery of having children one could not support. In later editions, however, Malthus was to argue that men exercised moral restraint in not getting married, a virtue not a vice, and did so *not* to avoid misery but to maintain and possibly advance their living standards. Once this is admitted, then man can in fact aim to perfect the society in which he lives; at least the superior power of population is not an immutable obstacle to such a goal, and thus the basis of Malthus' attack on his father falls to the ground. Furthermore, as Malthus had to admit, looking back over the history of mankind, living standards had tended to rise.

If we look at the other of Malthus's '*postulata*' – the provision of food – history again appears to have proved him wrong, though the current 'population explosion' does revive some of his fears. Malthus, not surprisingly, failed to recognize the effect new agricultural methods would have on the rate of increase of food output. Nor did he envisage – how could he? – the effect of transport improvements on opening up new areas of supply. But on this question, a more serious objection to Malthus's argument is that he failed to consider the possibility that an increase in population might occur for reasons unconnected with subsistence, or the converse, that population might be checked by forces unconnected with the supply of food. This is a question we shall take up particularly in Unit 7, *La crise démographique*. Finally Malthus did not recognise that an increase in population might lead to the development of new techniques and new methods of organizing the labour force which could lead to *increases* in *per capita* output. This is one way out of the Malthusian trap. Indeed it has been argued forcibly that most populations only seek to increase output when they have to; that is when their needs are outgrowing the output of their present technology (Boserup 1965; Clark 1967; Wilkinson 1973) and the main reason for their rising needs is rising population.

Another criticism of Malthus' theory is that he never really managed to marry its deductive and inductive elements. We have already noted that in the first edition of the *Essay*, the theory was essentially of a deductive nature. He chose, however, to make it inductive by collecting data and drawing his theory *out* of them. The economist Alfred Marshall (1842–1924) believed he succeeded in doing this, crediting his work with 'the merit of being the first thorough application of the inductive method in social science' (cited in Petersen 1965 p 45). But was this so? To go some way towards answering the question let us look at a part of Malthus' data collecting, namely that which he carried out during the Norwegian part of his 1799 tour of Scandinavia and Russia, already referred to. We are fortunate in knowing a great deal about this because a journal which Malthus kept has been recently discovered and published (James 1966). This is not the place to pursue the matter in all its detail (for this see Drake 1966 or Drake 1969), but a couple of comments are appropriate.

First Malthus appears to have done all that one might reasonably expect to find the data to support or refute his thesis. He spent six weeks in Norway; he travelled 600 miles; he had a large number of letters of introduction which gave him access to military, civil and business leaders, though he appears not to have met a single clergyman – a curious omission since the clergy were responsible for making returns of births, marriage and deaths. He also visited Thaarup, a former Professor of Statistics at the University of Copenhagen who had produced a volume of statistics on the Dano-Norwegian Kingdom. He spoke with farmers and post-house keepers, even a family of Lapps. Apart from these personal contacts Malthus kept his eyes open. His journal is full of comments on the changing landscape, the condition of the people he met, what they were eating, how they were dressed, what their houses were like, what was growing in their fields.

The second point to make about Malthus' enquiries is that despite his assiduity in data collecting his conclusions are suspect. For instance, almost before reaching Norway, Malthus was convinced that the main obstacle to population growth there

Figure 1 **Map showing route of Malthus in Norway.** Source: Michael Drake (1969).
Population and Society in Norway 1735-1865, Cambridge University Press

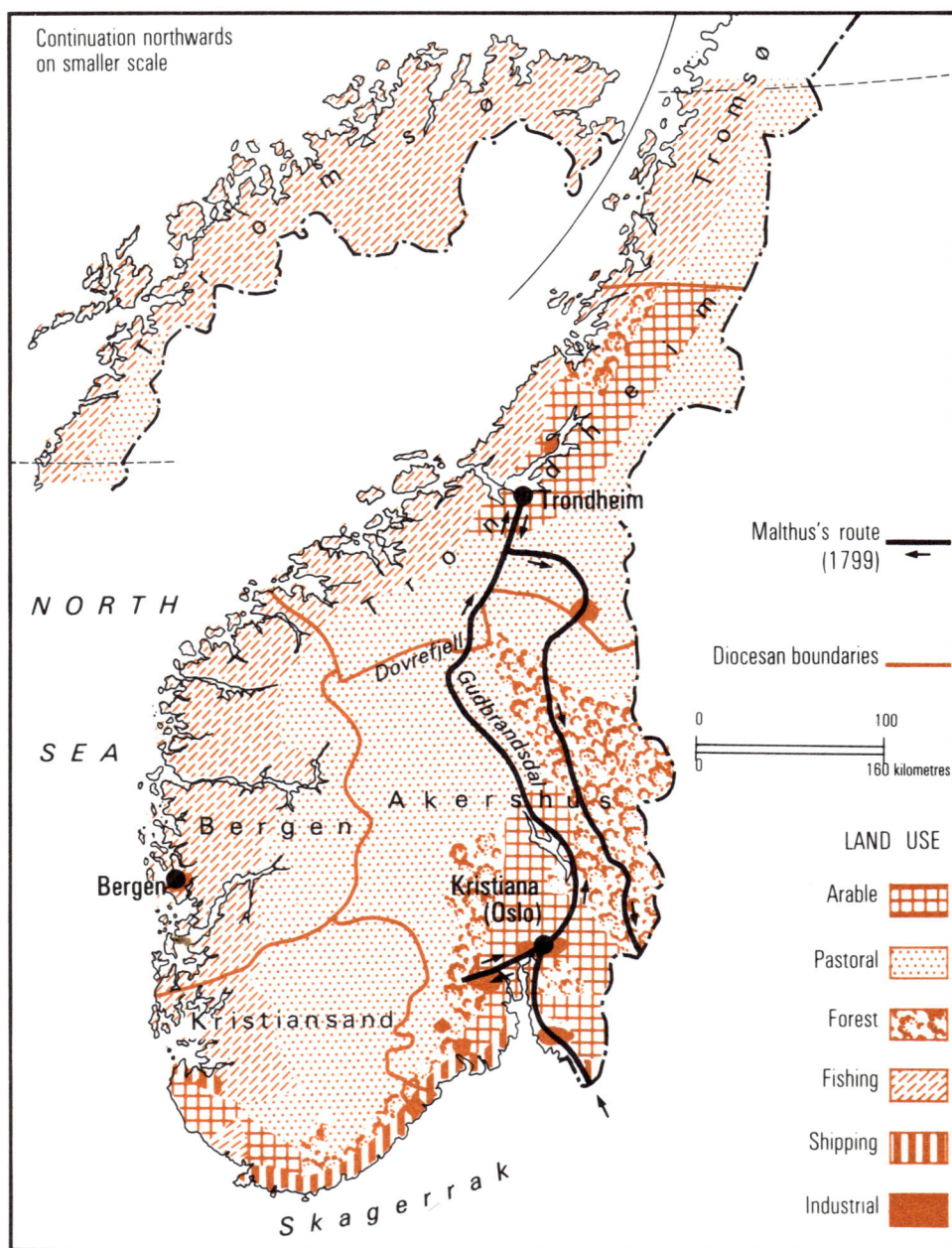

was 'the preventive check', for as he put it, the population 'increases so slowly though the people live so long' (James 1966 p 89). He, therefore, devoted most of his time to finding out about the 'preventive check', neglecting to enquire into the 'positive check'. The bias of his contacts and his itinerary, by chance, confirmed his initial preconceptions. For example, he met a lot of military officers who explained to him how, in their view, the method of conscription delayed entry into marriage. Again most of his 600 mile journey was through the richest parts of Norway with large farms staffed by *unmarried* male and female labourers who 'lived in'. Finally, drawing on the work of Thaarup, noted above, Malthus believed the ratio of deaths to the population was as 1 : 48, that is a crude death rate of 21 per 1000. Certainly by contemporary standards this was a very low rate and would support the view that the 'positive check' was weak. What Malthus failed to realize however was that this rate covered only the years 1775–84, which were years of below average mortality. Other years told a different story. For example in the very area through which Malthus travelled for

To calculate the crude death rate from the ratio of deaths to the population, simply multiply the ratio by 1,000. In this case, where the ratio is 1:48: $\frac{1}{48} \times 1,000 \fallingdotseq 21$ (ie the crude death rate is approximately 21 per 1,000). See Appendix, p 29.

Figure 2 Births and deaths per 1000 mean population in the Norwegian diocese of Akerhus, 1735–1865.
Source: Michael Drake (1969) *Population and Society in Norway 1735–1865*, Cambridge University Press

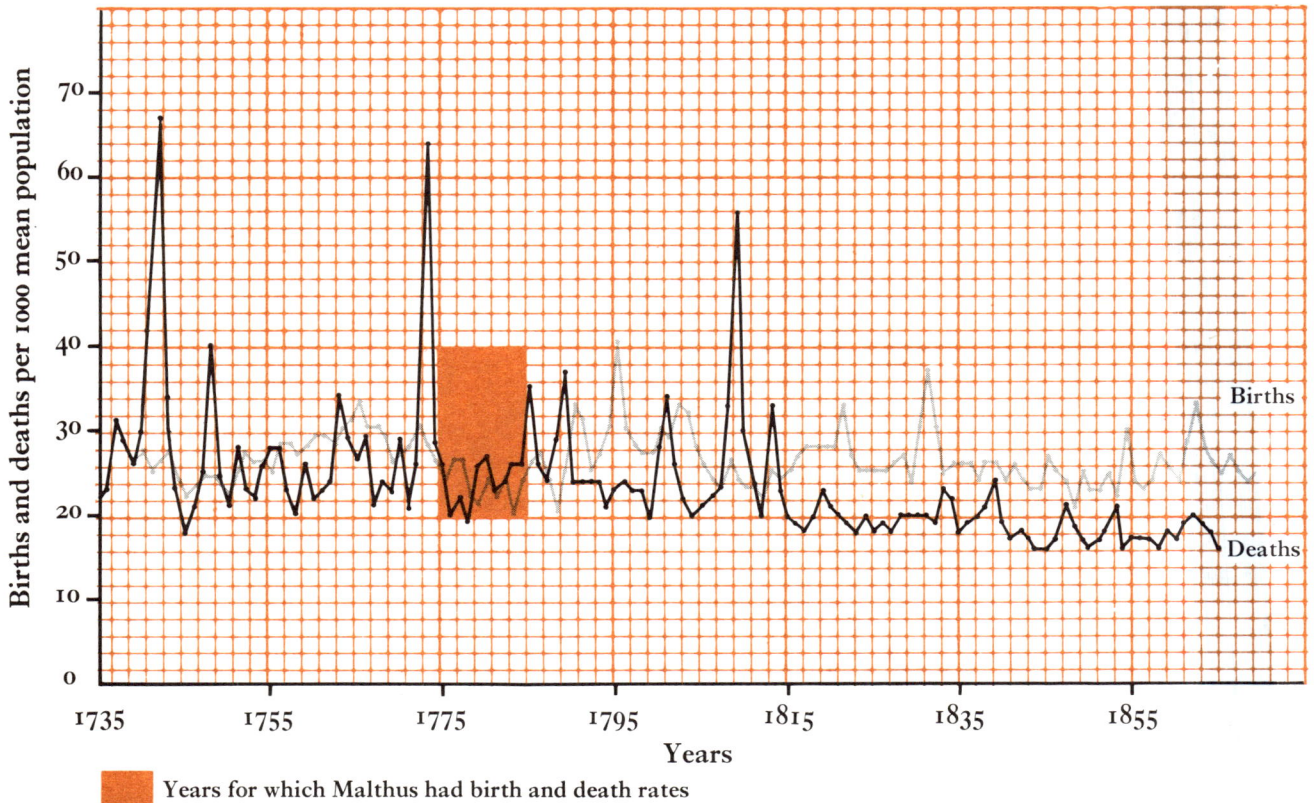

Years for which Malthus had birth and death rates

most of his stay (the diocese of Akerhus which contained 40% of the country's population), the crude death rate had been as high as 64 per 1000 in 1773 and was to rise to 56 per 1000 as late as 1809 (Drake 1969 pp 37–8).

5 Questions on the relevance of the *Essay*

It is now time to sum up what we have discussed to date. If you want this to be more than a passive exercise on your part have a try at some of the questions which follow. Otherwise turn to the answers at the end of the unit.

SAQ 1   I began this unit by suggesting that a discussion of the Malthusian population theory would provide one framework for these units on historical demography and, if you are so minded, for your projects. Looking back over the discussion, try to 'articulate topics of interest', to use the phrase introduced in Unit 1, which could form the beginnings of a project. For example, one of Malthus' two *postulata* was that 'food is necessary to the existence of man'. Obviously lack of food will blot out that existence. But it is possible that other factors may do so, eg war or disease, and that these may not be associated with the lack of food. One 'topic of interest' then would be to see the extent to which mortality was caused by food shortages, climatic variations, epidemic or endemic diseases, and to what extent it was reduced by changes in food supplies (eg potatoes instead of grain), more regular food distribution (resulting from transport and commercial changes), or improvements in medicine and hygiene. (Answer at end of unit.)

SAQ 2   We have argued that Malthus' *Essay* was very much an occasion piece, a product of the times in which he lived. It has been suggested (Wilkinson 1973 p 51) that 'there is no argument against the application of Malthusian theory to the populations of changing and disturbed societies . . .' (England at the time Malthus wrote, it must be remembered, was going through the Industrial Revolution) but 'Malthus does not make the necessary distinction between stable, coherent cultural systems and other, transitional cultures.' If this is true then perhaps Malthusian theory is relevant today to those underdeveloped countries whose traditional 'stable, coherent cultural systems' have been shaken by contact with the west. However, to get to the point of this question, can you think of other theories in the social sciences which are perhaps more firmly fixed in a particular time period than is sometimes recognized? (Answer at end of unit.)

SAQ 3   In considering objections to Malthus' theory some attention has been paid to weaknesses in his method of collecting information and in his way of using it. Looking back over the first four units of this course and the work you have done in previous courses, make a list of the pitfalls you may encounter. You could perhaps divide your list into three points; one on literary evidence, a second on statistical evidence and the third on the role of theory. (Answer at end of unit.)

6 A post-Malthusian population theory

Though Malthus wrote during the period of the English Industrial Revolution, we could hardly expect him to be conscious of its widespread ramifications. Essentially his theory seeks to explain the population experience of a pre-industrial world. For the period subsequent to that we have another theory. It is called *the theory of the demographic transition* (Davis 1945). Emerging in the 1930s and 1940s, it has aroused none of the passions associated with the Malthusian theory. Indeed until recently it was accorded widespread acceptance. In essence this theory seeks to explain the behaviour of birth and death rates in western countries from their pre-industrial stage down to the 1930s.

The theory of the demographic transition divides this period into four parts. Firstly, in the pre-industrial stage, countries experience high birth and death rates. Both these rates might be in the region of 35–45 per 1000 or possibly more. The picture is essentially a Malthusian one, with populations growing only slowly, say by under 5 per 1000 per year. A more graphic way of expressing this is to convert the rate of growth into the number of years it would take a population to double itself, assuming the particular rate continued. A quick way of doing this is as follows. Say we have a rate of 5 per 1000. This is the same as 0.5 per 100. Divide this figure into 70 (ie 70 ÷ 0.5). In this instance then the population would double in 140 years.

SAQ 4   How many years will elapse before a population expanding at the rate of *a*) 10 or *b*) 15 per 1000 *per annum* will double itself? (Answer at end of unit.)

The second stage commences with the advent of sustained economic growth. This, for a variety of reasons, brings about a fall in the death rate. Meantime the birthrate remains at its former high level, or only slightly under, with the result that populations expand rapidly – say by 10 or 15 per 1000. The third stage commences when continued economic growth brings about a fall in the birth rate. As by now the fall in the death rate is slowing down, this means that the rate of population growth declines. The fourth and final stage arrives when birth and death rates level off, producing a new equilibrium with population again growing by only 5 per 1000, or less, as in the first stage. A representation of these various stages appears in Figure 3. Table 1 shows a part of this process (Stages 2–4) in statistical terms, for a number of European countries.

In recent years the theory of the demographic transition has come under attack from various directions. For instance, Krause in the course reader (Drake 1973 pp 155–83) argues that Stage 1 of the theory is incorrect at least for some societies. Against the view that in this stage fertility was necessarily high and unlimited, in order to maintain societies constantly suffering the depredations of war, famine and

I have to admit that I don't know why the magic figure is 70!

Figure 3 The demographic transition

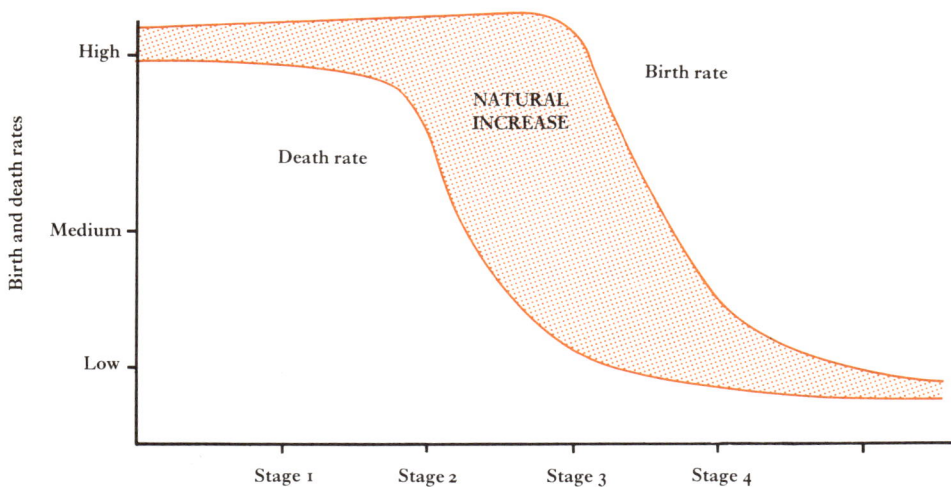

Table 1 Births and deaths per 1000 mean population in selected European countries at various dates from 1841–1950

	1841–50		1896–1900		1931–35		1946–50	
	Births	Deaths	Births	Deaths	Births	Deaths	Births	Deaths
Belgium	30.5	24.4	29.0	18.2	16.9	13.0	17.3	13.5
Denmark	30.5	20.5	29.9	16.4	17.8	10.9	21.6	9.6
Finland	35.5	23.5	33.5	19.5	18.4	12.6	27.0	11.7
France	27.3	23.2	21.9	20.6	16.5	15.7	20.7	13.8
Germany	36.1	26.8	36.0	21.3	16.6	11.2	16.6[1]	11.2[1]
Netherlands	33.0	26.2	32.2	17.2	21.1	8.9	25.9	9.5
Norway	30.7	18.2	30.3	15.6	15.2	10.4	20.8	9.3
Sweden	31.1	20.6	26.9	16.1	14.1	11.6	19.0	10.4
Switzerland	29.8	22.8	28.4	18.1	16.4	11.8	19.4	11.2
England and Wales	32.6	22.4	29.3	17.7	15.0	12.0	18.0	11.8

1 West Germany, 1946–9 only

Source: D. V. Glass and E. Grebenik 'World population 1800–1950' in H. J. Habakkuk and M. Postan (eds) (1966) *The Cambridge Economic History of Europe* Vol VI, pp 68–9, Cambridge University Press.

disease, Krause argued that levels of fertility and mortality were moderate. Since Krause wrote, this particular issue has been debated vigorously. The debate will be reported in more detail in Units 6 and 7. In passing, however, one might note that evidence has emerged of birth control within marriage as early as the seventeenth century (Wrigley 1966) and of long periods in English history of population stagnation which do not appear to have been caused by high mortality only (eg the years 1340–1450 and 1630–1730: see Wilkinson 1973 p 71).

Krause also argues that the population expansion in Stage 2 of the demographic transition came about through a rise in the birth rate rather than a fall in the death rate. According to the theory of the demographic transition, death rates fell as economic development brought higher productivity, especially in agriculture. Improved transportation and distribution systems spread the results of this widely, so regularizing food supplies and reducing famines and the effects of famine-induced disease. Also economic development permitted better welfare provisions for the poor and ushered in a society more willing and able to devote resources to medical and sanitary improvements. Against this Krause argued that economic development had more effect on fertility since it increased the number of jobs and so permitted earlier marriage and the production of more children. Other writers, (eg McKeown and Brown 1955 and 1972, McKeown, Brown and Record 1962) whilst believing mortality decline triggered off Stage 2 have denied that medical changes had much effect.

Unfortunately the discussion of Stages 1 and 2 of the demographic transition is inhibited by the paucity of reliable statistics – a matter to which we shall return in Units 6 and 7. You will note that the figures in Table 1 (p 19), which include the earliest reliable ones, only go back to the 1840s, which so far as these countries are concerned is well into Stage 2. Only the Scandinavian countries have data, on which we can depend, as early as the mid-eighteenth century: one reason why they have become something of a Mecca for historical demographers.

Other criticisms of the theory of the demographic transition concern its later stages. First, the onset of Stage 3 is supposed to have been brought about by the declining value of children. In an agrarian pre-industrial setting large numbers of children were begotten partly, it has been suggested, to compensate for high mortality, which swept so many away before they reached adulthood, and partly because children could contribute to family earnings at an early age and were a support, perhaps the only one, for their aged parents. Industrialization and urbanization, however, not only reduced job opportunities at an early age (partly through legislation designed to protect children) but ushered in a more mobile society. This took children out of their parents' orbit, with the result that fewer were around to take care of them when they could no longer support themselves. As a result, children became less desirable, and since technology was now producing cheaper and more reliable contraceptives, parents were able, that much more easily, to have fewer.

The theory is plausible, but, of course, is not necessarily correct for all that. As we have already noted, it has been suggested that birth control was not dependent upon modern technology to be effective, at the societal level if not at the individual level. Also, more recently it has been argued that the role of kin was not destroyed by industrialization and urbanization. Indeed kin may have become more important. One study has shown there was actually an increase in the 'co-residence of married couples and their parents' with increasing industrialization (Anderson in Laslett 1972 p 216).

Two final criticisms are worthy of a brief mention. Both involve the predictive power of the theory. The first of these concerns the relevance of the theory to societies outside Europe. Krause in the reader article not only criticises the theory on its home ground as it were, but also denies its applicability to the countries of the so-called underdeveloped world. Secondly, since Landry (1934) first propounded the theory, most western countries have experienced an upsurge in fertility, in some cases of quite considerable proportions. This can be explained partly in terms of a recovery from the very low levels of the 1930s and the years of the Second World War, and partly in terms of a tendency not so much to have more children but to have them earlier and closer together. The effect of this latter tendency towards earlier family completion dates would be a once and for all rise in the crude birth rate. However there does seem also to have been a change in attitudes towards children. Using the terminology and logic of the theory of the demographic transition we might argue that though industrialization, urbanization and the growth of the welfare state may have reduced the value of children as a *production good*, it may have increased their value as a *consumption good*. In other words today one no longer has children because they can contribute to family incomes (they now leave home, or even marry, almost as soon as their education is over); nor because they provide a form of social security for their parents (the state together with private pension schemes does that). Instead one has children solely for the pleasure they bring – like such other consumption goods as colour televisions, yachts or swimming pools in the back garden.

7 The importance of population mechanics

Joseph Schumpeter once remarked that 'the only valuable things about Malthus's law of population are its qualifications' (Schumpeter 1950 p 115 cited by Peacock in Glass 1953 p 66). One might almost say the same about the theory of the demographic transition. In fact, however, the criticism is a little harsh. Firstly it suggests that the 'qualifications' are well founded, that we can place greater reliance upon them than upon those components of the theory which they seek to qualify. This is not always so. As Krause admits – 'the tentative hypothesis that fertility was the primary determinant of economic growth in the pre-industrial and early industrial West is far from having been proved, and it may be incorrect' (Drake 1973 p 182). There is still a great deal to be done. Many of the findings we shall be reporting on in Units 6 and 7 need to be tested further; this is one reason why this aspect of historical demography finds a place in the course.

The discussion on the preceding pages may have raised another issue in your mind. We may formulate it like this. Is the discovery of the mechanism of population growth in pre-industrial and early industrial societies of significance outside itself? That is to say, does it help us explain other phenomena? One might expect it would because of the close relationship we posited at the beginning of this unit, between demographic conditions and other features of society. One such relationship appears to be between population growth and economic growth. Unfortunately the relationship is not always in the same direction. It can be argued that a rising population may stimulate economic growth. Alternatively, it may retard it. We'll examine the contrary arguments briefly.

Three arguments have been put forward, each suggesting that rising populations stimulate economic growth. The first is that if the growth of population is translated into *effective demand*, this encourages investment. The second is that if a rising population leads to a fall in the cost of labour this will increase profits and so provide investment funds. A third argument is that a rising population will lead to an increased density of population. This may lead to a greater division of labour and to a rise in productivity, whether it be in agricultural or industrial employment, as a result of greater specialization. Also an increasing density of population allows economies of scale, particularly in transport, manufacturing and various service industries. Each of these operates under the law of increasing returns, ie the bigger they are (and their size is a function of population size suitably modified by the level of its effective demand) the more efficient they are likely to be.

Against these three arguments can be set the following counter-arguments. Firstly a rising population in an underdeveloped economy may not lead to much of an increase in effective demand. By definition income per head will be low in an underdeveloped economy. A rising population will diminish it still further and so reduce whatever savings the mass of the population are capable of making, thus decreasing the supply of investment funds. Secondly, though a rising population may increase the supply of labour and thereby cut its cost, the amount in either case is likely to be small since there is possibly already a large pool of unemployed or under-employed labour. Furthermore, any rise in incomes is not likely to be transformed into investment funds. This is because in an underdeveloped economy the main recipients are either landowners, whose life style leads them to spend it on immediate and conspicuous consumption; or small traders who get it through their money lending and short-term credit operations and who are more than likely to use it to purchase land. A third counter-argument is that a rising population in an underdeveloped economy is more likely to see the operation of the law of diminishing rather than that of increasing returns. This is because land, being the main resource in such an underdeveloped economy, will be sub-divided; over-cropping will ensue, soil will become exhausted more quickly and the diminishing size of holdings will militate against the use of machinery.

Several other arguments have also been brought forward to suggest that a rising population hinders the economic growth of an underdeveloped economy. First, such an economy will have a high *burden of dependency*, that is to say the number of children will be large relative to the working population which has to support them. (See the

Effective demand **for an economic good refers not to the amount that people would like to be able to buy, but to the amount actually purchased at a given price.**

discussion of population pyramids in the Appendix, for a graphical representation of this.) A rise in population will *increase* this burden, since it will lead to a rise in the number of children. This will mean that even more labour (particularly female labour) will be tied up in caring for them. Furthermore, resources which might have been used for investment purposes will be needed to satisfy current consumption. Linked with this, funds which might have been used to raise the amount of capital per worker will instead be needed merely to *duplicate* existing facilities, whether these be productive capital (ie another plough rather than a better plough) or social overhead capital (ie another house rather than a better house). It has been demonstrated that the faster a population grows the more investment is needed to keep constant the amount of working capital per worker. Put in numerical terms it is reckoned that if a population is increasing by 1% per annum, one needs to invest $2\frac{1}{2}\%$ to 5% of national income merely to keep constant the amount of equipment per worker. If a population is growing by, say, $2\frac{1}{2}\%$ per annum, then the amount of national income one needs to invest to maintain the *status quo* rises to between $6\frac{1}{4}\%$ and $12\frac{1}{2}\%$: a sizeable amount.

Whether a rising population stimulates or inhibits economic growth is then a question without an obvious answer. As with so much in the subject matter of the social sciences, 'it all depends . . .' One possible way of resolving the paradox may lie in the mechanism of population growth, since this bears within it, encapsulates one might say, many of the factors which make one society more likely to experience economic growth than another. I am thinking of such factors as the attitude towards the future; the concept of achievement (see McClelland in Drake 1973); the willingness to forgo present for future gratification; a fatalistic or a rational approach to life and so on. If this is true, then whether we accept or reject the Malthusian theory or the theory of the demographic transition, or various aspects of them, becomes very important. To show this let us consider two alternative mechanisms of population growth.

Country A is an underdeveloped agrarian economy. It has a crude birth rate of 45 per 1000 and a crude death rate of 40 per 1000. Marriage is universal for women at an early age (mean age at marriage is 18 years) and there is no deliberate control of births within marriage. The high level of mortality is largely produced by endemic and epidemic disease, sometimes assisted by floods, famine and war. Some external agency enters this country and brings about a sharp fall in mortality. Within twenty years the crude death rate has fallen from 40 to 20 per 1000. The agency might be a better transport system which alleviates local food shortages, or it may be some new medical discovery which gets rid of a particularly destructive disease, eg smallpox or malaria. However, there is *no change* in the economy.

Country B is also an underdeveloped agrarian economy. It has a crude birth rate of 30 per 1000 and a crude death rate of 25 per 1000. Although 80% of its female population marry eventually, their mean age at first marriage is about 25 years. They spend, therefore, on average not much more than half their fertile period actually exposed to child bearing; a period consciously cut down at times by the practice of birth control within marriage. Marriage is comparatively late and fertility restricted in order to maintain living standards. Suppose now that into such a society there comes some technological change, or some greater demand for its products, which together, perhaps, lead to an increased demand for labour which makes itself felt through higher wages. This permits people to marry earlier and to support larger families. Over a period of twenty years the crude birth rate rises to 40 per 1000, the death rate remaining at 25 per 1000.

Country A then is experiencing a population growth of 25 per 1000 (ie $2\frac{1}{2}\%$ *per annum*); Country B one of 15 per 1000 (ie $1\frac{1}{2}\%$ *per annum*). But whereas Country A has a growing population because its death rate has been cut by some exogenous factor, Country B's population is rising because a growing economy is allowing population to grow and living standards, measured in terms of *per capita* income, to rise or at least be maintained. Country A had a higher burden of dependency than Country B and a lower income per head. There is nothing in the mechanism bringing about *its* growth of population that will stimulate economic growth. Country B, however, starts its economic growth from a stronger economic base, ie a lower burden of dependency, a higher income per head, a population already limiting its growth in order to maintain its living standards.

It is against this background that we now turn to Unit 6 to examine the mechanism of growth in a particular country. The question we ask is – was the demographic experience of Britain in the pre-industrial and early industrial periods more like that of Country A or closer to that of Country B?

Appendix: The measurement of populations*

Here I shall focus attention first of all on the two basic sets of measurements that the demographer takes.

The census

First the demographer draws up a kind of inventory of the population; a list of the characteristics of the individual members of the population, such as age, sex, occupation, address, race, whether native or foreign born, religious affiliation, whether married, single or widowed, place of birth and relationship to the head of the household (eg wife, son, daughter, mother, etc) in which he or she normally lives. Sometimes the demographer seeks more information than this, sometimes less.

In drawing up this inventory, or *census* (the Latin word for count), the demographer is very much aware that the population to which it refers is changing even as he makes a note of it. Individuals are being born, or are dying; losing their jobs or getting new jobs; sometimes getting rid of their spouses and taking new ones, and so on and so forth. He tries therefore to draw up his inventory, to enumerate his population, over as short an interval as possible – say notionally, at midnight on 25 April 1971 (the date of the most recent United Kingdom census), so as to reduce as much as possible the error of double counting.

Vital registration

The second way by which a demographer seeks to measure population is to record the events that cause it to change. The two most important events are births and deaths and these one might term the primary factors of change. Then there are the secondary factors, for example marriages, which obviously affect the number of births, or diseases which affect the number of deaths, or migration (both within and between countries) which affect both.

Many demographers are concerned solely with acquiring and manipulating the data provided by the census and by the vital registration system. Increasingly, however, demographers are concerning themselves with what might be called the tertiary factors of population change; tertiary because they act on the population firstly through marriage, disease, or migration, and secondly, at one remove as it were, on births and deaths. The list of these tertiary factors is virtually endless and, in our increasingly complex society, continues to grow at an alarming rate. Here are some, taken at random: the change in the number of jobs; the change in the number of doctors, nurses, hospitals and clinics; the change in the number of women taking the contraceptive pill; the change in the number of houses being built; the change in the number of teachers in schools; the change in wages and taxes; the change in the

---

* Originally published in Unit 32 of the Social Science Foundation course D100: *Understanding Society*.

quantity and type of food available; the change in the amount of coal, oil or electricity produced; the change in the number of cars on the road.

SAQ 5   Imagine a maternity ward in a Midlands town. Of the ten women in the ward, eight are coloured, two are white. These proportions could reflect a number of factors. Below is a list of some of them. Examine the list and suggest the ways in which each factor might contribute to the scene in the maternity ward. (Coming at this point, this question may seem a little unfair. If you cannot answer it now, leave it and come back to it after you have read the whole unit.)

1 age structure of the white and coloured population
2 sex ratios of the two populations
3 family size
4 age at marriage
5 racial composition of the community served by the hospital
6 racial segregation
7 attitudes towards maternity hospitals
8 housing conditions
9 immigration policy
10 the position in the country as a whole, with regard to all the above factors
   (Answer at end of unit.)

Much of what we shall be examining over the next 4 weeks is focused on these secondary and tertiary factors. Before we can understand the impact of these on population change, however, we need to examine the basic or primary ones, which, as I have said, form the core of demographic studies. I shall begin by examining one or two ways in which the demographer examines the structure of populations and then at some ways by which he measures population change.

The structure of population
The sex ratio

One of the first calculations made by the demographer on receiving the findings of a census is the so-called *sex ratio*. To calculate this, one relates the number of men in the population to the number of women, expressing the answer in terms of 100 or 1,000 women.[1] Thus if a population numbers 950, of which 500 are women and 450 are men, the sex ratio is 450 divided by 500, multiplied by 100, that is to say 90 per 100 women. Sex ratios vary widely between national communities, rural and urban areas, and within different age groups. It is an important measure because not only is it a vital element in any calculations of fertility and mortality trends, but it also has interesting implications for a variety of social and economic matters.

SAQ 6   1 A population consists of 18,000 men and 15,000 women. What is the sex ratio?
            2 Below are the sex ratios of four different populations. Match them up.
            A   1507 females per 1000 males
            B   939 females per 1000 males
            C   30,000 males per 1000 females
            D   1063 males per 1000 females

            (a) Gosport (near Portsmouth)
            (b) India in 1961
            (c) Worthing (on the Sussex coast) in 1951
            (d) Her Majesty's Prisons, average daily population in United Kingdom
                 (Answer at end of unit.)

1 Alternatively one can also express the ratio in terms of men. It is, therefore, very important to check carefully whenever you see a sex ratio.

The population pyramid

The age composition of a population is of great interest to the demographer. At most censuses, each individual is asked his precise age, either on his last birthday or on the one subsequent to the census. There is, however, so much misreporting of ages, even in the so-called advanced societies, that the demographer is normally content if he can allocate people to age groups comprising ten, or preferably five years. To show the age composition of a population in a simple and graphic form, the demographer frequently builds a *population pyramid*. The shape of the pyramid not only represents, in a striking fashion, the age composition of the population, but also gives a number of clues as to the processes that have gone into producing the particular age and sex structure of the population.

In building his pyramid, the demographer represents each age group by a horizontal bar. Males occupy the left of this bar, females the right. The actual length of each bar and the point at which it is divided between males and females depends on the number of people in each age group and on their sex. So as to be able to compare, quickly, populations of different sizes, it is usual to represent the number of men or women in each age group according to the proportion they bear to an average 100, 1,000 or 10,000 of the population as a whole.

Most populations have a classic pyramid-like structure – like those of Ancient Egypt – that is to say they will be wider at the base than at the top due to the process of attrition, through death, which usually occurs more frequently at the higher than the lower ages. The pyramid-like structure is, however, not universal and in sizeable populations, those of a whole country or a province for example, one can get a wide variety of shapes, whilst if one looks at smaller populations, such as one finds in an asylum, a college or even a town, one gets a greater variety still.

The pyramid represents the past mortality, fertility and migration experience of the community and can be used to forecast future changes in the population. Here are five pyramids, each representing countries at different stages of demographic development.

Figure 4 Population pyramids

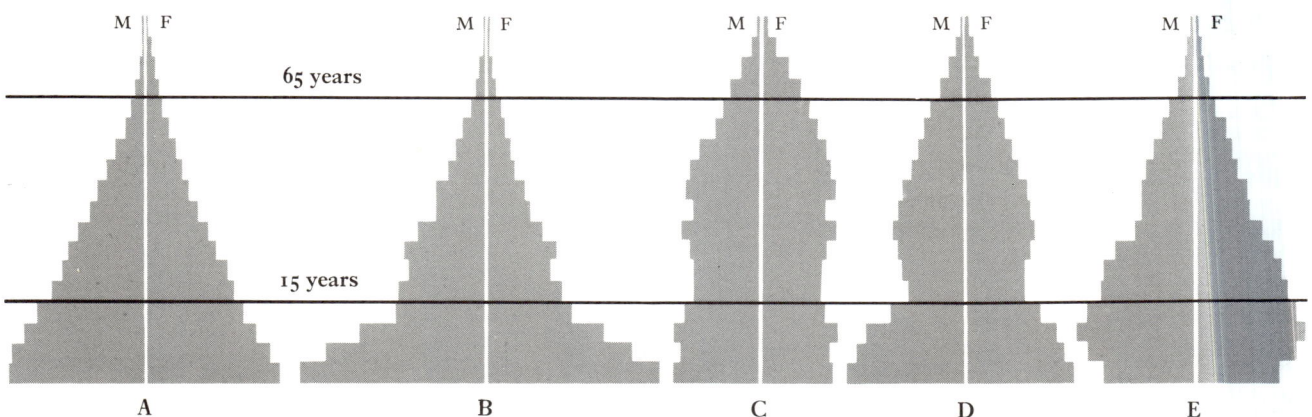

Pyramid A represents an underdeveloped country with high mortality and high fertility. Here the burden of dependency is heavy. By that I mean that the number of children is large relative to the number of people in the working age groups who have to support them. One notes, however, that the other dependent age group (the old and retired) is small in such a population, due to high mortality.

Pyramid B represents a population, with high fertility, that has recently experienced a cut in infant and child mortality. Again the burden of dependency is high because of the recent cut in infant and child mortality not being compensated for by an increase in the working population.

Pyramid C which looks rather like an artillery shell represents a population which has experienced low birth and death rates over, say, the past thirty to forty years. In such a community, of those that are born, very few die before they are at least forty years of age; or to put it another way, ninety-five per cent of the population lives to be forty or more years old, which is the situation in most western countries. Here the burden of dependency is low and of the two components of that burden the greater is to be found increasingly at the higher ages.

Pyramid D, which again looks rather like an artillery shell this time with a flared mini-skirt, represents countries like the United States that had relatively low birth and death rates during the twenty years up to the Second World War but had a sudden upsurge in fertility in the twenty years after it. As few of the newly born have died, such a society has had a growing burden of dependency particularly in the younger age groups.

Finally we have Pyramid E which represents a population that has recently experienced a drastic cut in its fertility, eg as Japan has done since the war. This sharp fall in fertility has meant a sharp reduction of the burden of dependency. It is for this reason that most underdeveloped countries are seeking to cut their fertility.

There are, of course, other measures of the structure of the population used by the demographer. But the basic ones are those that we have discussed, for it is the age and sex composition of a population which, taken together, are responsible for the primary processes of change, whilst the total size of the population and the size of its constituent parts is needed by the demographer to measure the rate of change of the population and by other social scientists who endeavour to explain such a change.

SAQ 7

Opposite and overleaf you will see a number of population pyramids.
Below are the populations they represent.
Try matching the pyramids to the populations.

(a) Hong Kong, 1967
(b) West Berlin, 1967
(c) a central business district
(d) Hungary, 1967
(e) Ghana, 1960

Some clues:

1 commercial travellers
2 First World War
3 birth control campaigns
4 Japanese occupation
5 emigration of young people
6 age reporting
7 abortion laws
(Answer at end of unit.)

Population change

Here the demographer is primarily concerned with the measurement of fertility and mortality over time. The most elementary of these measures are the crude birth and death rates.

The crude birth rate

The *crude birth rate* is the ratio between the number of births and the population producing those births over a period of time – conventionally fixed at one year. It is called 'crude' because it relates the frequency of births to the entire population and is therefore a blunter, less precise measure than one which relates the number of births

Figure 5 A

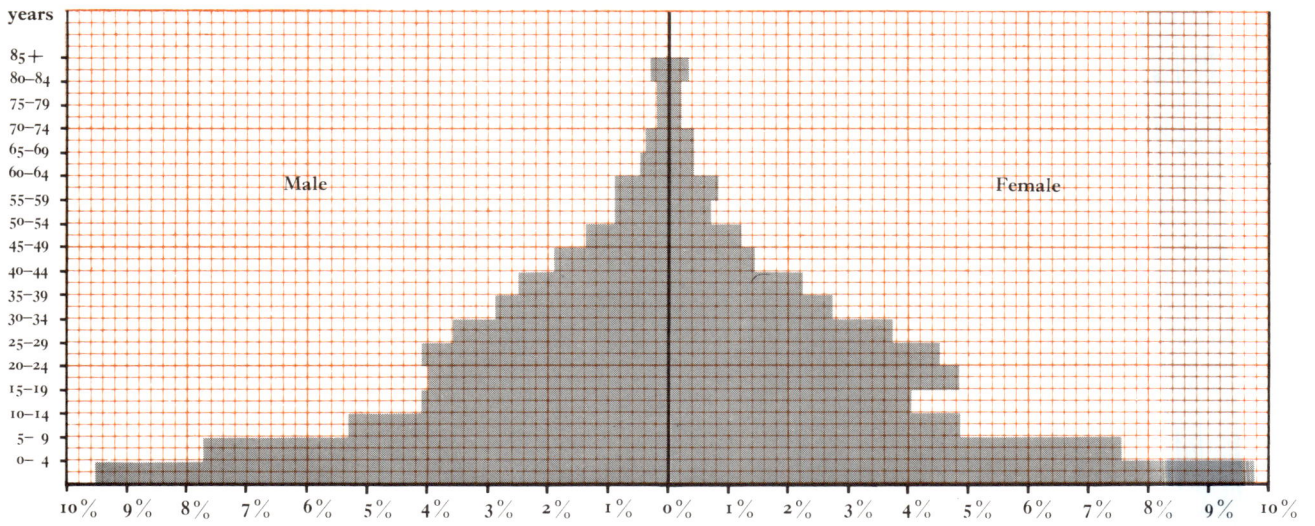

Figure 6 B

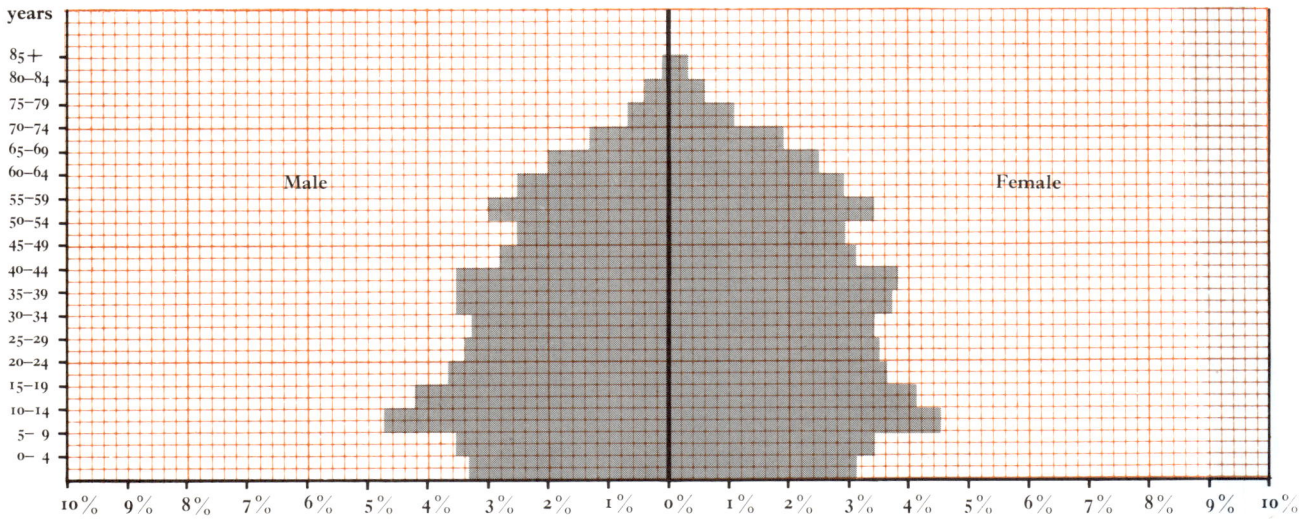

Figure 7 C

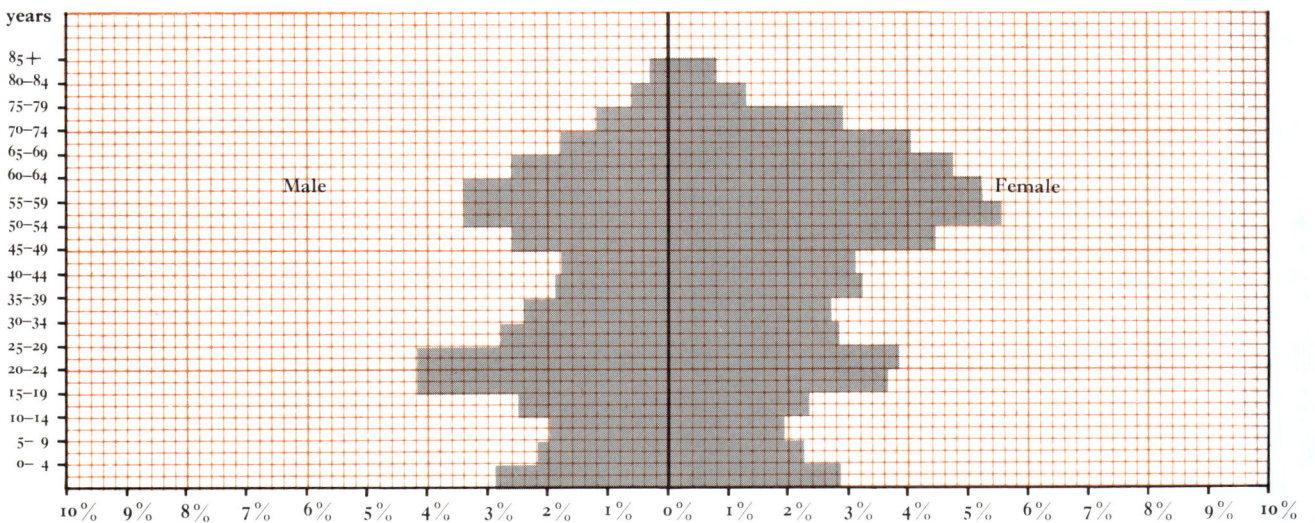

Figure 8   D

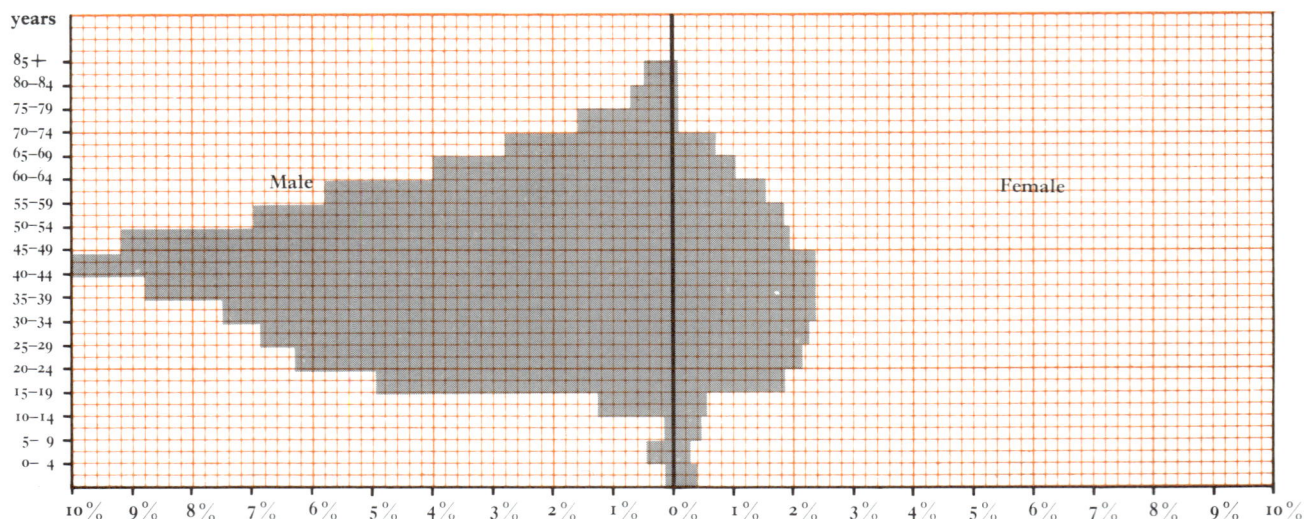

Figure 9   E

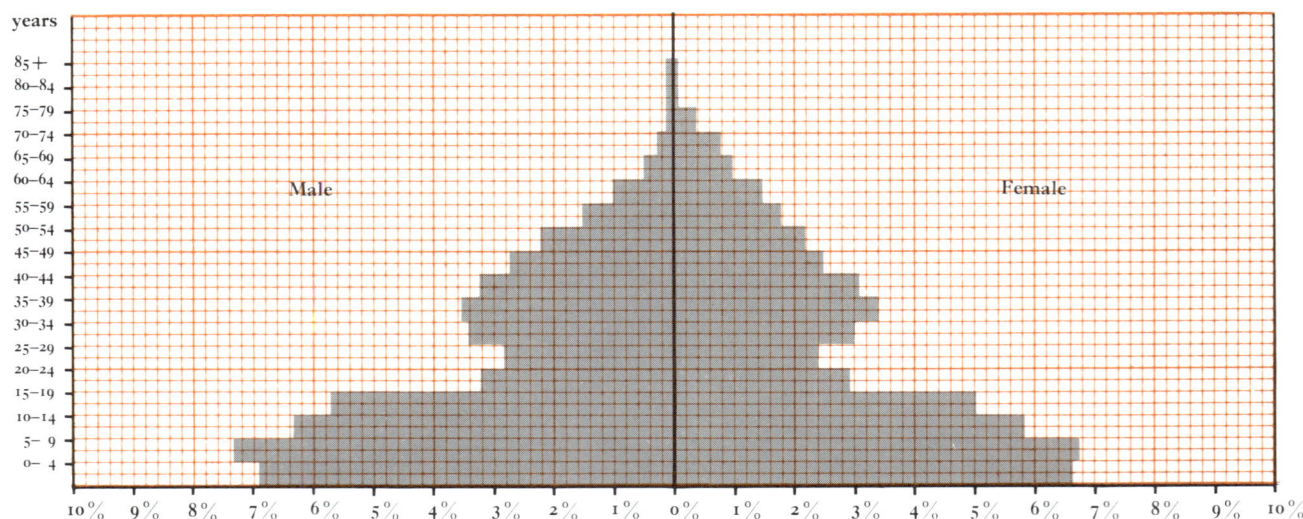

(or deaths or marriages) to a smaller, more directly relevant portion of the population, such as women of child-bearing age, married and so on. To calculate the crude birth rate one requires three pieces of information. First, one needs the number of births; second, the number of people in the area for which the birth rate is being calculated; and third, when the births occurred, so that one has the time over which the measurement is to be made. Usually we express the crude birth rate as so many births per 1,000 persons per year.

The crude birth rate is then a measure of fertility: the crude death rate, which we calculate in precisely the same way, is a measure of mortality. The difference between the two rates is called the rate of *natural increase*. In most countries the difference between the natural increase of population and the actual increase is small. But, if a country experiences a good deal of immigration or emigration, there can be quite a marked difference. Incidentally, the crude marriage rate is also calculated in this way. That is to say, it is the relationship between the size of the population, the number of marriages and the period of exposure which, as we have already said, is traditionally taken as one year. These crude rates are the ones that are found most frequently. This is partly because the basic data required for the calculation is relatively easily accessible, and also because the calculation is an easy one.

The crude death rate

The trouble with crude rates, however, is that they often hide as much about the fertility or mortality or nuptiality – nuptiality is just another way of saying the frequency of marriage – as they reveal. Let me give an example. According to the *United Nations Demographic Yearbook 1969*, the crude death rate for Singapore in 1967 was about six per 1,000: that for Scotland, twelve per 1,000. Now it is quite obvious that these figures give a misleading impression of the mortality experience of these two countries. The question of accuracy in the statistics obviously plays a part here, since there is little doubt that the Scottish registration system is more reliable than that of Singapore. But the main reason for the difference is not that the Scots, in any particular age group, are more exposed to the chance of death than the inhabitants of Singapore, but that the age composition of the population of the two countries is very different. Scotland has a population pyramid rather like that of type D on p 25, Singapore like type E[1]. And, as noted above, when one calculates the crude

Figure 10a   Population pyramid showing the population of Scotland

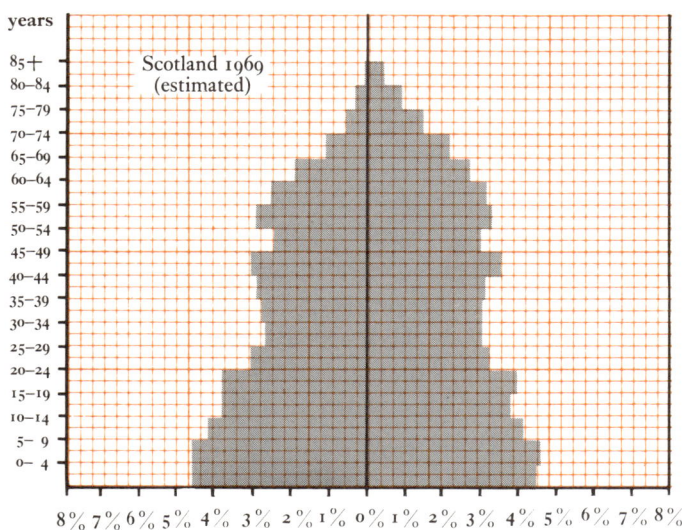

Figure 10b   Population pyramid showing the population of Singapore

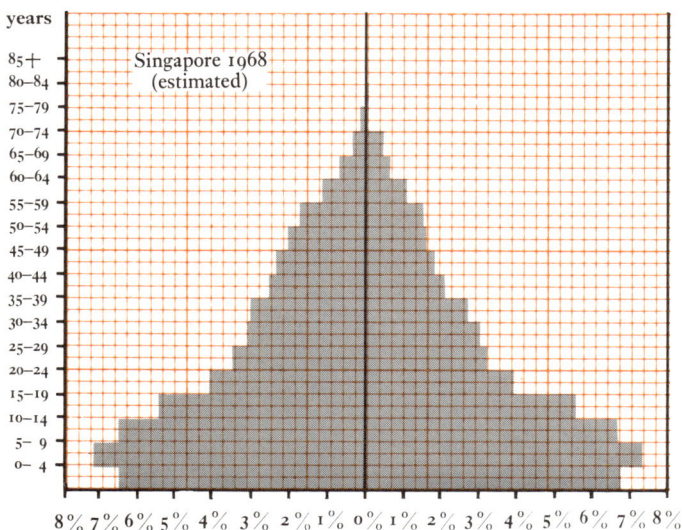

Source: The basic data for Scotland from 1969 and for Singapore from 1968 is to be found in the *United Nations Demographic Yearbook 1969*, pp 174–5 and 182–3.

1 Since the fall in fertility is of very recent origin, the structure of the pyramid, excepting the latest cohorts, is like type B.

death rate, one is unable to take account of differences in the age composition of the population. To get round this difficulty, we try to calculate what are called age specific death rates. We try, that is, to get the ages at which people die and relate these to the number of people living at that age. The calculation, once one has got the data, is quite a simple one. Here is an illustration.

Ages (years)	Mid-year Population 1970	Deaths in 1970	Deaths per 1,000 population
20–24	20,000	20	$\dfrac{20 \times 1,000}{20,000} = 1.0$
25–29	15,000	18	$\dfrac{18 \times 1,000}{15,000} = 1.2$

And so on for each age group. If we are able to work out age specific death rates for the populations we are interested in, then we can discover the extent to which differences in the crude death rates are the result of differences in the age composition. We can *isolate* one of the factors affecting mortality. For example, suppose we look again at the mortality experience of Scotland and Singapore. From the crude death rate it would appear that mortality in Scotland is twice that of Singapore, because the rate for the former is twelve per 1,000, for the latter only six. But what would the crude rates look like if both had the same age composition? We can discover this by calculating what is termed the *standardized mortality rate*.

The standardized mortality rate

To produce one kind of standardized mortality rate we need merely to calculate age specific death rates for each five-year age group of the populations we are interested in. We then decide what our standard population is to be and multiply the age specific death rates that we have calculated by the number of people in each of the corresponding age groups of the standard population. Let us take the Scottish population represented on the population pyramid above as our standard population, and work out

Table 2 Age standardized death rate for Singapore 1968

Ages	Age specific death rates in Singapore	Standard population (Scotland)	Expected deaths in Singapore
0– 4	9.6	462,400	4,439
5– 9	0.55	471,000	259
10–14	0.52	427,500	222
15–19	0.75	388,800	292
20–24	1.13	395,100	447
25–29	1.26	319,500	403
30–34	1.47	291,300	428
35–39	2.24	295,300	662
40–44	3.89	306,100	1,191
45–49	5.95	335,900	1,999
50–54	10.20	278,700	2,843
55–59	17.95	314,300	5,642
60–64	28.61	289,100	8,271
65–69	46.80	240,100	11,237
70–74	67.40	170,100	11,465
75–79	105.50	112,000	11,816
80–84	281.00	64,300	18,068
85+	413.00	32,900	13,588
		Total 5,194,400	Total 93,272

Age standardized death rate for Singapore, 18.0 per 1,000

Source: *United Nations Demographic Yearbook 1969* (1970), pp 174–5, 182–3, 606–7.

what the number of deaths would be in Singapore if that country had the same age structure as Scotland. This is done in the table on p 30. The calculation reveals that if Singapore had the same age structure as Scotland and the same age specific death rates as she had in 1968 then her crude death rate would be eighteen per 1,000 – which is some three times as great as she has now, with her present age structure. This shows that the 'population explosion' could become even greater if *age specific* mortality rates in countries like Singapore were reduced to western levels.

The general fertility rate

The search for more refined measures of mortality is paralleled in the case of fertility. The demographer is constantly trying to make his measures more specific by attempting to include in his calculation only those people who are really exposed to the event he is trying to measure. He knows, of course, that births are only produced by people during a certain age period which differs for men and women. It is shorter for women than for men, and since it is women who actually carry the children he may concentrate solely on women above the age of fifteen and below fifty, the child-bearing period. He will miss some women who are exposed to the risks of child-bearing above and below these ages, but they will be few in number.

The first measure the demographer may then calculate is the *general fertility rate*. The word 'general' here, like the word 'crude', is an indication that the demographer is not relating the events (in this case births) to precisely the group of individuals (the actual mothers) who produced them. If the requisite data is available, the calculation is simple. One merely takes the number of births in any particular year and relates this to the number of women in the appropriate age group, which may be fifteen to forty-four years or twenty to forty-nine or fifteen to forty-nine, depending upon the data available and one's particular predilections. Below is an illustration of this calculation.

Women aged 15–44 years on 1 July, 1970	Births in 1970	General fertility rate
800	120	$120 \div 800 \times 1,000 = 150$

The child-woman ratio

Often, particularly in underdeveloped countries, vital registration data is either unavailable or very unreliable. Since we do not have totals of births we cannot calculate a general fertility ratio. We must depend, therefore, upon the information we can glean from the census, always assuming, of course, that it is available and trustworthy. Using census material we can calculate what is known as the child-woman ratio. Here we take the number of children under, say, five years of age or under one year and relate it to the number of women in the child-bearing age group.

Women aged 15–44 years on 1 July, 1970	Children Under 1 year	Children Under 5 years	Children under 1 year per 1,000 women aged 15–44 years	Children under 5 years per 1,000 women 15–44 years
800	80	320	$80 \div 800 \times 1,000 = 100$	$320 \div 800 \times 1,000 = 400$

This particular measure is less satisfactory than the general fertility rate because it reflects not only fertility but also the mortality experience of children in the younger age groups. This can vary very greatly. Young children are particularly vulnerable to a series of infectious diseases. If they are inadequately fed they have little resistance. Thus if one society has greatly reduced the incidence of the major child killing diseases, whilst another society has not been so fortunate, the former might well have a higher child-woman ratio than the latter. This need not necessarily mean that it has higher fertility, just that more of its children survived long enough to be included in the calculation.

The total fertility rate

Both the general fertility rate and the child-woman ratio are obviously more specific than the crude birth rate, since they do relate births to the persons most likely to be exposed to producing children. However, they still reflect to some extent the age composition of the women within the fertile age group itself. This is an important drawback because we know that women are more likely to have children at certain ages than at others; for example, in some societies they are more likely to have them in their mid-twenties than in their mid-thirties and in almost all societies are more likely to have them at these ages than in, say, their mid-forties. To some extent, of course, the variation will depend upon the age of marriage, since in almost all societies the majority of children are produced by married rather than unmarried women. To overcome these particular snags we try to calculate what is called the *total fertility rate* (TFR). Again, assuming we have the data, the calculation is a simple one. An illustration appears below:

Years of age	Births per 1,000 women in each age group	Births per woman in each age group
15–19	15	.0150
20–24	150	.1500
25–29	250	.2500
30–34	180	.1800
35–39	110	.1100
40–44	40	.0400
45–49	25	.0250
	770	.770 × 5 = 3.850

You may wonder why I multiply the figure at the base of the right-hand column by 5. I do so in order to find the total fertility rate for a particular year, since each woman spends five years in the age groups represented in the left-hand column and is, therefore, exposed five times to this particular level of fertility. Ideally, we should calculate the rate for each individual year and then sum each of these rates, as we have done with rates for the five-year age group. But averaging in the first place and then multiplying is usually accepted as being good enough. This measure gives us an indication of the number of children the average woman in the particular population is likely to have, assuming the fertility pattern of each age group remains the same. Furthermore, of course, the measure does remove the distortion produced by variations in the age composition of the women in the fertile age groups.

Gross and net reproduction rates

Two other measures deserve at least a brief mention. The first of these is the *female gross reproduction rate*. This is a measure designed to indicate the number of female births likely to be produced by a particular population. It is, in other words, the total fertility rate with respect to female births and is usually approximately half the total fertility rate for males and females taken together. One quick way of calculating the gross reproduction rate is to multiply the fertility rate by the proportion of births that are female. For example, if I use the figure produced by the calculation above I would multiply 3.85 × 0.49 (there are almost invariably fewer girls born than boys), which will give us a gross reproduction rate of 1.89.

This is a useful indicator of whether or not a population is able to reproduce itself. If the figure is over 1, then it is possible; if it is under 1, it is impossible. There is, however, a complicating factor,[1] namely, that not all the female children born will survive to the ages at which they will contribute to replacing the population. We must, therefore, estimate the shortfall by examining the mortality experience of the population we are studying. Here is where we draw on the Life Table and by finding out the number of women who can expect to reach, and to pass through the fertile age group, we are able to calculate a more complex measure, known as the *net reproduction rate*. Here is an illustration. We have in column 2 of the table below the births per woman in each group (column 1) as given in our illustration of the total fertility rate on p 32. By multiplying each of the numbers in this column by 0.49 we arrive at the number of female births (column 3). To calculate the total fertility rate we multiplied each number by 5: that being the maximum number of years each woman could spend in each age group. To get at the net reproduction rate, however, we must multiply the numbers by the *actual* number of years spent in each age group. Obviously this will be smaller the older the age group since the population is progressively reduced by death. Column 4 gives, therefore, the average number of years spent in a particular age group by each of the women who enter it. Multiplying the numbers in column 3 by those in column 4 gives us the expected number of female births per woman. By adding these up we arrive at the female net reproduction rate.

1 Ages	2 Births per woman	3 Female births per woman	4 Average number of years per woman	5 Expected female births per woman
15–19	.0150	.0074	4.2	.0311
20–24	.1500	.0735	4.1	.3014
25–29	.2500	.1225	4.0	.4900
30–34	.1800	.0882	3.8	.3352
35–39	.1100	.0539	3.7	.1994
40–44	.0400	.0196	3.6	.0706
45–49	.0250	.0123	3.5	.0431
	.7700	.3774		1.4708

Net reproduction rate   1.4708

SAQ 8   Here is a certain amount of demographic information culled from the pages of the United Nations (1969) *Demographic Yearbook 1968*, New York.

1 A population classified by age and sex

Age group	Total males	Total females
0–4	2,158,000	2,073,000
5–9	1,893,000	1,824,000
10–14	2,094,000	2,021,000
15–19	2,201,000	2,102,000
20–24	1,748,000	1,605,000
25–29	1,587,000	1,400,000
30–34	1,702,000	1,570,000
35–39	1,722,000	1,662,000
40–44	1,660,000	1,660,000
45–49	1,238,000	1,266,000
50–54	1,193,000	1,266,000
55–59	1,349,000	1,469,000
60–64	1,240,000	1,416,000
65–69	992,000	1,264,000
70–74	618,000	1,045,000
75–79	418,000	780,000
80–84	233,000	498,000
85+	123,000	309,000
Total	24,169,000	25,230,000

1 Hence the use of the word 'possible' in the previous sentence rather than 'certain'.

2 The births produced by the population in the course of one year classified by age of mother.

Age of mother	Births
15–19	53,000
20–24	279,000
25–29	232,000
30–34	156,000
35–39	83,000
40–44	25,000
45–49	2,000
Total	830,000

3 The number of deaths in the population in the course of one year was 529,000.

4 The number of marriages in the population in the course of one year was 340,000.

Using this information
A Construct a population pyramid here.

Figure 11

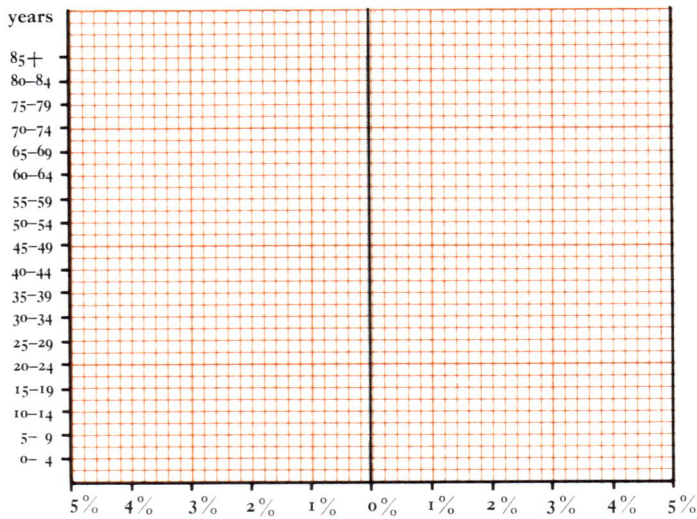

B When you have constructed the pyramid decide which of the following countries it represents.

Mexico   France   Korea

C Calculate a sex ratio for the population.

D Calculate   (i) the crude birth rate
                (ii) the crude death rate
                (iii) the crude marriage rate.

E Calculate a general fertility rate.

F Calculate a child-woman ratio.

G Calculate the total fertility rate.

H Calculate the net reproduction rate. For this you will need the average number of years per woman in the fertile age groups. For the purpose of the calculation use the following:

Years of age	Average number of years per woman
15–19	4.8
20–24	4.8
25–29	4.8
30–34	4.8
35–39	4.7
40–44	4.6
45–49	4.5

(Answer at end of unit.)

Answers to SAQs

Answer SAQ 1 'Topics' which are of interest, to me at least, include:

1 What are the implications of what Malthus calls 'the passion between the sexes'? It seems to me that he is here postulating a fairly straightforward relationship between 'passion' and 'children', the products of that passion. But may not other factors intervene to affect this? For instance, even if we ignore the question of contraception, there is that of fecundity, ie the ability of a couple who want children actually to produce them. In this country, over the past 100 years, about 7% of all couples have been physiologically wholly infertile. Sub-fecundity is however, much more widespread and, as Krause's article in the course reader suggests (Drake 1973 pp 175–8), in the sort of populations Malthus had in mind may account for great variations in fertility.

2 What determines the age at marriage and the proportion of a population which eventually marries? Malthus assumed that changes here were central to the rate of population growth. The mechanism he put forward was that as demand for labour increased, *men* could marry earlier and, as a result, being in the married state longer, would have larger families. But how far did this happen? Did an earlier age at marriage on the part of men result in a correspondingly large reduction in the age at marriage of women. In any case how much did the age at marriage change? (For one illustration see Floud 1973 p 83). Also what other factors affected the age at marriage and the choice of marriage partners? Was distance important? (For this see Küchemann *et al* in the course reader, Drake 1973 pp 211–14). What about the effect of changes in social security provisions? Malthus certainly thought the eighteenth-century English Poor Law encouraged early marriage and high fertility. But did it? (On this see Huzel 1969.) Also what about illegitimacy, the extent of extra-marital fertility? (See Laslett and Oosterveen 1973.)

Answer SAQ 2 We have already drawn attention to such a case. In Unit 2 where we quoted Thernstrom as noting that authors such as William F. Whyte in his *Street Corner Society* or Herbert Gans in his *The Urban Villagers* never really resolved the problem of how far what they wrote was, in the former case, rooted in Boston's North End of the 1930s, or, in the case of the latter, in Boston's West End in the 1950s.

In this country there was during the 1950s considerable discussion of what became known as the theory of *embourgeoisement*. Put crudely, this sought to explain certain social and political changes (eg the lack of Labour Party success in the Parliamentary elections of the 1950s) on the grounds that rising wages and changing occupational structure were turning sections of the working class into members of the middle class. (For a full discussion see Goldthorpe *et al* 1969.) Labour's return to power in the 1960s was thus a source of embarrassment to some but satisfaction to others who had not accepted the thesis. At a more sophisticated level, certain aspects of Marx's theories on the future of capitalist society now appear to owe a great deal to his understanding of the times in which he lived – much of it acquired, of course, in the library of the British Museum.

Answer SAQ 3 Pitfalls in:

Literary evidence

1 *Imprecision* Often literary evidence though couched in verbal terms is implicitly quantitative. Unless this is recognized serious misunderstandings may occur. In some cases this kind of evidence may have to be abandoned if it is not possible to clarify it sufficiently.

2 *Bias* Most of us in writing an account of anything are affected by a conscious or, more frequently, an unconscious bias. Questions which must, therefore, be asked of literary evidence, whether it be letters, diaries, newspaper accounts, or the

evidence reported to official or private committees of enquiry include the following:

a How far was the person making the statement in a position to make it?

b What factors in the circumstances in which the statement was made, in the person making it, could have affected the literal meaning of the statement?

c What factors in the reader's circumstances are likely to distort the meaning of the statement?

d For example, if it is 'just what we are looking for', is this because it fits some preconceived notion of ours; or because it occupies an objectively determined place in a research scheme?

Statistical evidence

What determines the value of any kind of statistics is the skill with which they are collected, processed and analysed. We'll look at each of these in turn.

1 Collection of population statistics

Demographers traditionally use two devices for collecting data; the census, whereby they get hold of various characteristics of a population at a particular point in time, and the register of births, marriages and deaths, which records these events as they happen (see Appendix). Since neither of these devices has been available for very long – for most western countries, neither was widespread before 1800 – historical demographers often seek out a variety of surrogate measures. These include tax returns (ie hearth taxes, poll taxes); ecclesiastical returns of the number of communicants; private enquiries by interested laymen, usually covering a parish or small town. (For a critique of some of these see Unit 6 and Hollingsworth 1969.) The trouble with these is that they are all subject to gross errors – usually in the direction of under-recording. Tax evasion, for instance, is not a twentieth-century phenomenon only. Even the official censuses have to be examined carefully. The population being counted was often suspicious and uncooperative – any count being regarded as a prelude to higher taxation or military conscription. Enumerators were frequently ill-educated and wanting in enthusiasm (Drake 1972). Their task was often exceedingly difficult, either because the population was scattered or, alternatively, crammed into a chaos of tenements in a nineteenth-century industrial slum. Often too the population was unable to give correct answers, simply through ignorance. This was particularly true of ages, which tended to be given in even numbers or to the nearest five or ten years.

The same strictures may be levelled at vital registration systems, especially those which preceded the advent of civil registration by the state; in England and Wales this was in 1837. Usually historical demographers must depend on church registers of baptisms (*not* births), marriages and burials (*not* deaths). In England such registers are available in some parishes for as far back as 1538. Sometimes they are incredibly detailed. For instance burial registers will give age and *supposed* cause of death; marriage registers may give the ages of bride and groom and the occupation of the latter. More commonly, however, the registers are obviously deficient, and as the article by Krause in the course reader (Drake 1973 pp 155–83) makes quite clear, have to be interpreted with great care and skill.

Theory

I argued in Unit 1 that one of the benefits of using theory explicitly in our enquiries is that it helps us formulate questions. Unfortunately it may also cause us to restrict the range of our questions. This is what, I have alleged, occurred in the case of Malthus on his Norwegian journey. Because he believed the preventive check was powerful in Norway, he neglected to consider the role of the positive check. That he did believe this is evidenced by the fact that the day *after* he set foot in Norway, he entered in his *Journal* this note: the population of Norway 'is increasing so slowly though the people live so long!' In terms of the theory as a whole this concentration on the preventive check was no bad thing since it countered his belief in the superior power of the positive check. Nevertheless in the context of the particular country it was unfortunate. One wonders what would have happened to his theory had the exigencies of war permitted him to go to France. For there the positive check, or its various manifestations, was currently more obvious than in Norway!

Answer SAQ 4   a 70 years (ie 70 ÷ 1.0 = 70)
                     b 47 years (ie 70 ÷ 1.5 = 47)

Answer SAQ 5
1 If the coloured population has a higher proportion of its members in the fertile age groups, one would expect it to have relatively more children than the white population, even if the average number of children per family was the same in both populations.
2 If the proportion of coloured men to coloured women is higher than that of white men to white women, it is likely that a higher proportion of coloured women will be married, and that they will marry earlier, than will white women. Other things being equal this would lead to higher fertility amongst coloured women than amongst white.
3 Although official policy is that all births should take place in hospital, pressure on space forces some hospitals to admit pregnant women only for their first birth or for their fourth and subsequent births. The relative proportion of white and coloured women in our ward could reflect this.
4 The earlier the age at marriage, the more children born to it – again, other things being equal.
5 Fertility of the white and coloured populations could be identical: the proportions of coloured and white could, therefore, reflect the racial composition of the community.
6 At first it might appear that the division in the ward between coloured and white women reflects a society segregated by colour. The conclusion could well be invalid, of course, if some of the white women were married to coloured men, and some of the coloured women to white men.
7 Many hospitals in Britain developed out of the old workhouses. Conditions were primitive and discipline strict – both being considered appropriate to the 'lower orders'. As a result many women only went into maternity hospitals as a last resort. It could be that the coloured women in our ward, if they were immigrants, did not have this attitude towards hospitals. This might, then, be part of the explanation of the position in the ward.
8 Many maternity hospitals admit pregnant women according to the condition of their houses: the poorer the housing, the better the chance of getting into the hospital. Coloured immigrants often have poorer accommodation than native whites.
9 Immigration policies change, often quickly. It may be that the position in our ward reflects a temporary situation arising shortly after a large number of coloured female immigrants have come to the town to join their husbands. Had we looked at the ward two years earlier, or again, two years later, the proportion of beds occupied by white and coloured women could well be very different.
10 The ward is obviously a small one. A sample of ten on one day tells us little about the position in the local community, let alone the country as a whole.

Answer SAQ 6
1 Either 1200 men per 1000 women ie $\frac{18,000 \times 1,000}{15,000}$

   or 833 women per 1000 men ie $\frac{15,000 \times 1,000}{18,000}$

2 A – (c) Worthing is a town to which many people retire. In 1951, 24.6% of its population was aged 65 years and over. This was a higher proportion than that of any other town in England and Wales with a population of 50,000 or more. (For all such towns 10.4% were over this age. Dagenham had the lowest proportion – 4.9%.) As it often happens that the men die first, the town contains a large number of widows. For these, and other data indicating socio-economic variations between the 157 largest towns of England and Wales, see C. A. Moser and Wolf Scott (1961) *British towns: a statistical study of their social and economic differences*, London, Centre for Urban Studies.

B – (a) Gosport is a naval base.

C – (d) Are women less criminal, more leniently treated by the courts, or more adept at avoiding arrest than men?

D – (b) In Ceylon, India and Pakistan – which between them contain 20% of the world's population – it appears that the female chances of survival are lower than those for males at almost all ages. This is contrary to the experience of most of the rest of the world and has not yet been explained satisfactorily.

Answer SAQ 7 *Ghana 1960 is A.*   Broad base reflects recent reduction in infant and child mortality, without any corresponding fall in a high fertility rate. The dent in the pyramid corresponding to the female 15–19 age group suggests a misreporting of ages: possibly some advantage in being 20 and over led to this.

Hungary 1976 is B. A European population: the clue being the shortfall of the 50–54 year age group due to a fall in fertility in the years of the First World War. No other participant in that war experienced as great a fall in fertility. The base of the pyramid reflects the large number of births in the years 1953–6 when abortion was prohibited and the subsequent repeal of anti-abortion legislation.

West Berlin is C. The clue here is the very high proportion of the population in the older groups – especially women. This reflects the 'artificial' nature of the city (it depends very heavily on subsidies from the west) and the emigration of young people to West Germany – both very much a legacy of the Second World War and its political aftermath.

The central business district is D. Here the main type of residential building is the hotel catering for business men.

Hong Kong is E. This pyramid shows a marked indentation corresponding with the years of the Second World War. The pyramid has a broad base, except for the youngest five-year age group. This latter phenomenon may partly be credited to the family planning movement.

Answer SAQ 8 A Figure 12 Population pyramid

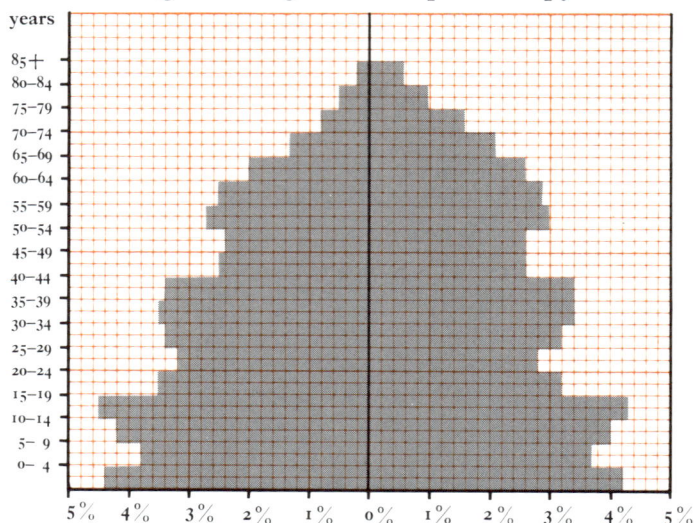

B   France

C   1044 women per 1000 men or
    958 men per 1000 women

D   (i) 16.8
    (ii) 10.7
    (iii) 6.9

E   74 births per 1000 women aged 15 to 49 years; alternatively 91 births per 1000 women aged 20–49 years, or 83 per 1000 women aged 15–44 years.

F   376 children aged 0–4 years per 1000 women aged 15–49; *or* 462 children aged 0–4 years per 1000 women aged 20–49 years *or* 423 children aged 0–4 years per 1000 women aged 15–45 years.

G

Ages	Women	Births	Births per 1000 women	Births per woman
15–19	2,102,000	53,000	25.2	.025
20–24	1,605,000	279,000	173.8	.174
25–29	1,400,000	232,000	165.7	.166
30–34	1,570,000	156,000	99.4	.099
35–39	1,662,000	83,000	49.9	.050
40–44	1,660,000	25,000	15.1	.015
45–49	1,266,000	2,000	1.6	.002
				.531 × 5

Total fertility rate = 2.655

H

Ages	Births per woman	Female births per woman	Average no of years per woman	Expected female births per woman
15–19	.025	.0123	4.8	.0590
20–24	.174	.0853	4.8	.4094
25–29	.166	.0813	4.8	.3902
30–34	.099	.0485	4.8	.2328
35–39	.050	.0245	4.7	.1152
40–44	.015	.0074	4.6	.0340
45–49	.002	.0010	4.5	.0045
				1.2451

Net reproduction rate = 1.2451

Notes

Page 28 ——— (The Year 1799 & 1800

No 138

Banns of Marriage between Michael Butler of the parish of Mentmore Bachelor and Elizabeth Tofield of this Parish Spinster were published on the three Sundays underwritten:

That is to say, On Sunday, the 17 Nov. 1799 by Cha. Ashfield
On Sunday, the 24 Nov. 1799 by Cha. Ashfield
On Sunday, the 1 Dec. 1799 by Cha. Ashfield

No 139

Banns of Marriage between Thomas Tofield of this parish Bachelor and Elizabeth Bates of this parish of Mentmore Spinster were published on the three Sundays underwritten:

That is to say, On Sunday, the 24 Nov. 1799 by Cha. Ashfield
On Sunday, the 1 Dec. 1799 by Cha. Ashfield
On Sunday, the 8 Dec. 1799 by Cha. Ashfield

No 140

Banns of Marriage between Joseph Capell of this parish Bachelor and Mary Timson of the parish of Tring Herts Spinster were published on the three Sundays underwritten:

That is to say, On Sunday, the 12 Jan. 1800 by Cha. Ashfield
On Sunday, the 19 Jan. 1800 by Cha. Ashfield
On Sunday, the 26 Jan. 1800 by Cha. Ashfield

No 141

Banns of Marriage between John Read of this parish Bachelor and Elizabeth Hodgins of this parish Spinster were published on the three Sundays underwritten:

That is to say, On Sunday, the 12 Jan. 1800 by Cha. Ashfield
On Sunday, the 19 Jan. 1800 by Cha. Ashfield
On Sunday, the 26 Jan. 1800 by Cha. Ashfield

No 142

Banns of Marriage between William Bandy of this parish Bachelor & Hannah Green of this parish Spinster were published on the three Sundays underwritten:

That is to say, On Sunday, the 13 July 1800 by Cha. Ashfield
On Sunday, the 20 July 1800 by Cha. Ashfield
On Sunday, the 27 July 1800 by Cha. Ashfield

Part cover: Page from Wing parish banns of marriage register, 1800. Source: Bucks County Record Office

Contents Unit 6

Objectives

After studying this unit and listening to the second radio programme, *No Safety in Numbers*, you should be able to:

1 Identify sources of error in the demographic data provided by parish registers and censuses.

2 Using the criteria provided in the unit, assess the value of a *particular* parish register for a *particular* demographic exercise.

3 Describe the main problems involved in using English historical sources to investigate the relationship between marriage and fertility in pre-industrial England.

4 Draw up a research proposal, using as a starting point some aspect of the articles by Krause or Küchemann *et al* in the course reader (Drake 1973), indicating the likely nature and problems of the source material, the techniques to be used and the hypothesis to be tested.

Population and Society

1 Introduction

In contrast to the previous unit which was necessarily generalized and somewhat abstract, this unit is both particular and concrete. We will attempt to show how appropriate techniques may be used to elicit demographic information from various kinds of historical data. The data to be explored will be drawn from western communities during the pre-industrial and industrial revolution periods and are of three kinds.

First, there is vital registration material drawn either from church registers of baptisms, marriages and burials or from secular governmental registers of births, marriages and deaths. Secondly, there is material taken from censuses or census-type listings. The former begin, for the most part, in the late eighteenth or early nineteenth centuries. The listings go back into the Middle Ages and are mainly the product of fiscal, military or ecclesiastical operations. Thirdly, there are literary accounts, such as travellers' tales, diaries, correspondence, reports of oral evidence before commissions of enquiry, completed questionnaires, newspaper articles and the like. We shall be discussing and demonstrating three kinds of technique applicable to the quantitative parts of this material.

The first of these embraces the methods used to convert census-type information (eg totals of communicants or men of military-service age) into population data. The second and third kinds of technique we shall describe as 'aggregative' and 'nominative'. Aggregative techniques are used to derive from, say, parish registers, *crude* rates of such demographic phenomena as births, marriages, deaths and migrants. Nominative techniques involve the bringing together of various pieces of demographic information using the *names* of individuals as the linking device. Such techniques (eg the reconstitution of families) can provide us with *specific* rates which, as the Appendix to Unit 5 sought to demonstrate, can give us the opportunity for more sophisticated analysis. Although some statistical skills are required for these various types of analysis, the skill of evaluating the reliability and validity of the evidence is even more important. This latter skill is, of course, also crucial in deciding on the merits of the various kinds of literary evidence noted above. The emphasis of this unit will then be on these non-quantitative skills.

In terms of the aims of Applied Historical Studies, there would be little point in explaining, *in vacuo*, these various techniques and sources. That is why, of course, Unit 5 was largely devoted to providing a theoretical framework and an appropriate array of concepts. I shall, then, structure this unit around a number of specific enquiries. These will be on fertility and nuptiality, since the two other major interests of the demographer, mortality and migration, are discussed in Units 7 and 8 respectively.

2 Population size

The amount of historical data which can reveal something about past populations is considerable. Hollingsworth (1969 pp 43–4) has summarized this. His list appears below. Note that the sources are listed in order of reliability, which in this area can be equated with usefulness.

1 Censuses, especially if given by name and age
2 Vital registration data
3 Bills of Mortality
4 Ecclesiastical records, such as parish registers and communicants' lists
5 Fiscal documents
6 Military records
7 Inventories of property
8 Genealogies
9 Wills
10 Marriage settlements

432 Chesham		
Names of persons returned	Occupations	Remarks
John Reading	Turners	
Wm Jones		
James Lewis		
Wm Lewis		
Jas Benham		
Wm East		
John Chapman		
Edw. Earl		Fits
John Hoare		
Richd Ware		
Chas Ware	Bakers	
Henry Sadler		
Joseph Bunker		Quaker
Benjn Deeley		
John Penny		
Thos Varney		
John Rotheram		
John Fowler		
Wm Andrews Senr		
Wm Andrews Junr		
Jos Chilton		
Wm Matthews		
Jno Matthews		
Thos Christmas		
Jno Potter		
Jesse East		
Jonathan Body	Carpenters	
Francis Weedon		
Richd Weedon		
Benjn Bunn		
Jno Woods		
Wm Woods		
Danl Chilton		
Stephen Woodbridge		
Thos Todd		
Nathaniel Priest		
Thomas Fern	Farrier	

11 Eye-witness estimates
12 Prices, over the long term
13 Number and extent of towns
14 Archaeological remains
15 Methods of agricultural economy
16 Ecclesiastical and administrative geography
17 New buildings
18 Colonization of new land
19 Cemetery data, both from skeletons and tombstone inscriptions

In bulk at least this list certainly appears promising. Paradoxically, though, its very size is a measure of the paucity of information. Most items give us no more than a broad indication of the size and geographical distribution of a population. And to get even that, much ingenuity is required. If, on the other hand, one wants to know something about fertility and nuptiality (the concerns of this particular unit), only items 1, 2, 4, 8, 10 and 11 are of very much use. Furthermore, so far as this country is concerned the most valuable items (1 and 2) appear only in the second quarter of the nineteenth century; hence the position is even less promising than might appear at first sight. However, before we begin to despair altogether, two remarks are pertinent. First, it is rare in the social sciences to get absolute precision. Both historians and social scientists deal in probabilities, and the fact that our sources are not perfect does not mean that they are of no value. Secondly, unless we use this data, we must abandon any hope of fully understanding one of the world's present concerns – the 'population explosion'. The societies undergoing this have, for the most part, very little quantitative or qualitative information about themselves *prior* to the recent surge in population growth. What is more, it is now too late to collect it, for there are few societies in the world today that have not been 'contaminated' by the west: some small tribes in the jungles of South America are perhaps the only exceptions. Therefore, whatever the risk of fallacious analogies, of behaviour being judged outside its societal and historical context, of too much being made out of too little evidence, I think we should try to do what we can with the material available. So, in trying to discover something about fertility and nuptiality prior to the period of civil registration and modern censuses, the first step would appear to be to calculate base populations at various dates. As the Appendix to Unit 5 shows, in order to calculate, say, the crude birth rate, one needs to know not only the number of births over a given period, but also the mean population size during that period. A first step would, therefore, appear to be to produce, from whatever material is to hand, population estimates. In fact, such material is abundant and the quality of much of it has already been assessed by other writers.

However, as the details given in Appendix 1 show, it rarely provides *the* answer to a historical demographer's prayer. In only a few cases has an attempt been made to enumerate the entire population. One usually has to estimate what proportion of it has been counted, then decide upon some multiplier to derive a total population figure. Much effort and a great deal of ingenuity have gone into this task. The cumulative result of it all, however, is to make one doubt whether such figures can ever play more than a supporting role.

3 The parish registers, 1538–1837

The strength of that supportive role will emerge in the course of our examination of the registers of baptisms, marriages and burials kept by the Anglican clergy in England and Wales. Such registers were ordered to be kept in 1538 by Thomas Cromwell, one of Henry VIII's chief advisers. Some parishes have an unbroken series of registers from that date to this, but they are few in number. Many others, however, do have registers which begin later in the sixteenth century. They are of value to the historical demographer for 300 years, being his main source for evidence of vital events until 1837, when civil registration began in England. Since then their value has diminished as more and more births, marriages and deaths have been registered by the State rather than by the Church.

Before we determine how we can use the information in these registers we must first attempt to discover what was registered and, equally important, what was not. The various steps in this process have been set out in the form of an *algorithm* in Appendix 2. How seriously one takes this is a matter for individual decision. I have, perhaps, been rather too cautious, especially where, at various points, I have suggested that a particular line of enquiry be reconsidered. For the historical record is a rich one and there are many instances where my 'playing safe' advice would lead to the neglect of potentially valuable data. However, only the student on the spot can decide in such instances.

You will note that at various stages of the algorithm, the words '**Note**', '**Exercise**' or '**Test**' appear. These indicate various steps in the analysis. I will go through each of these now.

An algorithm is 'a means of reaching a decision by considering only those factors which are relevant to that particular decision' (Wheatley and Unwin 1972 p 10). It is often presented in the form of a flow-chart. Followed step by step, the desired result will be achieved.

Exercise 1 Locate a Church of England Parish Register

In the period 1538–1837 the Church of England had between 10,000 and 11,000 parishes. The number varied from time to time as new ones were created or existing ones amalgamated with each other. The obvious place to look for registers covering this period would appear to be the local parish church. The care of parish registers is the responsibility of the local incumbent and his church wardens. Permission to use them must be sought from them. The church is, however, not the only place in which one can find parish registers. Because of their interest to genealogists, many have been transcribed. These transcripts are to be found, in manuscript form, in local libraries, county record offices or the headquarters of archaeological and historical societies. Such transcripts are usually easier to work with than the original registers, though there is always the possibility of their being copied inaccurately. Easier still, of course, are printed transcripts. Again there are many of these. Usually they are to be found in the same places as the manuscript transcripts.[1] Many county record offices now hold large numbers of registers or register transcripts and are usually able to say where those they do not have are to be found. For instance, the Dorset County Record Office at Dorchester has all this information conveniently displayed on a map in its search room.

[1] According to Lynda Ovenall (see Wrigley (ed) 1966A p 263) the principal series of printed parish register transcripts are as follows:
Bedfordshire Parish Registers (Bedford 1931–)
Cumberland and Westmorland Antiquarian and Archaeological Society : Parish Register Section (1912–)
Devon and Cornwall Record Society (Exeter 1910–)
Durham and Northumberland Parish Register Society (Sunderland, Newcastle-upon-Tyne 1898–1926)
Dwelly's Parish Records (Herne Bay 1913–26)
Harleian Society – Registers of London Parishes (London 1877–)
Lancashire Parish Register Society (Rochdale, etc. 1898–)
Lincoln Record Society – Parish Register Section (Lincoln 1914–25)
Parish Register Society (London 1896–)
Shropshire Parish Register Society (1900–)
Staffordshire Parish Register Society (London 1902–)
Sussex Record Society (Lewes 1911–)
Worcestershire Parish Register Society (Worcester 1913–)
Yorkshire Parish Register Society (Leeds 1899–)
Phillimore Series of Marriage Registers (ed. successively by Phillimore, W. P. W., Blagg, T. M. and Ridge, C. H. from 1897) for the counties of Berkshire, Buckingham, Cambridge, Chester, Cornwall, Cumberland, Derby, Dorset, Essex, Gloucester, Hampshire, Hertford, Huntingdon, Kent, Leicester, Lincoln, Middlesex, Norfolk, Northampton, Nottingham, Oxford, Somerset, Suffolk, Warwick, Wiltshire, Worcester and Yorkshire. In addition there are a number of registers printed privately, often by their transcribers. See also D. J. Steel, (compiler) 1968.

Note 1 Has the register a mean of at least 100 entries per year?

A register with 100 entries annually might, in the period 1538–1837, be expected to show a burial total of from 25–65, a baptism total in the same range, and a marriage total varying from 5–10. The figure of 100 is an arbitrary one. Much of value can undoubtedly be learned from registers with fewer entries. Just how much is indicated by the work of Küchemann *et al* on the Oxfordshire parish of Charlton-on-Otmoor (see Drake 1973 pp 195–219). There are, however, two main reasons for being chary about using registers whose entries total much below this figure. One is that if the mean number of entries per year falls below 100, it is often difficult to tell whether below average entries in any particular year are due to under-registration, or to actual changes in the number of events (baptisms, marriages and burials) being recorded. Deciding on this particular question is always difficult, as we shall see in a moment. Wherever possible, then, it seems sensible not to make the task more problematical. The second reason for sticking with the figure of 100 is that often, even if only for relatively short periods of time, a register will specify such matters as whether a baptism is of an illegitimate child or not, what the presumed cause of death is, or what the ages of brides and bridegrooms are. Much can be made of such information (see Exercise 2 below) *if* there is enough of it. This is more likely to be the case when the mean number of entries is at least 100, than when it is under this figure.

Note 2 Are there registers in adjoining parishes which together with the original register produce 100 entries a year?

One may have little choice here, since the registers of at least some adjoining parishes are likely to have either disappeared or be inaccessible. If a choice is possible, however, it is worth taking some care over it. The reason for this goes back to what one always hopes the registers will provide, namely a reliable picture of population change in the *area*. One reason why they may not is because inhabitants of the parish they supposedly serve may have some of their vital events recorded in neighbouring parishes. For instance, a man may marry a woman in an adjoining parish. The ceremony may well take place there even though the couple return to settle in the husband's parish. Again, it may be that families living further from their own parish church than from that of a neighbouring parish would baptize their children and bury their dead in the latter, for the sake of convenience. Sometimes too the main settlement of a parish may be close to one of its boundaries. When this occurs there is invariably some seepage across it, so far as the recording of baptisms, marriages and burials is concerned. It is worthwhile, therefore, getting a map showing the parish boundaries (eg the Tithe Map; or the early nineteenth-century Greenwood series of maps; or even a modern one-inch ordnance survey), and then trying to find out where the main settlements appear to be and how far they are from the parish church. Some indication of this may be obtained from a contemporary map and the various listings described in Appendix 1: an example of their supportive role referred to above. Another clue may be obtained from entries in what we will call the 'home' register, ie the first one looked at. Dr Roger Schofield of the Cambridge Group for the History of Population and Social Structure has noted that a good indication of the likely direction of extra-parochial registration can be gained from the addresses of brides and bridegrooms given in the marriage register. This, incidentally, is very useful information in its own right (see Unit 8). Schofield has discovered that if, say, ten per cent of brides and bridegrooms married in Parish A come from Parish B and, say, three per cent from Parish C, then it is likely that roughly three times as many baptisms and three times as many burials of Parish A inhabitants will be registered in Parish B than in Parish C. Of course, there will be a certain compensation mechanism working here. That is to say, a higher proportion of Parish B than of Parish C inhabitants will appear in the registers of Parish A. It is, therefore, worth

For an excellent guide to maps as sources of historical data, see Harley (1964) and Harley (1972).

The Cambridge Group for the History of Population and Social Structure, 20 Silver Street, Cambridge was founded in 1964 by Mr Peter Laslett and Dr E. A. Wrigley. It has a small professional staff at Cambridge and enjoys the co-operation of over 200 amateur historians scattered across the country, who have conducted various analyses of parish registers and census-type listings, on its behalf. Publications of the group include E. A. Wrigley (ed) 1966A and 1972 and Laslett (ed) 1972. The Group also helped to found the journal, *Local Population Studies* (1968–). Enquiries from anyone interested in historical demography are welcomed.

taking a quick one-in-five sample of the entries in the marriage register to get some indication of the *de facto* registration area as opposed to the *de jure* one. One should then choose one's area of study accordingly.

Test 1 Are there any obvious gaps in the register(s)?

There are few parish registers which do not exhibit quite clear breaks in the registration process. Their extent varies from register to register and from period to period. How one deals with such gaps will vary, depending upon their duration (both absolutely, and relatively to the total number of years under study) as well as upon the aims of the enquiry. Some years ago I went through a number of the registers of the parishes marked on Figure 2 from their first entries up to 1700. Since they revealed much of the promise, and the problems, of the registers you are likely to deal with, should you choose to do a project in historical demography, I think it is worthwhile looking at each of them here. The years listed below are those in which no baptisms, marriages or burials were registered. In passing you might note the wide variety of places where I obtained this information.

Batley (1559) Source: Sheard, M. (1894) *Records of Batley* pp 37–38.

The date in brackets marks the beginning of the earliest surviving register I have found.

Sheard had done my work for me, having gone through the register and totalled the baptisms, marriages and burials for each year. According to him the gaps were as follows:

Baptisms:	1596–1604; 1606–7; 1610–13; 1642; 1645; 1647.
Marriages:	1568–9; 1596–1604; 1606–7; 1610–13; 1626–27; 1631–33; 1636; 1639–42; 1645–52.
Burials:	1595–1604; 1606–7; 1609–13; 1631–33; 1636; 1641–42; 1645–52.

Bingley (1578) Source: *Yorkshire Parish Register Society*, Vol ix.

Marriages:	1654–62; 1687–1700.
Burials:	1654–62; 1687–1700.

Birstall (1559) Source: Manuscript registers in Birstall Parish Church.

Marriages:	1578–80; 1654–55.
Burials:	1578–80.

Bradford (1596) Source: Manuscript transcripts in Bradford Free Library. Burials and marriages from a transcript printed in the *Bradford Antiquarian Journal* Vols 5 and 6.

Baptisms:	1596–97.

Calverley (1574) Source: From a transcript made by Samuel Margerison and published privately by him in three volumes.

Baptisms:	1644–48.
Marriages:	1574–96; 1608–26; 1645–48.
Burials:	1574–96; 1608–26; 1645–48.

Dewsbury (1538) Source: For the years 1538–1653 a transcript made and published privately in 1898 by S. J. Chadwick; for the years 1653–98, a manuscript transcript in the library of the Yorkshire Archaeological Society at Leeds; for the years 1699–1700, the Bishop's Transcripts in the Borthwick Institute, York.

Baptisms:	1554–55; 1559; 1568–70; 1581.
Marriages:	1554–55; 1559; 1568–70; 1581.
Burials:	1554–55; 1559; 1568–70; 1581.

East Ardsley (1598) Source: Manuscript transcript in the library of the Yorkshire Archaeological Society at Leeds.

Baptisms:	1599–1601; 1605–6; 1612–62.
Marriages:	1599–1601; 1605–6; 1612–53; 1657; 1659; 1676; 1680; 1682–83; 1687.
Burials:	1599–1601; 1605–6; 1612–53; 1674; 1677; 1686.

The Bishop's Transcripts are copies of the registers made by the incumbent and sent by him to the Bishop's Registry at stated intervals. The procedure appears to have started towards the end of the sixteenth century. Although there are often discrepancies between them and the registers, and they sometimes lack the detail of the original registers, they are useful for

Figure 2 Location of Yorkshire parishes discussed in Units 6 and 7

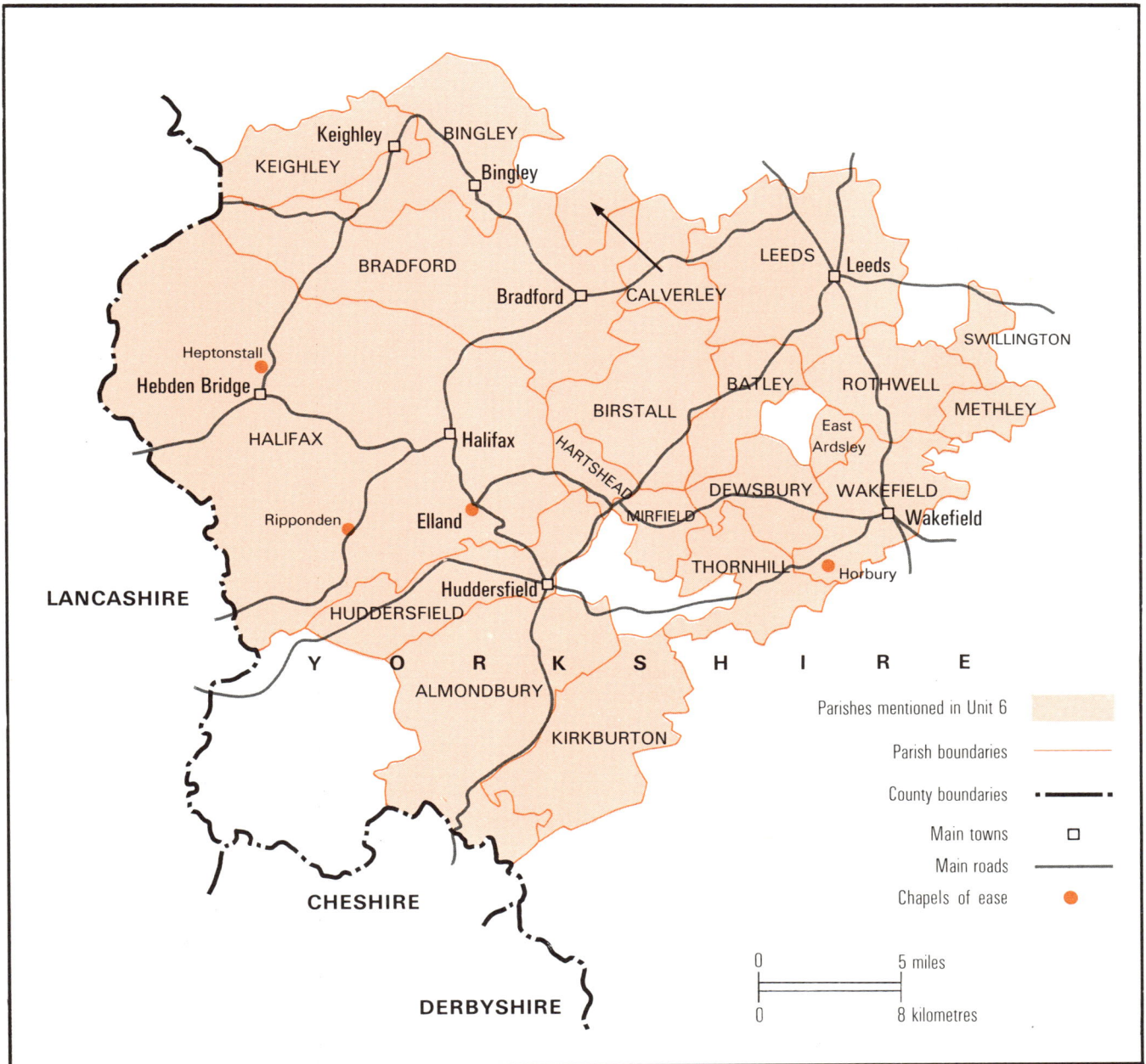

Elland (1559) Source: For the years 1559–1639 transcribed and published privately by J. W. Clay; for the years 1640–1700 by H. Ormerod.

Baptisms: 1642; 1648.

Marriages: 1642; 1648.

Burials: 1642; 1648.

Halifax (1540) Source: For the years 1540–93, a published transcript by the *Yorkshire Parish Register Society* Vol xxxvii; for the years 1594–1700 the manuscript Register in Halifax Parish Church.

Marriages: 1647–52.

Hartshead (1612) Source: *Yorkshire Parish Register Society*, Vol xvii.

Marriages: 1622; 1654.

filling in gaps in the registers. Chambers (1957 p 19) used them extensively for his Vale of Trent study and speaks highly of them. They are usually to be found in Diocesan or County Record Offices. The Bishop's Transcripts for all the Welsh dioceses are available in one collection at the National Library of Wales in Aberystwyth. This library also has most of the older parish registers – much to the annoyance of local archivists.

Table 1 Mean annual number of entries in twenty-two Yorkshire parish registers in the years[1] 1600–04 and 1690–94

Parish	1600–4	1690–94
Batley	49 (1590–94)	49
Bingley	98	131 (1680–4)
Birstall	159	208
Bradford	321	297
Calverley	83	137
Dewsbury	91	143
East Ardsley	17 (1607–11)	18
Elland[2]	293 (1604–08)	297
Halifax	891	601
Hartshead	30 (1612–16)	38
Heptonstall[2]	178	250
Horbury[2]	27	51
Huddersfield	214 (1606–10)	279
Keighley	71	80
Kirkburton	148	185
Leeds	573	686
Methley	39	46
Mirfield	40	65
Rothwell	114	115 (1685–89)
Swillington	16	18
Thornhill	71	81
Wakefield	325 (1613–17)	297

1 Except where gaps in the register have caused other years to be chosen.
2 Elland and Heptonstall were chapels within Halifax parish; Horbury, a chapel within Wakefield parish.

Table 2 Number of one-year gaps in twenty-two Yorkshire parish registers, by decade, 1540–1699

Parish	1540 -49	1550 -59	1560 -69	1570 -79	1580 -89	1590 -99	1600 -09	1610 -19	1620 -29	1630 -39	1640 -49	1650 -59	1660 -69	1670 -79	1680 -89	1690 -99	1540 -1699
Batley	—	—	2	0	0	4	7	4	2	5	8	2	0	0	0	0	34
Bingley	—	—	—	—	—	0	0	0	0	0	0	6	3	0	3	10	22
Birstall	—	—	0	2	0	0	0	0	0	0	0	2	0	0	0	0	4
Bradford	—	—	—	—	—	2	0	0	0	0	0	0	0	0	0	0	2
Calverley	—	—	6	10	7	2	10	9	0	4	0	0	0	0	0	0	48
Dewsbury	0	3	2	1	1	0	0	0	0	0	0	0	0	0	0	0	7
East Ardsley	—	—	—	—	—	1	4	8	10	10	10	10	3	3	5	0	64
Elland	—	—	0	0	0	0	0	0	0	0	2	0	0	0	0	0	2
Halifax	0	0	0	0	0	0	0	0	0	0	3	3	0	0	0	0	6
Hartshead	—	—	—	—	—	—	—	0	1	0	0	1	0	0	0	0	2
Heptonstall	—	—	—	—	—	5	0	0	0	0	0	0	0	0	2	0	7
Horbury	—	—	—	—	—	—	0	1	0	0	0	0	0	0	0	0	1
Huddersfield	—	—	—	—	—	—	0	0	0	0	0	0	0	0	0	0	0
Keighley	—	—	0	0	1	0	0	0	0	0	0	2	0	0	0	0	3
Kirkburton	0	1	0	1	0	0	0	6	7	4	0	0	0	0	0	0	19
Leeds	—	—	0	0	1	0	0	0	0	0	0	0	0	0	0	0	1
Methley	—	—	0	0	0	0	0	0	0	0	0	0	0	1	0	0	1
Mirfield	—	—	0	0	0	0	0	0	0	0	0	0	0	0	0	0	0
Rothwell	3	4	4	2	0	2	0	1	0	0	0	0	0	0	0	0	16
Swillington	3	3	3	1	1	7	0	1	2	1	7	6	2	0	1	1	39
Thornhill	—	—	—	—	3	5	0	0	0	0	0	0	0	0	0	0'	8
Wakefield	—	—	—	—	—	—	0	0	0	0	0	1	0	0	0	0	1
All parishes	**6**	**11**	**11**	**13**	**16**	**34**	**13**	**31**	**31**	**20**	**34**	**33**	**8**	**4**	**11**	**11**	**287**

1 See note to Table 1.

Heptonstall (1594) Source: For the years 1594–1652, *Yorkshire Parish Register Society* Vol lxxviii; for the years 1653–1700 from the manuscript Register in Heptonstall Parish Church.

Baptisms: 1594–98; 1686–87.
Marriages: 1686.
Burials: 1686–87.

Horbury (1598) Source: *Yorkshire Parish Register Society* Vol iii.

Baptisms: 1613.
Burials: 1613.
Marriages: 1613.

Huddersfield (1606) Source: Microfilm of the register in Huddersfield Public Library.

No gaps.

Keighley (1562) Source: *Yorkshire Parish Register Society* Vol lxxvii.

Marriages: 1587; 1651; 1653.

Kirkburton (1540) Source: Transcribed and published privately by F. A. Collins (1887).

Baptisms: 1555; 1576; 1611–12; 1614; 1617–26; 1630–32; 1636.
Marriages: 1555; 1576; 1611–12; 1614; 1617–26; 1630–32; 1636.
Burials: 1555; 1576; 1611–12; 1614; 1617–26; 1630–32; 1636.

Leeds (1572) Source: *Thoresby Society Publications* Vols i, iii, vii, x, xiii.

Marriages: 1592.

Methley (1559) Source: *Thoresby Society Publications* Vol xii.

Marriages: 1677.

Mirfield (1560) Source: *Yorkshire Parish Register Society* Vol lxiv.

No gaps.

Rothwell (1540) Source: For the years 1540–1689, *Yorkshire Parish Register Society* Vol xxvii, for the years 1691–1700, the Bishop's Transcripts in the Borthwick Institute, York.

Baptisms: 1545–46; 1551; 1556–58; 1563–64; 1568–69; 1676; 1690; 1693.
Marriages: 1545–46; 1556–58; 1563–64; 1568–69; 1676; 1690; 1693.
Burials: 1540; 1545–46; 1551; 1556–58; 1563–64; 1568–69; 1676–77; 1690; 1693.

Swillington (1543) Source: *Yorkshire Parish Register Society* Vol cxv.

Baptisms: 1545; 1554–55; 1560–61; 1643–50; 1657–61; 1663.
Marriages: 1544–46; 1553–55; 1560–61; 1575; 1582; 1591–97; 1614; 1629; 1633; 1644–51; 1656–61; 1663; 1669; 1688; 1691.
Burials: 1545–46; 1553–55; 1560; 1562; 1628; 1641; 1644–51; 1657–61; 1663.

Thornhill (1580) Source: *Yorkshire Parish Register Society* Vol xxx.

Baptisms: 1584–86; 1594–98.
Burials: 1584–86; 1594–98.
Marriages: 1584–86; 1594–98.

Wakefield (1613) Source: Manuscript transcript in the library of the Yorkshire Archaeological Society, Leeds.

Marriages: 1654.

SAQ 1 Suppose you had the above information on the twenty-two Yorkshire registers, which would you choose to work on? For the purposes of the exercise imagine that you lived in the area; that your time is limited to the 160 hours allotted for the project part of this course and that none of the registers had any special characteristic which the others did not have, eg information on age at marriage, cause of death, births as well as baptisms. I suggest you examine the question in the light of the first six steps of the algorithm and in your answer give reasons for your choice.

Having decided upon a register, or registers, we now take step 7 of the algorithm. *'Is there any other evidence of under-registration?'* To answer this question we need to run a series of further tests.

Test 2 The first involves going through each register month by month, to see whether there are any suspiciously large gaps. Here again one draws benefit from taking a register with a 100 or so entries a year, since a gap of, say, a couple of months between entries of any sort would suggest under-registration. If, on the other hand, a register had only fifty entries a year, such a gap would quite possibly be due to lack of business, as it were. One should make a preliminary assessment of the situation by taking a sample of years (every fifth would do) and going through them carefully. After that, assuming the gaps are in not more than about ten per cent of the years and do not extend over more than two to three months, one should total each month's events (baptisms, marriages and burials) and enter them on a schedule. The ones shown in Appendix 3, which were designed by the Cambridge Group for the History of Population and Social Structure, provide a convenient model.

After the preliminary test of the register's fullness noted above, one might decide to abandon it. This could well have happened with what appeared to be a leading contender for my favours after steps one to six of the algorithm, namely Kirkburton. Here are my notes on the breaks, *within* years, in that register.

1545 Register ends on 30 March and begins again on 30 October
1546 Register ends 10 October
1547 Register begins 9 December 1547
1556 Register begins in August
1558 Register ends 2 November
1566 Burials begin 7 July
1577 Begins 19 April
1581 Ends 8 October
1587 Gap in register 29 July to 7 October
1639 Begins 1 July
1645 No entries in November, February or March
1648 No entries in July: the word 'nothinge' appears instead.
1650 Register mutilated: possibly ten entries missing.

One can overcome these deficiencies to some degree by *interpolation*. If a gap appears in a particular month or months one can take the mean number of entries in the same month or months in the five years on either side, and take this to be as near an approximation as one can get to what should have been registered. There is, of course, the possibility that one is going to be wildly out, but if it is a matter of a month or two, the effect on the series as a whole is likely to be slight. If one comes across an entry like that noted above for July 1648, interpolation is best avoided. I take it that a 'nothinge' entered in the registers indicated, quite literally, that in that month there were no baptisms, marriages or burials.

The tests we have suggested so far can be carried out on any register. One has merely to locate the gaps and then decide whether they are too many for the purposes of the study one has in mind, and, if not, how to accommodate them. With the other tests I am about to turn to, the problems are not so easily dealt with, for in each case carrying out the test depends upon having ancillary information which, in the case of the parish or parishes of your choice, may simply not exist.

The Church year in this period ran from 25 March to 24 March. Since most registers used it, there was an obvious advantage in my doing so. It was also useful because it meant that all the winter months were included in the one year. Burial peaks in any one winter could thus be more easily spotted, than if they were split between two calendar years. The Church year has also been used by the late Professor J. D. Chambers (1957) and so to make comparison with his work easier, the same periodization has been followed here. Since then other writers have used the 'harvest year' (Michaelmas – 29 September – to Michaelmas, or 1 August to 31 July) as well as the calendar year. Eversley in Wrigley (1966 p 31) suggests that what year one chooses is unimportant, except presumably in any particular study embracing a number of parishes, where one should stick to the same one for standardization purposes.

Interpolation is most dangerous in the case of burials, because a gap can easily occur at the time of a major crisis. It is particularly difficult to keep corrections standard, and ideally one would like two versions of each return, one before and one after correction.

Test 3 The first of this category of tests concerns those who were responsible both for entering items in the register and for preserving the registers themselves. By law the vicar was responsible, though in practice the dual task seems to have fallen on curates and church wardens in many cases. Sometimes a register will, in a marginal note, give an indication of what was happening. Here are some examples from the registers (and the transcripts) listed in Tables 1 and 2 above.

Going through the Methley register I counted the following number of entries:

Year	Baptisms	Marriages	Burials
1683	23	6	31
1684	23	9	30
1685	29	8	36
1686	27	4	12
1687	14	3	16
1688	20	4	17

I also noted a marginal comment in the register to the effect that a new parson was inducted in 1687. Could it be that the quite sharp fall in baptisms in that year (and of burials in the previous one) was due to the changeover?

Another example of the same thing comes from the Kirkburton register:

Year	Baptisms	Marriages	Burials
1560	70	15	36
1561	48	15	48
1562	44	19	19
1563	25	3	15
1564	55	10	33

Henry Suthel, the vicar of Kirkburton for fifty-six years, from 1506–1562, died in the latter year. The new vicar also held the living of Methley, 14 miles away as the crow flies. It is possible that here again the changeover had an adverse effect on the registration. Incidentally, in 1564, a fresh handwriting appears in the register, suggesting the end of an interim period.

From 1653 to 1660 registration was taken out of the hands of the clergy and secular registrars were appointed. In very many parishes this led to a deterioration in the system. Of the twenty-two registers in Table 2 as many as nine had at least a one-year gap in the 1650s. In other parishes both the quality of the registration and the coverage increased during this period. In Halifax for example, from 1654 to 58, the age of bride and bridegroom was given in 564 marriages and from 1654 to 57, the occupation of the bridegroom in 422 out of 465 marriages. Frances Anne Collins, the transcriber of the Kirkburton register, noted that from 1653 to 1660 the sworn registrar was one William Hepworth. He was a layman, and she writes (pp 39–40), 'his fitness for the office as a writer is shown by his handwriting, which is clearer and better than any in the Kirkburton registers'.

Sometimes the break in registration caused by the changeover in the registrar, whether civil or secular, was quite dramatic. For instance, on a flyleaf in the Heptonstall register for 1631 is written: 'In the year 1631 the Minister of this place, his wife, his son and the Parish Clerk all died of the plague in August, October and November'. Not surprisingly the totals of baptisms and marriages for that year show a pronounced fall, compared to neighbouring years (see over).

The marriage register in 1631 ends on 8 June; the baptism register on 14 August. The burial register does not show a gap and the number entered in it is higher than for the surrounding years. Nevertheless, here too there may have been under-registration. For the register contains the comment 'theise parsones dead of the plague

Year	Baptisms	Marriages	Burials
1628	110	20	77
1629	81	28	71
1630	109	26	82
1631	48	8	117
1632	114	20	62

or supposed to dy of that disease within the parish of Heptonstall to the number of one hundreth and seven'. Some are said to have been 'buried at home'. Others, one can but surmise, may have been buried in like manner, and not registered.

Whilst the efficiency of any registration system depends a good deal on the conscientiousness of the registrars, one must also keep an eye on the extent of the public's demand for registration. Occasionally one comes upon comments in the registers indicating a very great concern on the part of certain people that they should appear in the register. Note this cry of anguish from the Keighley register:

> February 1590 Richard Holmes the son of Francis Holmes was baptised the second day of this moneth above written and was left unsett [ie in the register] to my greatt harts greife but I pray to the O Lord that I be found in the booke of lyfe. . . .

It is, of course, impossible to generalize from individual statements like that. One can, however, narrow the range of probabilities a little more when it comes to considering the number of those who, for one reason or another, were reluctant to use the services of the Church of England, and to the extent that they avoided using them were not registered.

Test 4 The assumption has been made, up to this point, that the register, or registers, under analysis cover the *entire* population of the area, at least officially, for the *entire* period under examination. That is to say, it is assumed that the parish (or parishes as the case may be) is not reduced in size and that new registers for different parts of the parish are not begun. In fact, with rising populations, many parishes did set up *chapels* and 'daughter' churches within their boundaries and, sometimes, baptisms, marriages and burials performed at them, were recorded in separate registers. Local enquiries of the vicar, library or County Record Office will normally elicit whether or not such registers were kept, from what date and whether or not they are accessible. An alternative starting point is the return printed in Vol III of the *1831 Population Census*. This says what registers were believed to be in existence at that time and gives the date they began.

Naturally the commencement of new registers within existing parishes varies widely from one part of the country to another. In the area covered by the registers listed in Table 2, the number of new registers was probably atypically high. This was because in the sixteenth and seventeenth centuries, not to speak of the eighteenth, the woollen cloth industry was growing rapidly and there are a number of indications that the population was increasing accordingly.

It should be emphasized that the dates given on pp 50-3 and Table 3 refer to the earliest registers known to have existed in 1831. Others could have been started and lost. What is more, it is known that sometimes items were recorded on separate slips of paper, to be entered in the register at some later date. If a parish were between registers, as it were, it is not unlikely that some of these slips were lost before they could be copied into the new register. When one notes what happened to some registers, the misplacing of such odd slips of paper appears even more likely. The smaller the parish or chapel, the fewer the number of entries, the greater the likelihood that such *ad hoc* methods operated. Larger parishes probably had a more efficient system.

See Institute of Heraldic and Genealogical Studies (nd) for maps showing the chapelries, as well as the parishes, specifying for all the date that the registers commence.
See also Steel (1968).

For example, in 1859 a Mr John Nowell transcribed the register of Almondbury parish (near Huddersfield). After completing this task he

Figure 3 Page from a burial register of Simpson, 1763–65. Source: Bucks County Record Office

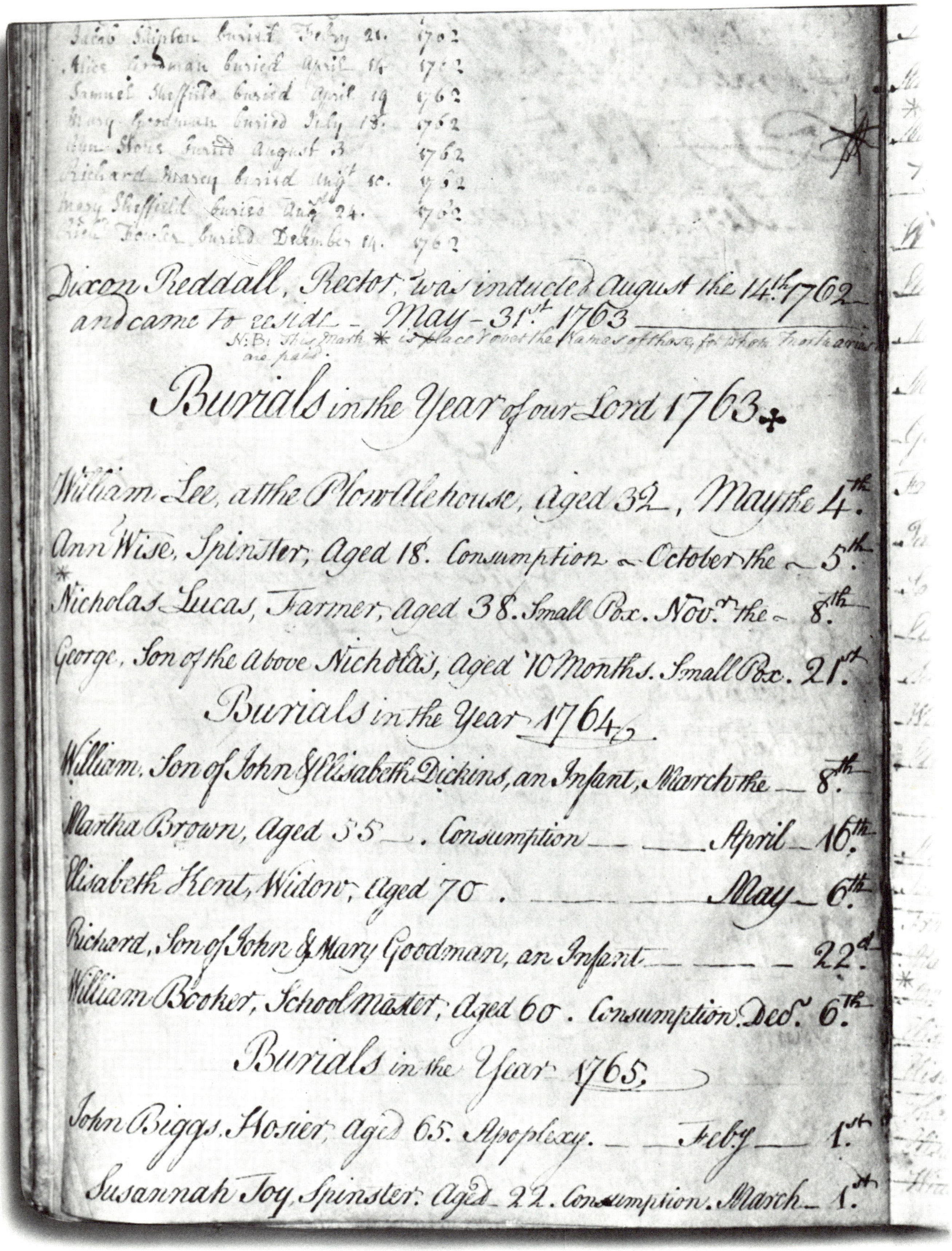

John Simpson buried Feby 20.   1762
Alice Goodman buried April 14.   1762
Samuel Sheffield buried April 19   1762
Mary Goodman buried July 18.   1762
Ann Stores buried August 3   1762
Richard Marey buried Augt 10.   1762
Mary Sheffield buried Aug 24.   1762
Rich Fowler buried December 14.   1762

Dixon Reddall, Rector, was inducted August the 14th 1762 and came to reside – May 31st 1763

N:B: This Mark * is Placed over the Names of those, for whom Mortuaries are paid.

Burials in the Year of our Lord 1763 ✠

William Lee, at the Plowttle house, Aged 32, May the 4th.

Ann Wise, Spinster, Aged 18. Consumption – October the 5th.

Nicholas Lucas, Farmer, Aged 38. Small Pox. Novr the 8th

George, Son of the Above Nicholas, Aged 10 Months. Small Pox. 21st.

Burials in the Year 1764

William, Son of John & Elisabeth Dickins, an Infant, March the 8th.

Martha Brown, Aged 55. Consumption   April 16th.

Elisabeth Kent, Widow, Aged 70.   May 6th.

Richard, Son of John & Mary Goodman, an Infant   22d.

William Booker, School Master, Aged 60. Consumption. Decr 6th.

Burials in the Year 1765.

John Biggs. Hosier, Aged 65. Apoplexy.   Feby 1st.

Susannah Joy, Spinster. Aged 22. Consumption. March 1st.

Table 3 Dates and places at which registers of baptisms, marriages and burials were begun in parts of twenty-two Yorkshire parishes up to 1700

Parish	Chapelry	Register commenced
Birstall	Tong	1550
Bradford	Haworth	1645
	Thornton	1678
	Wibsey	1640
Halifax	Elland	1559
	Heptonstall	1593
	Cross Stone	1640
	Todmorden	1666
	Ripponden	1684
	Rastrick	1614
	Luddenden	1653
	Illingworth	1695
	Sowerby	1643
Huddersfield	Slaithwaite	1684
	Armley	1665
Leeds	Hunslet	1686
Wakefield	Horbury	1598

Source: Population Census 1831.

The setting up of a chapel subordinate to a church did not necessarily mean that a new register was begun. Nor did it follow that such a chapel performed the full range of rites. For example, we learn from a note at the end of the Kirkburton register entries for 1695 that it was 'a true register of all baptisms, marriages and burials in the church and churchyard of Kirkburton and of *all the baptisms* in the chappell of Holmfirth'. A similar note appeared after the 1699 register entries, though note the cautionary last phrase 'a true register of all baptisms, burials and marriages which have happened in the parish church of Kirkburton and in the chappell of Holmfirth *to our best knowledge*'.

One of the problems with chapels within a parish is knowing when they were, and when they were not, supposed to register whatever rites they performed, in the register of the mother church. So far as Halifax (pp 51-3) is concerned, it seems that the chapelries of Heptonstall and Elland probably kept registers from 1538–58 and 1538–93 respectively, but that the earlier volumes have not survived. Certainly there is no reduction in the number of entries in the Halifax register at the time the registers we do have for Heptonstall and Elland begin.[1] In the course of the seventeenth century other chapels were opened in Halifax and appear to have started their own registers (Table 3). Sometimes these were under Elland or Heptonstall and, it appears, should have reported whatever baptisms etc they performed to these more ancient chapels. Thus, to take an example, the chapel of Cross Stone has a register (or had in 1831) dating from 1640. Yet in the Heptonstall register for 1685, at the end of the marriage entries, there is a letter from the then Archbishop of York complaining that the 'curate or chappell wardens of the Chappell of Crosstone have carelessly and wilfully omitted and neglected to make returns of the names of all such persons as have been married baptised and buried as aforesaid to the curate and clerke of

noted: 'Thus ends the labour of reading and collecting these ancient papers, all tattered, torn and mutilated, covered with dirt, defaced and the writing nearly in many cases illegible and the contractions in the words made after a manner now quite obsolete . . . the mutilated register comprised in about 350 detached leaves which evidently once formed a book – the back gone and the margins frittered away by time, bad usage or both. They have been tramped under feet of careless churchwardens, soiled perhaps in their imputed orgies and certainly the succession of vicars have "set no store upon them" or their mutilation at least would have been prevented.' Referring to another register Nowell writes: 'I have seen the entries of half a century cut away in shreds from a register by a parish clerk to subserve the purposes of his trade as a tailor'. (The transcript by Nowell is in the church chest of Almondbury Parish Church.) The editor of the Richmond (Surrey) parish register transcript writes in a similar vein: '. . . [Richmond's] parish clerks were for about two centuries members of one family who passed on, each generation to the next, a tradition of slovenliness and neglect in regard to their duty. The "method" adopted during the whole of the period mentioned would seem to have been to compile the Register at intervals of many years from such memoranda and notes as had not been mislaid or lost. There are some hundreds of instances in which Christian names or surnames or both are unrecorded . . .'
(J. Chancellor C. Smith 1903, Preface.)

---

1 The transcriber of the Halifax register notes in his introduction (Crossley 1910 pp iii–iv) that 'the ancient parish of Halifax covered a wide area, and in addition to the mother church was served by two chapels, Elland and Heptonstall, which though dependent upon it had certain parochial rights and *registers of their own*' [my italics]. He then lists separately the townships under the mother church and the two chapels and remarks that other pre-Reformation chapels were gradually resuscitated but if weddings, baptisms and burials took place there the events were noted in the Halifax register until 1812.

Heptonstall'. He goes on to point out that this has meant a financial loss to the said curate and clerke as the appropriate fees had not been handed over. It does not follow, of course, that because baptisms etc should have been returned to Heptonstall, they were supposed to be registered there too. We have already noted that Cross Stone was under Heptonstall, not Halifax: a chapel under the jurisdiction, apparently, of another chapel. This same phenomenon was repeated in the case of the chapel of Ripponden, which reported to Elland. From 1687, the Elland register lists the entries from Ripponden separately, suggesting that in this case there was a dual registration, for Ripponden appears to have its own register from 1684 (Table 3).

Leeds Parish Church registration seems to have suffered increasingly, from the 1630s to the end of the seventeenth century, as a result of baptisms and marriages being conducted in chapels and private houses, within the parish, which were not reported to the mother church. Notes complaining of this appear again and again. This one made at the end of the December 1631 entries is typical: 'There were divers children for these 2 or 3 yeares last past, baptized at severall chappels within this Parish whose names were not made knowne to us and therfore if you find them not registered according to your expectation, blame not the clarke'.

The importance of these developments for the use of parish registers for demographic analysis is twofold. First it may lead one to believe erroneously that a decline in the number of entries in a parish register, or even a slowing down in the rate of increase of such entries, is due to demographic changes, when it may be a product of jurisdictional ones. And, of course, it may happen that the entries of baptisms, marriages and burials are affected differentially. It seems more likely, for instance, that baptisms failed to be recorded, even though burials were, as the chapelries were perhaps less likely to have their own burial grounds, at least in the sixteenth and seventeenth centuries. Certainly I would imagine that some part at least of the excess of burials over baptisms recorded in the Leeds parish register, in all but four of the years 1660–99, was due to this cause. The second important matter raised by this kind of situation concerns the decision whether or not to analyse a particular register. Unfortunately, it seems likely that the bigger parishes, whose registers we believe offer the best opportunities for demographic analysis for reasons given above, are likely to be just the ones which may suffer from the development of chapels, either nonconformist or Anglican, with the consequent problems we have outlined. One should, therefore, make as sure as possible, in any *particular* case, that one understands what is happening at any *particular* time to the church–chapel relationship so far as the registration of baptisms, marriages and burials is concerned.

Test 5 One of the reasons commonly put forward for under-registration is that nonconformists boycotted Church of England services, particularly baptisms. After checking on the arrival and departure dates of incumbents (Test 3), it is then worthwhile finding out what one can of the existence of nonconformity in a parish. Much attention has been paid to this, so far as the late eighteenth and early nineteenth century registers are concerned (see Krause 1963). It is possible that earlier registers were similarly affected. For instance, in the registers listed above (Table 2), notes to the effect that nonconformists are not entering their baptisms, marriages and burials in the Church of England parish registers are particularly noticeable after 1660. One example is a note in the Leeds baptism register for 31 January 1694 which reads, 'Mr Mawde, curat at the Old Church hath baptised children in many men's houses, and neither he nor ye parents acquainted me therewith, and likewise many children att the severall Chappels, and as for Presbiterian children not one ingrost because of their obstinacy and let others blame them that are blameworthy'.

One way in which some indication of the extent of nonconformity (though not necessarily of its impact on the registration system) can be obtained from the various

Table 4 Batley: religious allegiance of 819 families

	The Church	Presbyterians	Anabaptists	Independents	Quakers	Moravians	Methodists
In the Township of:							
Batley	224		1	51	1		49
Morley	72	129	4	1		6	47
Gildersome	65	6	60		11	1	23
Churwell	40	22	1		1		4
	401	157	66	52	13	7	123

Source: Archbishop Drummond's Visitation Returns (1764). Cited in Stephens (1971) p 31.

ecclesiastical censuses is noted in Appendix 1. For example, Archbishop Herring's Visitation Return made in 1743 includes the parishes listed in Table 2. For each of them it gives the number of families in the parish and the number of dissenting families (indicating of what kind) and also states whether the Church of England incumbent resided in the parish or not. This latter fact is useful for Test 3. It appears that about ten per cent of families in the area were dissenters though this varied from nil in Thornhill ('not a dissenter of any sort in ye parish' according to the informant) to over a third (233 out of 622) in Batley. At first sight the difference is somewhat startling, especially as Batley was only about four miles from Thornhill. Two additional pieces of information suggest that at least so far as the Batley figures are concerned they may not be wholly spurious. One is the report that the Church of England chapel in Morley (a township in Batley Parish) was taken over by the Presbyterians during the Civil War and never restored to the Church. Secondly, Archbishop Drummond's Visitation Return of 1764 for the parish of Batley is broadly in line with the 1743 return. Furthermore, the detail of the return suggests it was more than mere guesswork on the part of the informant. The figures given in Table 4 were in answer to the questions: 'What number of families have you in your Parish? Of these, how many are dissenters? And of what sort of denomination are they?'

It does not, of course, follow that because a parish has dissenting families within it, registration of baptisms, marriages and burials by the Church of England was bound to be less than complete. The dissenters could, after all, accept these rites. Sometimes one gets direct evidence of this. For example in the same Visitation Return (Archbishop Drummond's) as provided the information for Table 4 above, the vicar of Birstall remarked 'I cannot tell how many [families] are Dissenters as most of them bring their children to be christened at the Church'. Despite this, however, one must I think assume that, other things being equal, the registers of parishes with a high proportion of dissenters would be less complete than those with a small one. It is, therefore, worthwhile searching local histories (particularly the volumes of the *Victoria County History*) for evidence of dissenting congregations.

Quite apart from what might be termed ideological objections to accepting the rites of the Church of England, it is not unlikely that others objected to their cost and inconvenience. Take the latter point first. If the parish church was five or six miles from one's home, taking a child for baptism could be quite a chore, no matter how committed one was to the Church of England. If the weather was bad, the roads difficult, or if one was sick (a not unlikely occurrence just after childbirth), such a journey might well be delayed. Sometimes, too, baptisms were delayed because a custom had developed of conducting them at special times of the year, partly so that one could get one's friends together perhaps, and make it more than just a private event (Mills 1973). Whatever the cause of the delay, the effect was to increase the number of children who were buried *unbaptized* and, therefore, unentered in the baptism registers. The registers were, it should always be remembered, registers of baptisms, not of births (except in some cases during the period of secular registration from 1653 to 60).

In addition to the *Victoria County History*, a useful source is the list of non-parochial registers published by the Registrar General in 1859. Also, in Dr Williams's Library in London, there are two lists of dissenting congregations at two dates – 1715 and 1772. The only realistic test of whether dissenters were registered is to take one of the early registers or a list of those deposited by the church for absenting themselves from communion, and see exactly how many of them turn up in the Anglican registers. (See Arkell in *Local Population Studies*, 9, for an example of such a study.)

Test 6 We now need to search the register for any indication that baptisms were delayed. Chambers (1966 p 19) suggests that 'in the marsh parishes of Lincolnshire, for instance, where the Church may be five miles from the outlying farms, the failure to baptize the newly born was a much more common occurrence than to bury the dead, and this was reflected in the greater frequency with which burials outstripped baptisms'. Here again the quasi-censuses listed in Appendix 1 may give some indication of the settlement pattern within a parish. Sometimes a burial register will indicate whether a child is unbaptized or not. One example of this occurs in the Rothwell register. There, from 1634 to 38, some 135 out of 1,231 entries in the burial register bear the description 'infants not baptized'. This figure represents eleven per cent of the total registered burials and ten per cent of the total registered baptisms. Among the registers listed in Table 2 one notes the appearance of unbaptized children in the burial registers of Kirkburton, Dewsbury, Horbury, Thornhill, Mirfield and Keighley as well as Rothwell. The Kirkburton registers are interesting in this connection because they contain large numbers of burials of so-called 'chrisom' children. One use of the term is to describe a child buried within one month of birth. The actual form of the entry in the Kirkburton register, however, suggests it referred to *unbaptized* children. For example, the following two entries appeared next to each other:

January 28 1698:   'Martha daughter of William Littlewood of Scholes, a twin, baptized the 28th day'.

January 28 1698:   'A crisom child of the said William Lockwood, another twin, buried the 28th day'.

An earlier entry reads:

January 1655–6:   'A crisom child of George Killner borne and buried the first day'.

If no direct indication is given of the baptismal status of persons appearing in the burial register, one should keep an eye open for entries like this: 'An infant of John Smith buried . . .' This could mean unbaptized, though it may mean no more than that the person keeping the register had forgotten the name.

It was once supposed that the burial registers reflected the number of deaths more accurately than baptismal registers did the number of births, because disposing of a body was more difficult than neglecting to baptize one. Work by Krause (1958), however, has shown that many private burial grounds existed, particularly in London and the industrialized areas of the North. He does not, however, think that such burial grounds existed on any scale elsewhere, or outside London, much before the last decade of the eighteenth century.

The presumed reason for the existence of these private burial grounds is that burial there was cheaper than in those belonging to the Church of England. Charges varied even within the Church, and this it was alleged led to some people choosing the cheaper ones, even if it meant going out of their home parish. Information on these matters for the early nineteenth century can be obtained from two large folio manuscript volumes in the British Museum (BM Additional Manuscripts 6896 and 6897). One illustration will serve to show the type of entry. It refers to a part of Birstall, one of the parishes in Table 2. The date is 1811.

Cleckheaton: The number of baptisms and burials is unknown. The marriages take place at Birstall, Cleckheaton being a Chapel of Ease under it. At one small village, Lower Wike, in this Chapelry there is a chapel and seminary of United Bretheren. Upper Wike is situated near Wibsey Chapel, which is in the parish of Bradford, to which chapel more, I suppose, are taken than to Cleckheaton Chapel; the dues are also less, our dues being double, one half is passed to Birstall, namely 10d each baptism and 10d each burial.

When considering the inadequacy of registration, one should bear in mind that it affected different events (ie baptisms, marriages and burials) at different times.

The impact of dissent on baptismal registers was probably increasing in the mid-seventeenth century and in the second half of the eighteenth century. The impact of the inconvenience of travelling long distances to the church, which in rural parishes may have been constant, probably increased in industrializing areas in the north and in Wales during the late eighteenth and early nineteenth centuries. This was because new areas were settled (eg around coal mines and water-driven spinning mills) which were not well served by churches built in earlier centuries for different settlement patterns, though some industrialists, like Richard Arkwright, built churches or chapels. So, too, the patronage of private (ie non Church of England) burial grounds was probably greater in industrializing areas in the late eighteenth and early nineteenth centuries than at any other time.

So far as marriages are concerned one can distinguish between the period prior to 1753 and the period after it. In that year Hardwicke's Marriage Act was passed. This made it virtually impossible to contract a valid marriage unless it were carried out in a church according to an Anglican ceremony. The act was passed because it was alleged that many clandestine marriages were being contracted which, of course, was

Figure 4 Extract from an Act of Parliament aimed at improving the registering of births, marriages and burials, 1695.

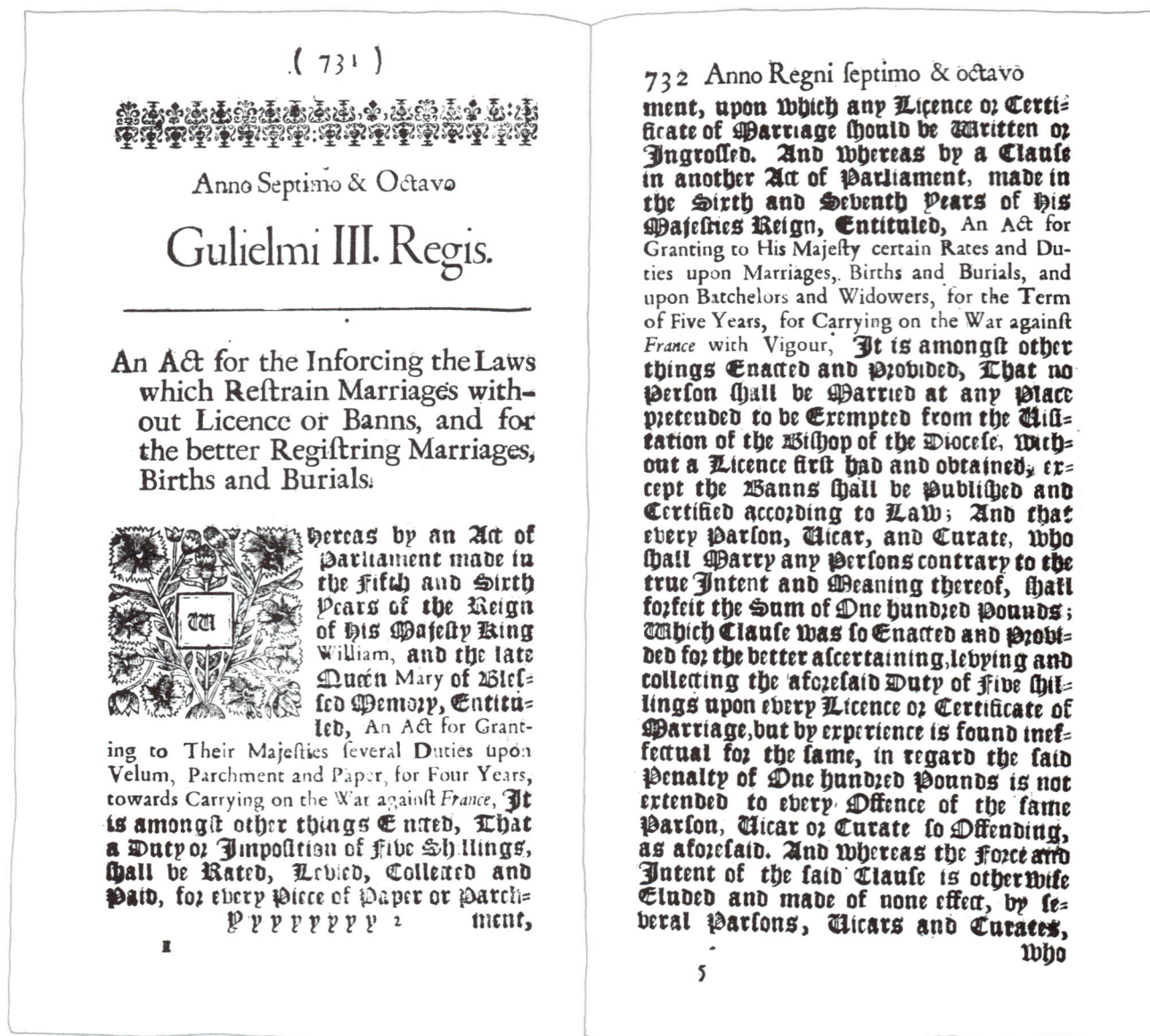

(731)

Anno Septimo & Octavo

Gulielmi III. Regis.

An Act for the Inforcing the Laws which Restrain Marriages without Licence or Banns, and for the better Registring Marriages, Births and Burials.

Whereas by an Act of Parliament made in the Fifth and Sixth Years of the Reign of His Majesty King William, and the late Queen Mary of Blessed Memory, Entituled, An Act for Granting to Their Majesties several Duties upon Velum, Parchment and Paper, for Four Years, towards Carrying on the War against *France*, It is amongst other things Enacted, That a Duty or Imposition of Five Shillings, shall be Rated, Levied, Collected and Paid, for every Piece of Paper or Parchment,

Pppppppp 2

732 Anno Regni septimo & octavo ment, upon which any Licence or Certificate of Marriage should be Written or Ingrossed. And whereas by a Clause in another Act of Parliament, made in the Sixth and Seventh Years of His Majesties Reign, Entituled, An Act for Granting to His Majesty certain Rates and Duties upon Marriages, Births and Burials, and upon Batchelors and Widowers, for the Term of Five Years, for Carrying on the War against *France* with Vigour, It is amongst other things Enacted and Provided, That no Person shall be Married at any Place pretended to be Exempted from the Visitation of the Bishop of the Diocese, without a Licence first had and obtained, except the Banns shall be Published and Certified according to Law; And that every Parson, Vicar, and Curate, who shall Marry any Persons contrary to the true Intent and Meaning thereof, shall forfeit the Sum of One hundred Pounds; Which Clause was so Enacted and Provided for the better ascertaining, levying and collecting the aforesaid Duty of Five Shillings upon every Licence or Certificate of Marriage, but by experience is found ineffectual for the same, in regard the said Penalty of One hundred Pounds is not extended to every Offence of the same Parson, Vicar or Curate so Offending, as aforesaid. And whereas the Force and Intent of the said Clause is otherwise Eluded and made of none effect, by several Parsons, Vicars and Curates, who

5

a source both of scandal and of loss of income for the Church. There is certainly evidence of these marriages. Sometimes it is explicit and can be quantified. Wrigley, for instance, (1973) has analysed a marriage register from the Gloucestershire parish of Tetbury. Here the vicar differentiated between marriages which were contracted in his parish according to the proper form and those that were not. Of the sixty-eight marriages occurring there in the years 1696–9, some thirty-three were irregular and of these, fourteen were termed 'clandestine' (Wrigley 1973 p 16). Though it is rare to find such direct evidence, a test can be carried out which would indicate under-registration of marriages. This consists of totalling the number of baptisms in, say, a five-year period and dividing it by the number of marriages in the same period, or in the immediately preceding five years. The ratio should be about 1:4 or 1:5. If it is as high as 1:7 or 1:8 (in other words if there are eight baptisms for every marriage) then the registration of marriages is almost certain to be defective. The reason for this is that to have a ratio as high as 1:7 or 1:8 would mean a rate of marital fertility far higher than any other evidence we have would suggest was possible.

4 Exercises in parish register demography

Before turning to some specific exercises let me make two introductory points. The first of these concerns the registers on which the exercises are to be done. In the previous section I have suggested a number of tests to be carried out before demographic analysis begins. The tests are severe ones, deliberately so. For although much useful work can and has been done on registers which would not have passed all the tests, exposing a register to them puts the researcher into that cautious frame of mind so necessary for work of this kind.

The second point worth reiterating here concerns the aim of the exercises. For the purposes of this block we have limited these to elucidating the demographic experience of pre-industrial and early industrial societies, as defined in Unit 5. Furthermore within this area of interest we are primarily concerned with the relationships between economic change and population change. Admittedly this encompasses a great deal. Nevertheless, having such a framework is an important first step for exercises in Applied Historical Studies, for it helps us structure the hypotheses to be tested and to relate our findings to one another. Hopefully we shall end up with a coherent corpus of knowledge, rather than a collection of disparate findings.

In discussing the various exercises I shall adopt the strategy for research in Applied Historical Studies that I sketched out in Unit 1.

Exercise 2 TOPIC OF INTEREST The determinants of the age at marriage in pre-industrial and industrializing societies.

ARTICULATE PROBLEM Interest in the age at marriage takes us back to Malthus's preoccupation with the 'positive' and 'preventive' checks to population growth. Ever since Malthus, age at marriage has been considered an important regulator of fertility: the earlier the age at marriage, the longer the time available for procreation, and the greater the number of births. Furthermore, again following Malthus, the most important cause of fluctuations in the age at marriage is said to have been the extent and nature of economic opportunity.

If you pause for a moment and reflect on the last three sentences, a number of questions may occur to you, concerning the validity of the various assumptions underlying them. I shall express my queries in the form of hypotheses which can be tested.

FORMULATE HYPOTHESES

Hypothesis 1: Age at marriage was not an important regulator of fertility because changes in it were slight.

Hypothesis 2: Age at marriage was not an important regulator of fertility because differences in the age at marriage of men did not correspond with differences in the age at marriage of women. Since it is the length of time a woman is exposed to the possibility of having children that determines the fertility of a marriage, the fertility period of women being shorter than that of men, the age at marriage of men is not particularly important. So differences in the age at marriage of men associated with differences in employment and earnings need *not* affect fertility levels.

Hypothesis 3: Age at marriage was not necessarily an important determinant of fertility because of the practice of birth control within marriage.

Hypothesis 4: A rise in the age at marriage did not mean a fall in fertility because its effect was countered by a rise in illegitimate births and in pre-marital conceptions.

DEVISE TESTS

Hypothesis 1: Find ages at marriage of pre-industrial and industrializing populations at different times.

Hypothesis 2: Find ages at marriage of men and women classified according to the occupation of the men.

Hypothesis 3: To test for the practice of birth control within marriage, measure the length of the 'mean interval between the penultimate and last births. A marked rise in this interval is typical of a community beginning to practice family limitation. It rises in these circumstances, because even after reaching an intended final family size additions are nevertheless occasionally made, either from accident (failure of whatever system of restriction is in use), from a reversal of an earlier decision not to increase family size, or from a desire to replace a child which has died' (Wrigley 1966 p 173).

Hypothesis 4: Find a series of births which can be classified, first by whether the births are legitimate or illegitimate, and then, for legitimate births, according to the date of the marriage which produced them.

COLLECT DATA

Hypothesis 1: Ages at marriage are sometimes given in parish registers and sometimes in registers of people married by licence. They may also be obtained from some registers using the *reconstitution of families* technique. For an account of this see below.

Hypothesis 2: Ages of bridegroom and bride, together with the occupation (at marriage) of the former, are sometimes given in parish registers and sometimes in registers of people married by licence.

Hypothesis 3: To link the date at which a woman married with the date of birth of *each* of her children is possible, if the entries of marriages and baptisms in a parish register are detailed and complete. This is relatively rare with English parish registers. If the registers are good enough, the *reconstitution of families* technique may be used.

Hypothesis 4: Some registers give baptisms classified according to whether they are legitimate or illegitimate. Some registers are so complete that one can unequivocally link the date of baptism of a child with the date of marriage of its mother.

TESTS

In this section I shall report on a number of studies that have been carried out, each of which provides a test of the hypotheses under discussion.

Test of Hypothesis 1: There are several ways of getting information relating to age at marriage. Four main sources will be examined here.

Some parish registers give the ages of bride and bridegroom. This is unusual, however, especially in the sixteenth and seventeenth centuries. Of the twenty-two, registers listed in Table 2 above, only one gave ages at marriage in the period up to 1700. This was the Halifax register during the years of civil registration 1654–8. Ages at marriage appear more frequently in late eighteenth- and early nineteenth-century registers. Even when ages are given, however, their value might be flawed by two factors. The first of these arises from the fact that many people in pre-literate or semi-literate societies were not too sure of their age. When asked to give it they commonly chose an even number, especially one ending with a nought. This lack of precision also meant that if asked their age on two separate occasions people were likely to give two different answers. For example in a study Carol Pearce and I did on the Kent town of Ashford as late as the years 1840–70, we discovered wide variations in age reporting. Of the 1,741 individuals enumerated both at the 1851 census and that of 1861, only 58.9 per cent gave ages that were the expected ten years apart. Some 26.2 per cent gave ages with a difference of nine to eleven years between them. Over one eighth of the population (14.9 per cent) gave their age in 1861 as being less than nine or more than eleven years greater than what they had said it was in 1851. There is little one can do about such discrepancies. They are a warning, however, against taking too seriously relatively small changes in age at marriage, especially if these are derived from a small number of observations.

SAQ 2 In view of my comments about age reporting, what strikes you about Table 5 ?

Table 5 Age of bridegrooms and brides married at Halifax Parish Church, 1654–8

Age	Bridegrooms	Brides[1]
18	2	5 (2)
19	1	8 (4)
20	16	25 (14)
21	37	56 (38)
22	46	58 (31)
23	42	41 (21)
24	52	36 (16)
25	28	34 (15)
26	42	36 (22)
27	19	17 (9)
28	29	34 (20)
29	14	9 (3)
30	43	39 (16)
31	6	5 (—)
32	13	12 (6)
33	10	9 (4)
34	13	11 (5)
35	5	7 (2)
36	16	5 (2)
37	6	3 (—)
38	8	7 (6)
39	1	2 (1)
40	21	25 (14)
41	6	1 (—)
42	3	12 (4)
43	1	9 (3)
44	4	6 (3)
45+	80	52 (21)
Total	564	564 (282)

1 The figures in brackets indicate the women said to be spinsters. In view of the comparatively small number of these relative to the total number of brides, one must assume that many not so designated were so in fact.

Source: Halifax Parish Church Registers.

The second problem with the age at marriage figures arises if the previous marital status of the bride and bridegroom is not given. For marriages can, of course, take place between previously unmarried couples (bachelor–spinster marriages); between a bachelor and a widow; a widower and a spinster; and a widow and widower. The most common type of marriage seems to have been between a bachelor and a spinster and in discussing the impact of economic opportunity on marriage age, it is this type one usually thinks of. In the pre-industrial period, with mortality higher than today, marriages of the other three types were not uncommon. Certainly twenty per cent of all marriages were likely to involve at least one partner who had been married previously. Differences, then, in the mean age at marriage over time, or between different occupational groups at any particular time, might either reflect differences in the proportion of first to second marriages or differences in the age at first marriage, or a combination of the two. Let me give an example.

This table shows the number and proportions marrying under twenty-one years of age in Halifax in the period 1654–8, 1861 and 1871.

	1654–8	1861	1871
Males	3.4% (19/564)	8.4% (110/1292)	11.9% (179/1494)
Females	6.7% (38/564)	20.9% (270/1292)	24.3% (365/1494)

Sources: For 1654–8, Halifax Parish Register: for 1861, *Twenty-Fourth Annual Report of Registrar General of Births, Deaths and Marriages*, London 1863 p 20; for 1871, *Thirty-Fourth Annual Report of Registrar General of Births, Deaths Marriages*, London 1873 p 20.

At first glance the table suggests quite a sharp fall in the age at *first* marriage of both men and women between the mid-seventeenth and late-nineteenth centuries. (One assumes here that the proportions marrying under twenty-one years are a good indicator of this.) But, for the reasons given above, it could be that what has happened is a change in the proportion of first to second marriages over the period.

Ideally one would wish for a series of registers, randomly distributed across the country, and giving age at marriage together with marital status at marriage, from the mid-sixteenth to the mid-nineteenth centuries. This we do not have and never will have. We must, therefore, try to piece together the scattered fragments of information we can glean from isolated registers. It is very possible, for instance, that some people taking this course may discover registers with a longer and more detailed coverage of age and status at marriage than I found. An alternative strategy is to use the *reconstitution of families* technique to derive age and status at marriage by bringing together the various entries in the registers (ie baptisms, marriages and burials).

It must be emphasized from the beginning that this is not a technique which students of *Historical data and the social sciences* can employ; at least not within the framework of the course. The reason for this is that it is incredibly time-consuming. Wrigley, the pioneer of the technique in this country (see Wrigley 1966, 1966A, 1972 and 1972A) estimates that to 'reconstitute' all the families in a parish, averaging 100 entries in the register a year, for a period of three centuries would take some 1,500 hours!

The reconstitution of families was first carried out in France by Louis Henry (1956; with Gautier 1958 and with Fleury 1965). The technique is essentially simple, at least in conception. Imagine a community which for, say, 300 years faithfully baptizes all its children, solemnizes all its marriages in the parish church, buries all its dead in the churchyard. Imagine too that a succession of vicars and their church wardens record, accurately, each one of these events. Finally, imagine that during the 300 years, the community was a closed one, no one coming into it and no one leaving it. In such a community, everyone would appear in the parish register at least twice;

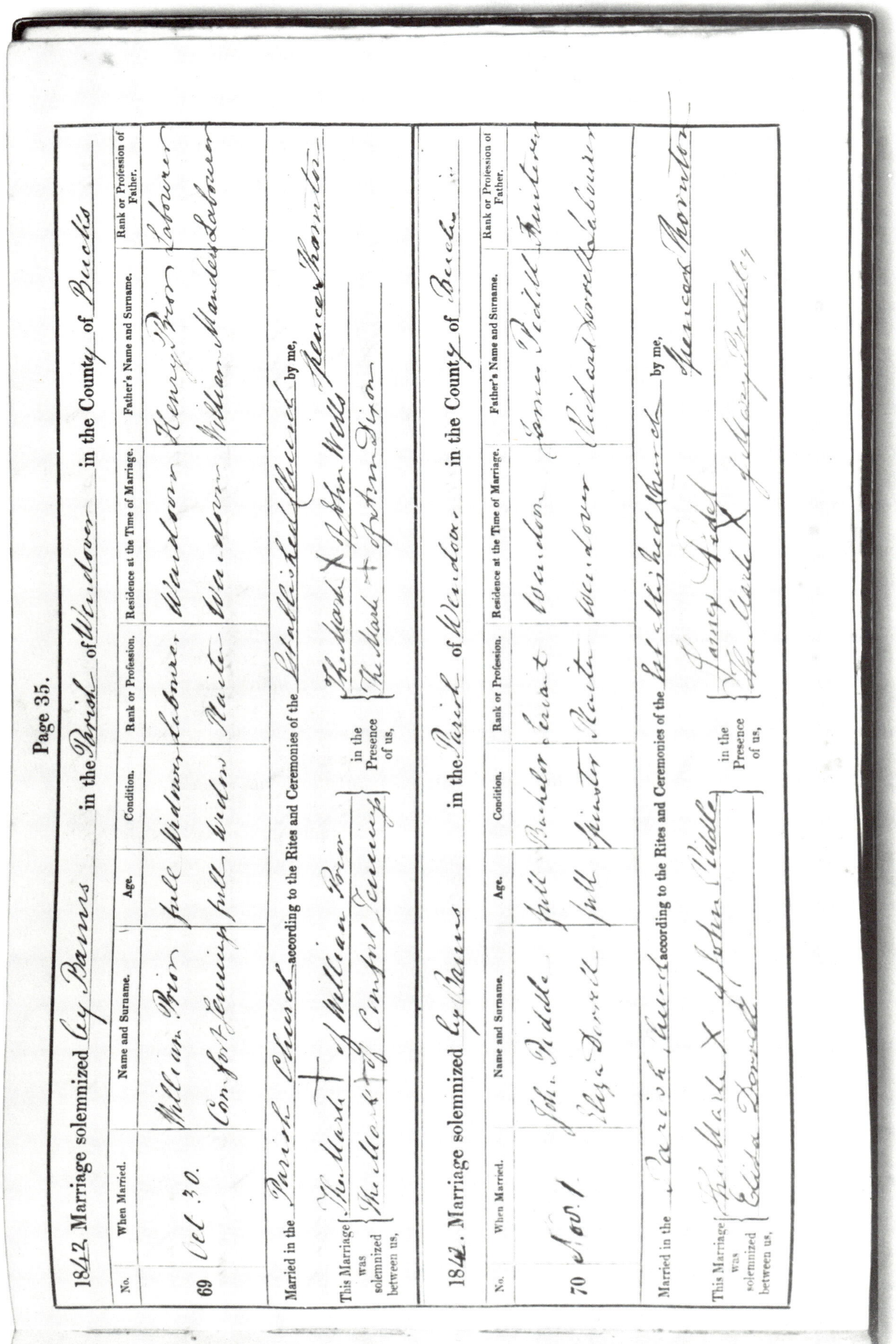

Page 35.

1842. Marriage solemnized by Banns in the Parish of Wendover in the County of Bucks

No.	When Married.	Name and Surname.	Age.	Condition.	Rank or Profession.	Residence at the Time of Marriage.	Father's Name and Surname.	Rank or Profession of Father.
69	Oct 30.	William Prior	full	Widower	Labourer	Wendover	Henry Prior	Labourer
		Comfort Jennings	full	Widow	Plaiter	Wendover	William Saunders	Labourer

Married in the Parish Church according to the Rites and Ceremonies of the Established Church by me, Spencer Thornton

This Marriage was solemnized between us, The Mark + of William Prior, The Mark + of Comfort Jennings; in the Presence of us, The Mark X of John Wells, The Mark + of John Dixon

1842. Marriage solemnized by Banns in the Parish of Wendover in the County of Bucks

No.	When Married.	Name and Surname.	Age.	Condition.	Rank or Profession.	Residence at the Time of Marriage.	Father's Name and Surname.	Rank or Profession of Father.
70	Nov 1	John Piddle	full	Bachelor	Servant	Wendover	James Piddle	Knitter
		Eliza Dorrell	full	Spinster	Plaiter	Wendover	Richard Dorrell	Labourer

Married in the Parish Church according to the Rites and Ceremonies of the Established Church by me, Spencer Thornton

This Marriage was solemnized between us, The Mark X of John Piddle, The Mark X of Eliza Dorrell; in the Presence of us, James Fidel, The Mark X of Mary Buckley

Figure 5 Page from a marriage register of Wendover, 1842. Source: Bucks County Record Office

on being baptized and on being buried. Most people, however, would appear on a number of occasions; as a bride or bridegroom, as parents baptizing their children, burying them or witnessing their marriages. To find a person's age at marriage in such a community, given such data, involves linking up the entries in the baptism and marriage registers. The difference between the two dates (assuming baptism took place shortly after birth which is not always the case; see Mills 1973), would be the age at marriage of the individual. It follows from this that one can also calculate age at death; the age of a mother at the birth of each of her children; the number of second marriages, illegitimate births, pre-marital conceptions, etc, etc. From this information one can go on to calculate specific rates, because one can associate particular people with the particular events they are responsible for, rather than crude rates where one has to associate these events with a larger population. For the distinction between crude and specific rates see the Appendix in Unit 5.

In sketching the essentials of the reconstitution of families technique, I have stressed its possibilities. The problems involved in making it a reality are, however, formidable. In Appendix 4 are reproduced the five forms designed by the Cambridge Group for the History of Population and Social Structure. Each has to be completed before any analysis can begin. First, one completes the form for each baptism; then for each burial; then for each marriage (two forms here, one for the wife and one for the husband) and finally after sorting the forms into numerous piles, one transfers all the accumulated information on to the Family Reconstitution Form. Quite apart from the effort involved in filling out each of these forms and then repeatedly shuffling them into different piles (eg all the baptisms of the children of one particular couple; all the burials; all the marriages), one has to tussle with the problem of identifying accurately each individual (especially difficult in Wales and the Scottish highlands with their plethora of common names!) and his links with other individuals. Experience so far suggests that only a few registers in England give sufficient details over a long enough period (Wrigley suggests a century is the minimum) to make a reconstitution exercise viable. And then, of course, few parishes in pre-industrial England were closed communities. Many people left; many arrived. This again reduces the effectiveness of the technique.

In spite of these difficulties a number of full scale reconstitution studies have been completed. Of these the most famous is that of Wrigley on the small Devonshire parish of Colyton (1966, 1966A, 1972, 1972A). Table 6 comes from one of his reports on that work.

Table 6 Age at first marriage in Colyton, Devon
1560–1837

Period	Number[1]	Mean	Median	Mode[2]
		Men		
1560–1646	258	27.2	25.8	23.0
1647–1719	109	27.7	26.4	23.8
1720–1769	90	25.7	25.1	23.9
1770–1837	219	26.9	25.8	24.4
		Women		
1560–1646	371	27.0	25.9	23.7
1647–1719	136	29.6	27.5	23.3
1720–1769	104	26.8	25.7	23.5
1770–1837	275	25.1	24.0	21.8

1 The total number of marriages in the four periods were 854, 379, 424 and 888 respectively.

2 The mode was calculated here from the mean and the median using Tippett's formula, Mean — Mode = 3 (Mean — Median). See L. H. C. Tippett (1952) *The Methods of Statistics*, Wiley, New York, 4th revised edition, p 35.

Source: Wrigley (1966); reprinted in Drake (1969) p 163.

A brief perusal of Table 6 suggests that the mean age at first marriage did fluctuate from two to five years over this period, though the median and mode show less variability. (For a discussion on which measure to use, in this particular context, see Floud 1973 pp 82–4).

Both this evidence and that provided by the parish registers (1654–8) and civil registers (1861 and 1871) of Halifax given above, suggest that our Hypothesis 1 is not correct. Note that Wrigley's evidence is 'harder' than that provided by the Halifax parish register, because his data are unambiguously of first marriages (ie bachelors to spinsters).

A second source of material which enables us to test Hypothesis 1 is provided by collections of *marriage allegations*, *bonds* and *licences*.

> When a couple wished to be married by licence, instead of by banns, the groom made an 'allegation', that is a statement that there was no impediment to the marriage. The allegation gave the names and ages (not always in precise terms) of the couple and the occupation of the groom. The bond was a surety for there being no impediment to the marriage. The allegations and bonds are usually to be found in Diocesan Registries. The licences were, of course, issued to the couples. (Bradley 1971 p 64)

These documents have been used to show that between the early sixteenth and the mid-nineteenth centuries there was little change in the mean age at first marriage of women. Razzell's findings to this effect appear in Table 7.

Table 7 The age at marriage of spinsters, 1615–1841

Period	Region	Mean age at marriage	Number in sample
1615–21	Wiltshire, Berkshire, Hampshire[1] and Dorset	24.6	280
1662–1714	Yorkshire[2]	23.76	7,242
1701–36	Nottinghamshire[3]	24.5	865
1741–5	Surrey[4]	24.9	333
1749–70	Nottinghamshire[3]	23.9	700
1796–9	Sussex[5]	24.1	275
1839–41	England and Wales[6]	24.3	14,311

1 Nevill, E. (ed) *Marriage Licences of Salisbury, 1615–1682.*
2 Drake, M. (1962) 'An elementary exercise in parish register demography' *The Economic History Review*, 2nd series, Vol. XIV p 444.
3 Blagg, T. M. and Wadsworth, F. A. (eds) 'Nottinghamshire marriage licences', *The Index Library*, British Record Society.
4 Bax, A. R. (ed) (1907) *Allegation for Marriage Licences Issued by the Commissary Court of Surrey, 1673–1770*, Norwich.
5 Macleod, D. (ed) (1929) 'Sussex marriage licences, 1775–1800', *Sussex Record Society*, Vol. XXXV.
6 *Fourth Annual Report of the Registrar General* (1842), p 10.

Source: Razzell (1965); reprinted in Drake (1969) p 132.

The figures in Table 7 lend support to Hypothesis 1. In comparing the ages at marriage contained in the marriage licences issued in many different parts of the country with the ages collected by the Registrar General in the early years of civil registration (the last line in the table) one is struck by the overriding similarity between them. However, the similarity may be an illusion. Only the Registrar General's entry covers the whole country and only it covers all types of marriages, ie those by banns and those by licence. It is possible that the selection of marriages from the licences only is biased in two ways. Firstly, the regional spread might have produced a fortuitous similarity of result. Secondly, it is possible that the clientele marrying by licence had a different age structure from that marrying by banns.

Nevertheless, despite these doubts, the evidence of the licences must be taken into account.

A third possible source of data with which to test Hypothesis 1 is the *civil registers* of marriages. These begin in 1837 and, unlike the Church of England registers, cover not only ecclesiastical parishes but registration districts which, taken together, make up the areas on which the Poor Law of 1834 was organized. Unlike the parish registers they are uniform in character. It is true that various attempts at standardizing the entries in parish registers had been made (eg Hardwicke's Marriages Act, 1753; Rose's Burial Act, 1812). From 1837 entries of births, marriages and deaths were made on printed forms. Fuller details too were required, though for some years they were not given universally. For instance, to take the present subject under discussion; the age and occupation of the bridegroom and bride were required, together with the name and occupation of both the bridegroom's and the bride's fathers.

The point of mentioning civil registers here is not to discuss their layout but to indicate how they may be used to test Hypothesis 1. It may be thought that since civil registration did not begin until 1837, they are ruled out of court in terms of time. Yet it is possible that much useful information can be culled from them, especially from those covering the more remote parts of England and Wales. For it could be argued that these areas were still pre-industrial, still influenced by, if no longer totally committed to, the social forms of an earlier age. One may, therefore, by examining the civil registers across space instead of across time discover whether or not age at marriage varied widely.

Access to the civil registers is unfortunately not easy. Although there is no legal bar equivalent to the rule which prohibits access to census enumerators' returns until 100 years have elapsed, the Registrar General appears reluctant to give general access to the registers. It is, of course, possible to get information on individual births, marriages and deaths by the payment of a fee. But this is of no value to the historical demographer. The bar seems to be partly financial and partly administrative. Some researchers, including myself, have had access to civil registers. The original approach in each case, must be made to the local registrar who, though he holds the registers, must refer each request to the Registrar General.

A fourth source of information on age at marriage in pre-industrial societies is *oral evidence*; sometimes called literary evidence, since it is normally presented in a literary rather than a numerical form. Often, too, it is impressionistic rather than statistical. Such evidence was discussed briefly in Unit 1. So far as age at marriage is concerned, this kind of evidence may come from diaries, letters, travellers' tales, or the oral reports given in evidence to official inquiries. Often the evidence takes an anecdotal form and in the case of age at marriage is moralistic in tone. For example, during my work on Norwegian population history (reported in Drake 1969) I came across this statement in a leading newspaper: 'it is shocking to behold so frequently young people of 18–20 years marrying without the least thought for the future'. As it happened, it was possible to check this statement against the statistical evidence. At the time the statement was made (1850), less than one per cent of bridegrooms and six per cent of brides were under twenty years of age. As it happened, the man making the statement, a dean of the State Church, lived in an area which had one of the lowest ages of marriage in the country (Drake 1969 p 152).

Coming nearer home it is possible to make the same kind of check on oral evidence given by local gentry, clergy, farmers, tradesmen and labourers to the Poor Inquiry Commission which conducted its enquiries in Ireland in the early 1830s. It put this question to large numbers of witnesses: 'What was the usual age at marriage of labourers?' The general opinion was nineteen years of age. The statistical evidence supplied in the 1841 Irish census suggests that the median age could have been no less than twenty-five years at any time in the 1830s.

The discrepancy is hardly surprising. For how can one possibly answer such a question meaningfully without statistical information? How in fact it was arrived at may be illustrated by the extract from the Poor Inquiry Commission report cited below:

> Labourers usually marry from sixteen or eighteen to twenty or thereabouts – *Davenport*. When asked did he remember any case of this early marriage, he did not remember one, but *Davison* stated that he himself married at twenty and also that his son had done so the other day. (Report of Poor Inquiry Commission . . . 1836 xxxi p 60)

Davenport and Davison were both labourers from County Down.

Peter Laslett in his *The World We Have Lost* (1965 p 81) notes that Juliet married Romeo, in Shakespeare's play, at about fourteen years of age; Miranda in the *Tempest* was married in her fifteenth year. Laslett goes on to say: 'It all seems clear and consistent enough. The women in Shakespeare's plays, and so presumably the English-women of Shakespeare's day, might marry in their early teens, or even before that and very often did so' (Laslett 1965 p 81). In fact when Laslett came to examine early seventeenth-century marriage licences from the diocese of Canterbury, he discovered that eighty-five per cent of the women getting married for the first time were over the age of nineteen; the mode being twenty-two, the median twenty-two and nine months and the mean about twenty-four (Laslett 1965 p 82). *One* woman did, however, give her age as thirteen, four women said they were fifteen and twelve that they were sixteen. One should perhaps note that Laslett may be creating something of an Aunt Sally here. Shakespeare was writing about Italians; inhabitants of Verona in one case, exiles from Milan and Naples in the other. The ages at marriages he gives could, then, be said to reflect *not* Elizabethan practice but Elizabethan beliefs about Italian practice. There is in any case no reason to compare the ages of Juliet and Miranda with the mode, median or mean, either in Italy or in England: there are literary and dramatic reasons in both cases for the emphasis on the heroine's youth. And the *Tempest* is very obviously *not* a realistic work. It seems possible then that in interpreting this particular piece of literary evidence, Laslett has ignored the literary conventions of the period. (I am indebted for these remarks to Dr Jean Lindsay.)

It will be apparent by now that none of the four sources we have looked at, nor the methods used to exploit them, provide an unequivocal test of Hypothesis 1. Each has its strengths, each its weaknesses. One major drawback is that, to date, relatively little work has been done on the parish registers or the marriage allegations and that the most promising technique (family reconstitution) has been exploited hardly at all. But the answer when it comes will depend upon local studies; that much is clear. There is, therefore, plenty of scope for projects here.

Test of Hypothesis 2: In examining possible tests of Hypothesis 1, much time was spent in introducing the various data sources and illustrating how they might be exploited. Having got this out of the way, our examination of the tests of Hypotheses 2, 3 and 4 can be that much briefer.

Both the parish registers and the marriage licences do, on occasion, give the occupations of bridegrooms. The late Professor J. D. Chambers in his *Vale of Trent* study (1957 pp 51–2) used the licences for Nottinghamshire in the years 1701–53 to examine differences in age at marriage both between occupations and over time (Table 8). Before saying anything about the results, it is necessary to say a word or two about the material in Table 8 itself. First you will note that there is no indication as to whether the marriages were first or second marriages. One must assume, therefore, they were a mixture of both. Secondly, in the calculation of the median, different numbers of bridegrooms and brides have been used, presumably because in some cases

Table 8 Ages and occupations recorded in the Nottinghamshire certificates of marriage

Occupation	1701–20	1721–40	1741–53		
Gentlemen					
No. of bridegrooms	168	118	55		
No. of brides	153	112	50		
Median age (bridegrooms)	26	28	25		
Median age (brides)	22	24	21		
Tailors, Clothiers, Weavers, Cordwainers					
No. of bridegrooms	57	133	119		
No. of brides	53	116	106		
Median age (bridegrooms)	25	25	24		
Median age (brides)	24	24	23		
Labourers					
No. of bridegrooms	138	89	85		
No. of brides	114	85	75		
Median age (bridegrooms)	26	27	25		
Median age (brides)	25	25	24		
Occupation	1701–10	1711–20	1721–30	1731–40	1741–53
Yeoman farmers					
No. of bridegrooms	96	45	43	143	412
No. of brides	93	45	36	130	370
Median age (bridegrooms)	25	27	30	26	25
Median age (brides)	23	24	25	24	22
Husbandmen					
No. of bridegrooms	169	318	428	267	275
No. of brides	144	291	379	205	254
Median age (bridegrooms)	26	27	26	26	26
Median age (brides)	23	23	24	24	23
Framework knitters					
No. of bridegrooms	93	133	190	124	173
No. of brides	149	103	168	119	74
Median age (bridegrooms)	24	24	24	23	23
Median age (brides)	23	22	23	23	24

Source: Chambers (1957 p 52) derived from Blagg and Wadsworth (1930 Vol II).

the age of the former was given but not that of the latter and vice versa. In most cases this may well not alter the size of the median, on the assumption that the missing observations were randomly distributed, so even had we had them all the distribution of ages would have been the same as, or similar to, what we do have. However, in one or two cases the discrepancy in numbers is quite large. This is particularly so, you will notice, in the case of the framework knitters (people who made stockings, scarves etc, on hand- and foot-operated knitting machines). Here the medians may not be strictly comparable.

Turning now to the substantive side of Table 8 we see a rather confused picture in the relationship between the median ages of bridegrooms and brides. Figure 6 suggests there is little correlation between them, if one takes them altogether. But what if one disaggregates the picture into its constituent occupational groupings?

SAQ 3 On the scatter diagram in Figure 6 draw the links between the points for each occupational group. Do any of the resulting lines suggest more of a correlation than the picture of all the groups would suggest?

Visual inspection of Table 8 and Figure 6 suggests that in most cases the median age of bridegrooms was above that of the corresponding set of brides. The 'age gap'

Figure 6 Median age of men married by licence in Nottinghamshire, 1701–53, plotted against median age of women. Source: See Table 8.

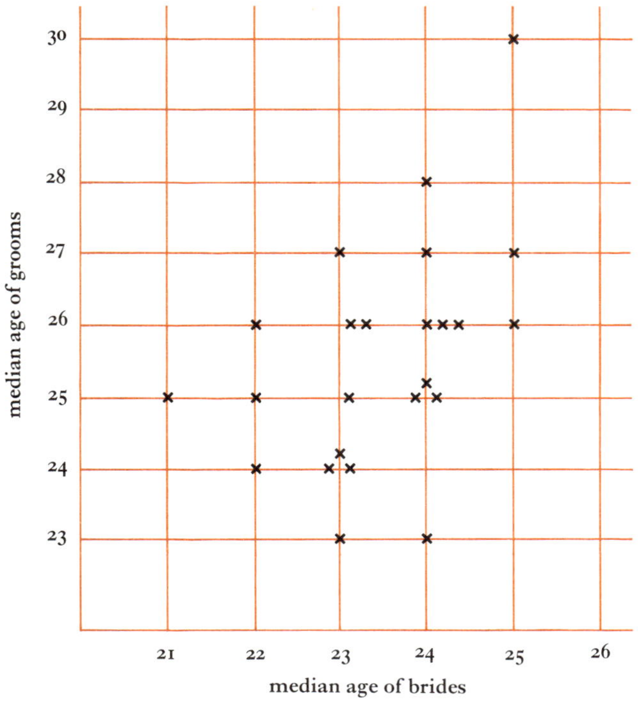

was greatest in the case of gentleman and yeoman farmer marriages. It was least in the case of framework knitters, where on one occasion it was nil (1731–40) and on another actually reversed (1741–53). One should note, in this latter instance, the point made above about the different numbers of bridegrooms and brides entering into the calculation of the respective medians. Another point to notice is that although framework knitters married earlier than the other groups, their brides were not markedly younger. Indeed, when compared with the ages of the brides of the gentlemen and yeoman farmers the difference was slight, though the bridegrooms of both these groups were older, on occasion five to six years older, than the framework knitters.

The evidence of Table 8 does, then, lend some support to Hypothesis 2, for 'differences in the age at marriage of men did not correspond with differences in the age at marriage of women'; at least not wholly.

To test Hypothesis 2 further we can draw on three other sources. These are parish registers, census enumerators' returns and literary evidence. I will deal with each of these in turn.

First, the parish registers: there are few registers which give age and occupation at marriage at all consistently until the late eighteenth and early nineteenth centuries. The Halifax register did do so, however, for the years 1654–7 and one assumes that other registers, as yet unanalysed, must have done so too. I have already noted that the information in this register is flawed because it does not differentiate between first and subsequent marriages in the case of men, and does so only partially in the case of women (see Table 5). Despite this, however, certain pointers may be derived from it.

Table 9 shows the mean, median and modal ages of the larger occupational groups represented in the Halifax Register from 1654–7. Two of these measures are not particularly useful in this context and are included as yet one more reminder of

Table 9 Mean, median and modal ages of brides and bridegrooms, by occupation of bridegrooms, married at Halifax Parish Church 1654–7

Occupation	Number of marriages	Mean		Median		Mode	
		Bridegroom	Bride	Bridegroom	Bride	Bridegroom	Bride
Clothiers	157	30.1	28.1	27.3	25.4	24.0	22.0
Labourers	72	36.3	33.7	31.0	30.3	22.0	26/40
Yeomen	39	30.7	27.6	26.9	23.3	22.0	21.0
Clothmakers; clothdressers and clothworkers	65	29.1	27.5	26.6	25.9	30.0	21.0
Tradesmen and craftsmen	74	31.2	30.1	27.2	26.3	22.0	21/22

Source: Halifax Parish Church Registers

the need for extreme care in interpreting statistics. These two measures are the mean and the mode. The mean is unsatisfactory because it gives a disproportionate weight to extreme values: in this case people marrying for a second or subsequent time (these being in the fifty to sixty-year-old age range). The mode is equally unsatisfactory, partly because the small numbers in each group can lead to a freak result and partly because, as noted earlier, the tendency to choose ages ending in an even number also biases the result. We are left, therefore, with the median. This is influenced less by the extreme ages and is also less affected by the even-number tendency.

A glance at the median ages given in Table 9 shows a range in the case of bridegrooms from 26.6 to 31.0 years and of brides from 23.3 to 30.3 years. It also shows that the median age of bridegrooms is not a good predictor of the median age of brides. Hypothesis 2 does, therefore, get some support here.

Table 10 Number of bridegrooms older than their brides, number of brides older than their bridegrooms, number of brides and bridegrooms of same age; classified by occupation of bridegroom, married at Halifax Parish Church 1654–7

Occupation	Bridegroom and bride same age		Bridegroom older		Bride older		Total
Clothiers	20	(12.8%)	93	(59.2%)	44	(28.0%)	157
Labourers	6	(8.3%)	39	(54.2%)	27	(37.5%)	72
Yeomen	4	(10.0%)	24	(61.6%)	11	(28.3%)	39
Clothmakers; clothdressers and clothworkers	11	(16.9%)	39	(59.9%)	15	(23.2%)	65
Tradesmen and craftsmen	8	(10.8%)	40	(54.0%)	26	(35.2%)	74

Source: Halifax Parish Church Registers

Another, somewhat oblique, way of approaching Hypothesis 2 is illustrated in Table 10. There you see I have divided the Halifax marriages into three sets: the first consists of those marriages where bride and bridegroom were the same age, the second where the bridegroom was older than the bride and the third where the bride was older than the bridegroom. This categorization can also be done on the material supplied in the enumerators' books of the British censuses from 1851 onwards, as these give the ages of married couples. In other countries one can go further back in time. In Norway, for instance, I was able to use the 1801 census (see Table 11).

The purpose of this exercise is to explore further into the nature of the marriage market. This is necessary because implicit in Hypothesis 2 is a crucial assumption about the basic feature of that market. This is that the 'natural' match was one where a man, having secured a livelihood sufficient to support a family, married a woman of his own age or slightly younger. However 'natural' that may seem today, the reality in pre-industrial western societies appears to have been somewhat different. First, the geographical area of the marriage market was relatively small. For some indication of this see the chapter by Küchemann *et al* in the course reader (Drake 1973 pp 209–14). This meant that the choice of partners was restricted in number and age range. Secondly, the at times high death rates, which were irregular in impact (see Unit 7), further disturbed the age structure, so that communities may have had comparatively large numbers of people in one age group and few in another. Sometimes, too, an epidemic might have affected women more seriously than men or vice versa, further disturbing the sex ratio of the community. A third point to note is that for some men the economic opportunity which enabled them to marry was not unconnected with their wife's position. 'Marrying for money' is usually associated with unions between rich people. In pre-industrial western Europe, however, it appears that men not only married widows for their *small* plots or *little* businesses, but also women previously unmarried and getting on in years who had managed to save a bit from their days in service or in some other employment. It was this which contributed to the situation of men marrying women who were older than they were. (There is also some evidence that they did so in order to keep down the size of their families. See Drake 1969A p 140.) How far it contributed, and how the factors of unbalanced age structures and narrowly confined marriage markets did so, is open to discussion. The point is that, as Table 10 shows, in some communities marriages where the bride was older than the bridegroom accounted for between a quarter and a third of all marriages. Wrigley at Colyton notes that:

> ... in the period 1560–1646 in forty-eight per cent of the first marriages in which the age of both parties is known the man was older than the woman, in forty-seven per cent the woman was older than the man, and in five per cent their ages were equal. In the period 1647–1719 the percentages were 40, 55 and 25, while by the period 1800–37 the figures were 59, 29 and 12. (Wrigley 1966 p 165)

To close the section, here are some figures from a study I did in Norway. Note that as with Wrigley's they refer to first marriages. It may be that in remoter parts of Wales, Scotland and Ireland even in the late nineteenth century some vestiges of the kind of marriage market indicated by the figures in Table 11 still existed. It would

This change in the proportion of brides older than grooms would seem to suggest that differences in employment and earning potential *did* affect marital fertility, because they determined not the age of the groom, but the age of the bride.

Table 11 Age gap separating farmers from their wives, where neither partner previously married, in parts of Norway in 1801, classified according to whether the bridegroom was a farmer or a crofter[1] and whether wife or husband the elder partner, shown in percentages

Age gap	Farmers		Crofters	
	% Husbands older	% Wives older	% Husbands older	% Wives older
Same age	7.1		6.3	
1–4 years	24.9	15.6	22.9	18.8
5–9 years	23.5	8.2	18.5	12.3
10–14 years	12.6	2.8	8.9	6.2
15+ years	4.5	0.8	3.7	2.4
	65.5	27.4	54.0	39.7
Total marriages	2,978		2,593	

1 Crofters worked for the farmers receiving in return a small money payment, a tied cottage and sometimes a plot of land. In one area I studied, 17.1% of the crofters were married to women who were at least 10 years older than they were, neither partner having been previously married.

Source: Drake (1969A) pp 131-2

be worth exploring this through the civil registers (if accessible) and the census enumerators' returns. It is also possible that local diaries, newspaper stories, or official reports may provide some comments that could enlighten us further.

The evidence presented here does lend some support to Hypothesis 2. But, as with Hypothesis 1, it is partial. More work is needed.

Test of Hypothesis 3: The practice of birth control is obviously now widespread in western societies. Until recently its emergence in them has been associated with the rise of urban industrial societies, various features of which were thought to discourage the production of large families (Banks 1954). The work of Henry (1956) on the bourgeoisie of Geneva and of Wrigley (1966) on the population of Colyton have now shown the existence of birth control within marriage for much earlier periods. Before examining the results themselves, it is worth noting that in both cases the findings were achieved through using the reconstitution of families technique. It is difficult to see how, for these early periods, any other analytical technique would prove successful. Certainly, there is little or no literary evidence as to the extent of birth control practices, although particular methods are sometimes remarked upon. Krause notes one, for instance, in the course reader (Drake 1973 pp 179–80 note 59).

Wrigley carries out a number of calculations to demonstrate the existence of the practice of birth control within marriage (Wrigley 1966). Only two will be shown here by way of illustration. The first of these (Table 12) is of age-specific marital fertility at different periods from 1560–1837. A study of Table 12 reveals a marked decline in fertility in the 1630–46 period as compared with the one preceding it. Fertility continues to decline in the period 1647–1719, recovers somewhat in the following period, and by the years 1770–1837 almost reaches its peak of the late sixteenth and early seventeenth centuries. Note that the period of lowest *marital* fertility is also that when the age at marriage was latest in Colyton (see above Table 6). The latter did not bring about the former, of course, because Table 12 gives *age-specific* marital fertility. Nevertheless, the coincidence is an interesting one, to which we shall return.

The second measure of Wrigley's to be shown here appears in the histograms in Figure 7. These show the final birth intervals of child-producing couples during

Table 12 Age-specific marital fertility (children born per 1,000 woman-years lived). The number of women-years on which the rate is based is shown in brackets.

| Colyton | Age in years | | | | | | |
	15–19	20–4	25–9	30–4	35–9	40–4	45–9
1560–1629	412	467	403	369	302	174	18
	(17.0)	(205.5)	(473.5)	(561.5)	(517.0)	(443.0)	(383.5)
1630–1646	500	378	382	298	234	128	0
	(4.0)	(63.5)	(120.5)	(107.5)	(55.5)	(23.5)	(16.0)
1647–1719	500	346	395	272	182	104	20
	(4.0)	(52.0)	(187.5)	(253.5)	(258.5)	(249.5)	(200.5)
1720–1769	462	362	342	292	227	160	0
	(19.5)	(69.0)	(164.0)	(216.0)	(203.0)	(156.0)	(138.0)
1770–1837	500	441	361	347	270	152	22
	(34.0)	(279.0)	(498.0)	(504.5)	(430.0)	(224.0)	(186.0)
Crulai[1]							
1647–1742	320	419	429	355	292	142	10
	(65.5)	(30.5)	(599.0)	(633.0)	(588.5)	(505.5)	(205.5)

1 The Crulai figures are taken from Gautier and Henry *La Population de Crulai*, pp 102 and 105, and Table vii, pp 249–54. The Colyton rates are derived from marriages formed during the years specified except that marriages which bridge the period 1630–1646 to 1671–1719 are divided at the end of 1646, data from before that date being allocated to the earlier period, beyond it to 1647–1719.

Source: Wrigley (1966) p 89; reprinted in Drake (1969) p 166

Figure 7 Number of months elapsing between the ultimate and penultimate births to married couples in Colyton in the periods 1560–1646 and 1647–1719.
Source: Wrigley (1966) p 93

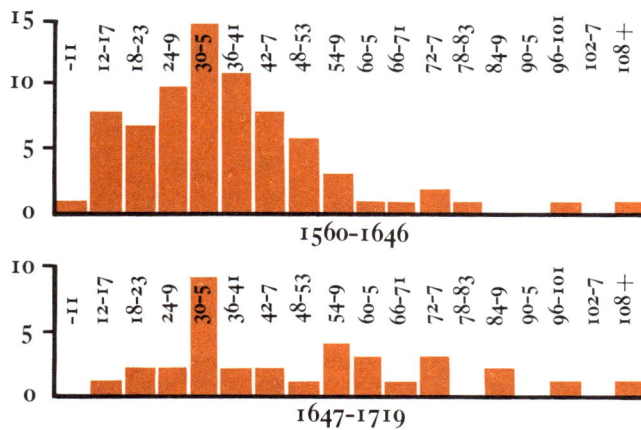

1560–1646

1647–1719

the period of high marital fertility (1560–1646) and of low marital fertility (1647–1719). Wrigley's comment on Figure 7 is:

> In the earlier period [1560–1646] the distribution is unimodal with a fairly clear peak about the 30–35 month interval. In the later period this peak is again apparent, but there is also a suspicion of a second peak in the 54–65 month intervals, suggesting that while the 'natural' distribution continued to occur in some cases, there was superimposed upon it a different pattern which might be the result of family limitation. (Wrigley 1966 p 94)

Although Wrigley and Henry (see Table 13) have demonstrated the existence of birth control within marriage in pre-industrial western Europe, it does not follow that it was widespread, or that it had much effect on fertility. At the moment, given the extent of variation in the age at marriage shown above, it would seem that it was unlikely to have been of key importance, certainly nothing like as important as at the present time. Indeed in Colyton it seems to have been a factor which helped to lower fertility at a time when the marriage age was rising. In other words, birth control was not adopted by couples who had married early and wished to avoid the burdens of child rearing, but by those who had married late (presumably for the

Table 13 Marital fertility of the bourgeoisie of Geneva (children born per 1,000 woman-years lived)

Age of wife at marriage	To wives of husbands born 1650–99						
	Under 20	20–4	25–9	30–4	35–9	40–4	45–9
Under 20	348	506	352	225	148	41	0
20–4		476	436	210	125	21	0
25–9			404	324	48	26	0
30 and over				323	195	54	18
All ages	348	493	400	244	130	35	5
Age of wife at marriage	To wives of husbands born 1700–49						
	Under 20	20–4	25–9	30–4	24–9	40–4	45–9
Under 20	358	335	142	75	26	0	0
20–4		461	271	130	63	25	0
25–9			505	223	153	55	0
30 and over				360	115	130	0
All ages	358	393	277	163	83	49	0

Source: Henry (1955) p 76

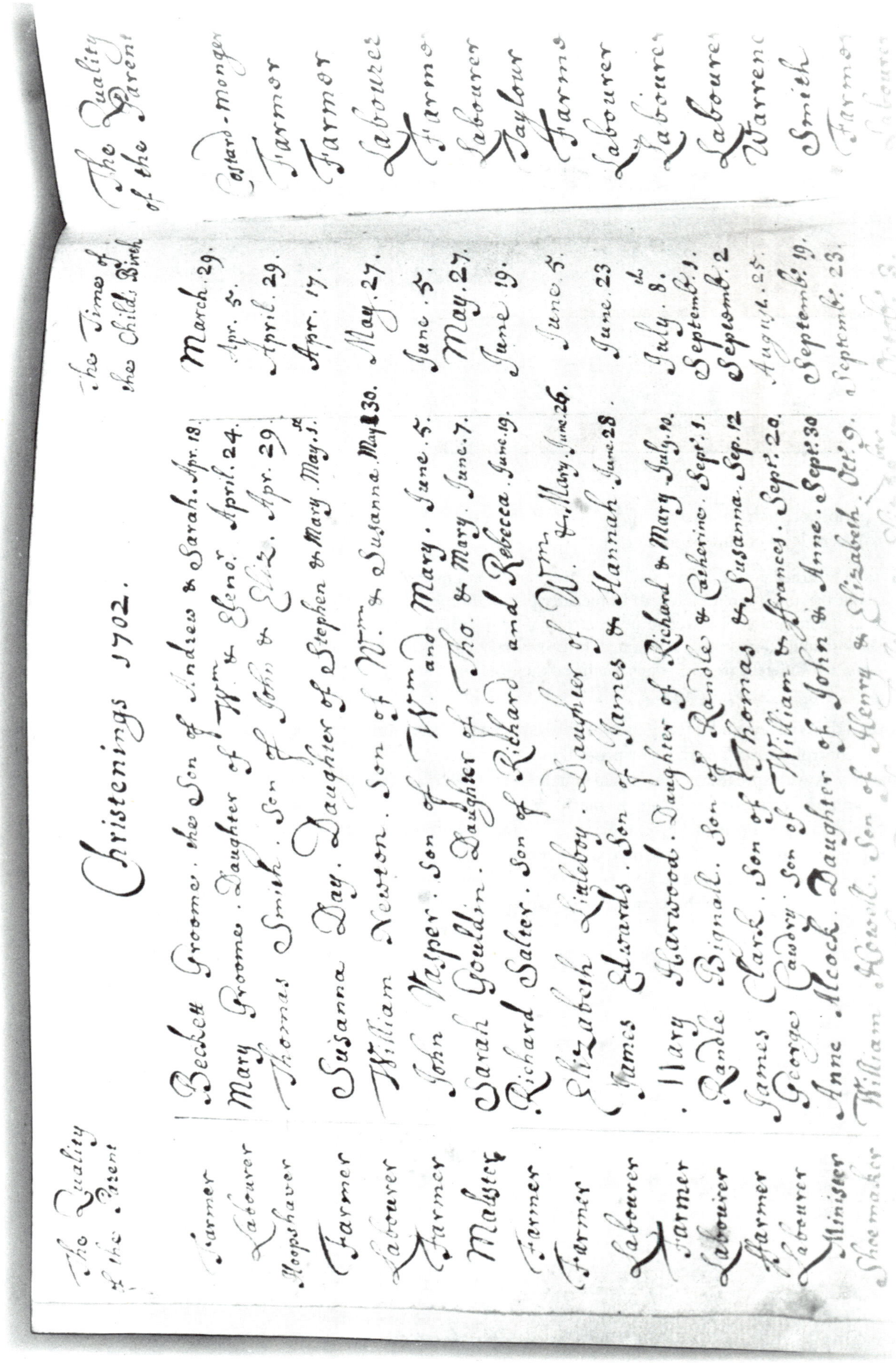

Christenings 1702.

The Quality of the Parent	Christenings 1702.	The Time of the Child's Birth	The Quality of the Parent
Farmer	Becket Groome, the Son of Andrew & Sarah. Apr. 18.	March. 29.	Costard-monger
Labourer	Mary Groome, Daughter of Wm & Elenor. April 24.	Apr. 5.	Farmer
Hoopshaver	Thomas Smith, Son of John & Eliz. Apr. 29.	April. 29.	Farmer
Farmer	Susanna Day, Daughter of Stephen & Mary. May. 5.	Apr. 17.	Labourer
Labourer	William Newton, Son of Wm & Susanna. May 30.	May. 27.	Farmer
Farmer	John Valper, Son of Wm and Mary. June. 5.	June. 5.	Labourer
Maltster	Sarah Gouldin, Daughter of Tho. & Mary. June 7.	May. 27.	Taylour
Farmer	Richard Salter, Son of Richard and Rebecca. June 19.	June 19.	Farmer
Farmer	Elizabeth Linkboy, Daughter of Wm & Mary. June. 26.	June. 5.	Labourer
Labourer	James Edwards, Son of James & Hannah. June 28.	June. 23	Labourer
Farmer	Mary Harwood, Daughter of Richard & Mary. July. 10.	July. 8.	Labourer
Labourer	Randle Bignall, Son of Randle & Catherine. Sept 1.	September 1.	Labourer
Farmer	James Clark, Son of Thomas & Susanna. Sep. 12	September. 2	Labourer
Labourer	George Cadby, Son of William & Frances. Sept. 20.	August. 25.	Warrener
Minister	Anne Alcock, Daughter of John & Anne. Sept. 30	September. 19.	Smith
Shoemaker	William Alcock, Son of Henry & Elizabeth. Oct. 9.	September. 23.	Farmer
			Labourer

Figure 8 Page from baptism register of Iver, 1702. Source: Bucks County Record Office

same reason) and who despite late marriage still believed that without birth control, they would produce more children than they wanted or could manage to support.

Test of Hypothesis 4: We come now to our final hypothesis. Evidence on illegitimacy and pre-marital conception is not so scarce as on birth control, but it is not, as yet, abundant. Many baptismal registers do discriminate between legitimate and illegitimate children on their being baptized, though it is usually impossible to tell whether they do so consistently. The higher mortality of illegitimate than of legitimate children, especially in the early days and weeks, would reduce the number reaching the baptismal font, and would, therefore, further distort the ratio. Despite these and many other problems, work has been done on illegitimacy using the parish registers. In a recent article, Laslett and Oosterveen (1973) have analysed some twenty-four registers which record the baptisms of illegitimate children relatively consistently from the second half of the sixteenth century to the first quarter of the nineteenth. These twenty-four represent the best of some 600 registers now on file in the offices of the Cambridge Group for the History of Population and Social Structure. This may seem a small proportion, but it must be remembered that these twenty-four registers do record illegitimate baptisms for almost a quarter of a millennium. Almost a quarter to a third of parish registers record illegitimate baptisms for shorter periods.

A graphical representation of the changes in the proportion of registered illegitimate baptisms to legitimate ones appears in Figure 9. One should discount the fluctuation in the 1650s and the 1800–1840 period, as here gaps in the material are considerable. On the general configuration, however, Laslett and Oosterveen appear quite confident.

It is interesting to note, as Laslett and Oosterveen (p 257) do, that:

. . . the Restoration, reckoned to be the most licentious in English *literary* history before our present permissive generation, was marked throughout its whole half century by a stable low [illegitimacy ratio], the longest interlude of unvarying illegitimacy so far identified'. [my italics]

More interesting, from the point of view of Hypothesis 4, is their view (p 269) that:

When the parishioners of pre-industrial England married early, illegitimacy amongst them was high, and when they married late, the number of bastards went down. This,

Figure 9 Illegitimacy ratios (% illegitimate to legitimate baptisms) England 1561–1960, by decade. Source: Laslett and Oosterveen 1973, Figure 1

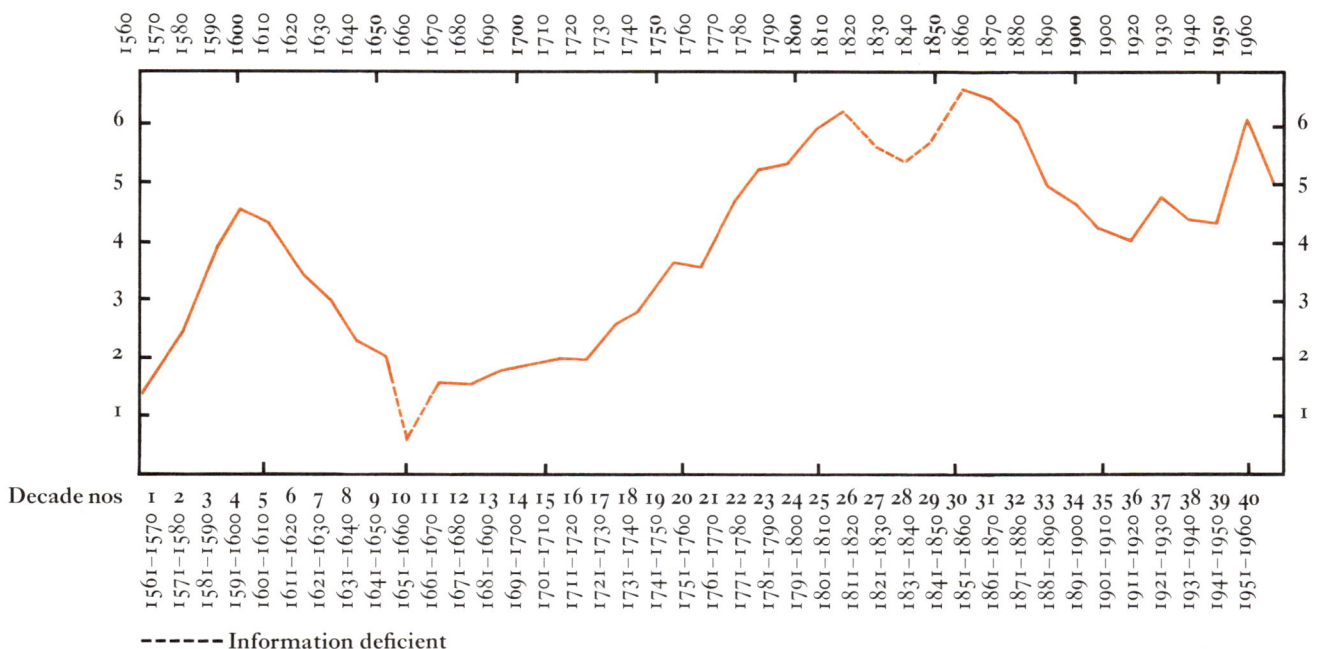

------- Information deficient

we believe, falsifies any argument which supposes a necessary positive connection between sexual deprivation and the procreation of children outside marriage.

If this view is confirmed by subsequent work, then Hypothesis 4 appears to be refuted, at least that part of it which suggests illegitimacy rose as the age of marriage rose. Of course, it may not be confirmed. There is evidence from other countries which supports Hypothesis 4. For example Bavarian laws restricting marriage were followed by a rise in illegitimate births, their repeal by a fall (Knodel 1967, 1970).

But what of pre-marital conceptions? It is possible to get at the incidence of these by adopting a partial reconstitution of families technique. If one links a baptism to a marriage occurring less than eight and a half months earlier, one can say that the child was pre-maritally conceived. Work in England by Hair (1966, 1970) suggests that about twenty per cent of all brides in the period 1540–1700 were pregnant at marriage and forty per cent in the years 1700–1820. There is some evidence, too that pre-marital pregnancy was less prevalent in the seventeenth century than in the sixteenth or eighteenth (Hair 1970 pp 60–1). This as Laslett and Oosterveen (1973 p 270) remark is 'our curve all over again'. It would seem, therefore, on the evidence before us at the moment, that both parts of Hypothesis 4 are refuted by, at least, the available English evidence. The two words to stress here are *available* and *English*. Further work in this country and elsewhere is called for.

RESULT

In testing our four hypotheses we have not been able to wholly confirm or refute any one of them. A number of points have, however, emerged which are relevant to the project work you are to undertake during this course.

Firstly, it is apparent that considerable attention has to be paid to the source material. Each source has its potential, each its problems.

Secondly, it seems to me at least, breaking down a problem into a series of linked hypotheses not only provides a focus for the work, but also enables one to associate in a credible fashion one set of findings with another. For instance, what does seem to have emerged from our tests is that the age at marriage, the rate of illegitimacy and the practice of birth control are associated, but in ways that would not strike one, unless empirical work had suggested them. For it appears that a late age at marriage is associated with *low* illegitimacy *and* the practice of birth control within marriage, and that earlier marriage is associated with an increase in the illegitimacy ratio and a relaxation in birth control.

Thirdly, our tests have shown just how little of the available material has been used in producing the results we have described. There remains a lot to be done.

Answers to SAQs

Answer SAQ 1 The first factor to be considered is that of time – your time that is! As this is limited to 160 hours, one should avoid the really large registers such as Halifax and Leeds and possibly even Elland, Bradford and Wakefield. One should also avoid registers or transcripts which are to be found in different places. For instance, the Dewsbury register has many admirable qualities. It is a convenient size; it covers the maximum time span (1538–1700); it has few gaps. Assuming, however, that it is accessible only in the places I found it, then a lot of time will have to be spent on travelling: ie Dewsbury Public Library for the published transcript covering the years 1538–1653; the Library of the Yorkshire Archaeological Society at Leeds for the manuscript transcript of the years 1653–98 and (if you must be a perfectionist!) a trip to the Borthwick Institute at York for the Bishop's Transcripts covering the years 1699–1700. Remember too that many Record Offices are closed on Saturdays!

It may be, of course, that the amount of time spent travelling is less than the time it takes to decipher the sixteenth- and seventeenth-century script of an original register, even though it is on your very doorstep. In an ideal world one would obviously work with the original register, since one can never be sure that a transcriber has done his job well. But in doing research one is not operating in an ideal world. There is a *Concorde* quality about it; the time needed shows a strong tendency to escalate. For this reason I would hesitate about the Birstall register and the Heptonstall one. The latter has the disadvantage of a split site too.

Having narrowed the field a bit, we move on to the second step of the algorithm. 'Has the register at least 100 entries a year?' Quite a number of the registers do not: Batley, East Ardsley, Hartshead, Horbury, Keighley, Methley, Mirfield, Swillington and Thornhill. If you turn to pp 50–3 you will notice that a number of these have years with no entries of either baptisms, marriages and burials, or indeed of all three. In some cases, of course, this was probably because the population served by the register was so small, that it produced no one to be baptized, married or buried. But with a small register there is no way of telling the difference between under registration and nothing to be registered.

One could adopt the strategy suggested in step three of the algorithm to overcome the problem of small registers. Here the neighbouring parishes of Horbury and Thornhill would make a good pair. Together they cover the whole of the seventeenth century with only a one year gap. Another possible combination would be Mirfield and Hartshead. Each of these four parishes appears in a published transcript which reduces the workload, though there is still the problem of bringing together the entries from two registers.

Of the remaining registers I would not use Calverley because of the large number of missing years (see Table 2), nor Bingley for the same reason. My argument is weaker in the latter case. We are left with Rothwell, Huddersfield and Kirkburton. Of these I would exclude Rothwell because, although it covers almost the entire period (1540–1700) it has a number of gaps in the early decades and may entail a trip to York to complete the last ten years. I say *may* because the original register could be accessible in the parish church. Huddersfield has an unbroken register, but it begins only in 1606; has rather a large number of entries and is on microfilm. Seventeenth-century script is often difficult to read; on microfilm, deciphering it can be a very trying task indeed, but for an aggregative study, this is not a major problem.

We are left with Kirkburton. It is in the form of a printed transcript; it covers almost the whole period (1540–1700); it is not too big. Unfortunately it has some rather large gaps in the 1620s. In fact, if we pick Kirkburton we must do so after consciously rejecting the advice in steps 5 and 6 of the algorithm; that is after going through the 'rethink necessary' step. Perhaps we should go back again over the ones we have rejected because of their size. Perhaps Elland would be a better bet. In the last analysis we must make a value judgement. All our algorithm can do is to help us ask the right questions.

Answer SAQ 2 The tendency to choose even numbers when reporting one's age. Of the 482 men aged from 19–44 years, some 306 gave an even numbered year, as against 176 who gave an odd one (ie 63.5 per cent to 36.5 per cent). For the same ages for women the numbers were respectively 306:201 (or 60.3 per cent:39.7 per cent).

Answer SAQ 3 Disaggregating the scatter diagram suggests to me a fairly high positive correlation between the age of gentlemen bridegrooms and their brides. That is to say the older the bridegrooms, the older the brides. The same is true, but to a lesser extent, for the tailors, clothiers etc. group and for the labourers and yeomen. For husbandmen there seems little or no correlation and for framework knitters a hint of a low negative correlation. It should be noted that this exercise is purely suggestive; the number of points being somewhat limited. If you want to check up on the interpretation of scatter diagrams see *The quantitative analysis of historical data* Unit 4, pp 103–5.

Appendix 1 Sources for estimating total population size

Population Count	Content	Areal coverage	Location of documents	Shortcomings	Bibliography	Multiplier to get total population
1547 Chantry Certificates	'Housling'people. Assumed to be totals of communicants.	English parishes	Public Record Office, London	Doubt as to whether covered people aged 14+ or 16+ : possibly much lower (see Cornwall 1970 p 32)	Thirsk (1959); Hollingsworth (1969); Cornwall (1970)	1⅔
1563 Ecclesiastical Census	Of families, or households.	English parishes in certain dioceses (11 in all)	British Museum: Harleian Manuscript 594, 595,618	Doubt as to whether families or householders	Thirsk (1959); Hollingsworth 1969: Cornwall (1959)	5 or 4
1603 Ecclesiastical census	Communicants and recusants	English parishes	British Museum: Harleian Manuscripts 280,594,595 Diocesan record offices.	Doubt as to age of communicants	Thirsk (1959): Hollingsworth 1969: Turner (1911)	1⅔
1641-7 Protestation Return	Involved an oath to defend, among other things the'true reformed Protestant religion'. Oath administered to all males over 18. Those refusing the oath to be listed separately.	English parishes	House of Lords Record Office	In some places administered to those over 15 year of age	Thirsk (1959): Hollingsworth 1969: Oxfordshire Record Society (1955)	2 (to include women) + 40% to include under 18 year olds.
1676 Compton Ecclesiastical Census	Communicants - assumed to be 16 + years old - and non-conformists	English parishes	Manuscript in Salt Library Stafford for dioceses in Province of Canterbury: Tanner Ms 150 No. 7 fol 27 seq. Bodleian, Oxford for Province of York.	Some incumbents returned number of inhabitants, some, the numbers of families and some the number of communicants. Did not always specify which; Nonconformists on occasion deliberately understated.	Thirsk(1959): Hollingsworth (1969) Guilford (1924): Marshall (1934); James (1952): Chalkin (1960): Bond (1973): Stephens (1958 and 1971): Forster (1961, 1967, 1969).	1⅔
1688/1690 Communicants list	Communicants, non-conformists catholics	Dioceses in Province of Canterbury	Dalrymple (1771-3)		Dalrymple (1771-3) Hollingsworth (1969)	1⅔
Bishops Visitation Returns. Sixteenth to Eighteenth Centuries.	Visits by Bishop's representatives to discover state of church buildings+ of religious life. Often included number of families in the parish and of what, denomination.	Parishes throughout England	Diocesan and County Record Offices.	Sometimes families given, sometimes householders or individuals.	Ollard and Walker (1928-31) Stephens (1971)	4 or 5
Muster Rolls Early sixteenth to mid seventeenth centuries.	Lists of able bodied men, assumed to be aged 15-60	Parishes throughout England	Public Record Office.	'Able' is a dubious definition: payment of a 'muster bounty' may have inflated lists.	Hollingsworth (1969); Rich (1950): Boynton (1967)	4 - 7
Hearth Tax Returns 1660-89	Lists of houses paying the tax (+ sometimes those not paying).	Parishes throughout England	Public Record Office	Unless charged and uncharged houses given are of little use.	Hollingsworth (1969)Marshall (1936): Patten(1971) Owen(1959); Thirsk (1959) Meekings (1940)	4 - 5
Poll Tax Late seventeenth century	All over 16 listed	Parishes throughout England	County Record Office.	Certain people exempted on grounds of poverty.No indication how many.	-	1⅔
1695 Marriage Duty Act	Complete listing of all inhabitants	English Parishes	County Record offices, parish chests; private collections	Few listings appear to have survived	Glass (1965) Laslett (1969) Wrigley (1966)	1
Local censuses	Varied: usually carried out by individuals	Limited coverage of parishes, villages and towns	County Record Offices	Unique , one-off events.	.Law (1969): Tranter (1967) Laslett (1969):Youngson (1961) Kyd (1952): Percival (1774-1776)	-

Appendix 2 Analysing a Parish Register

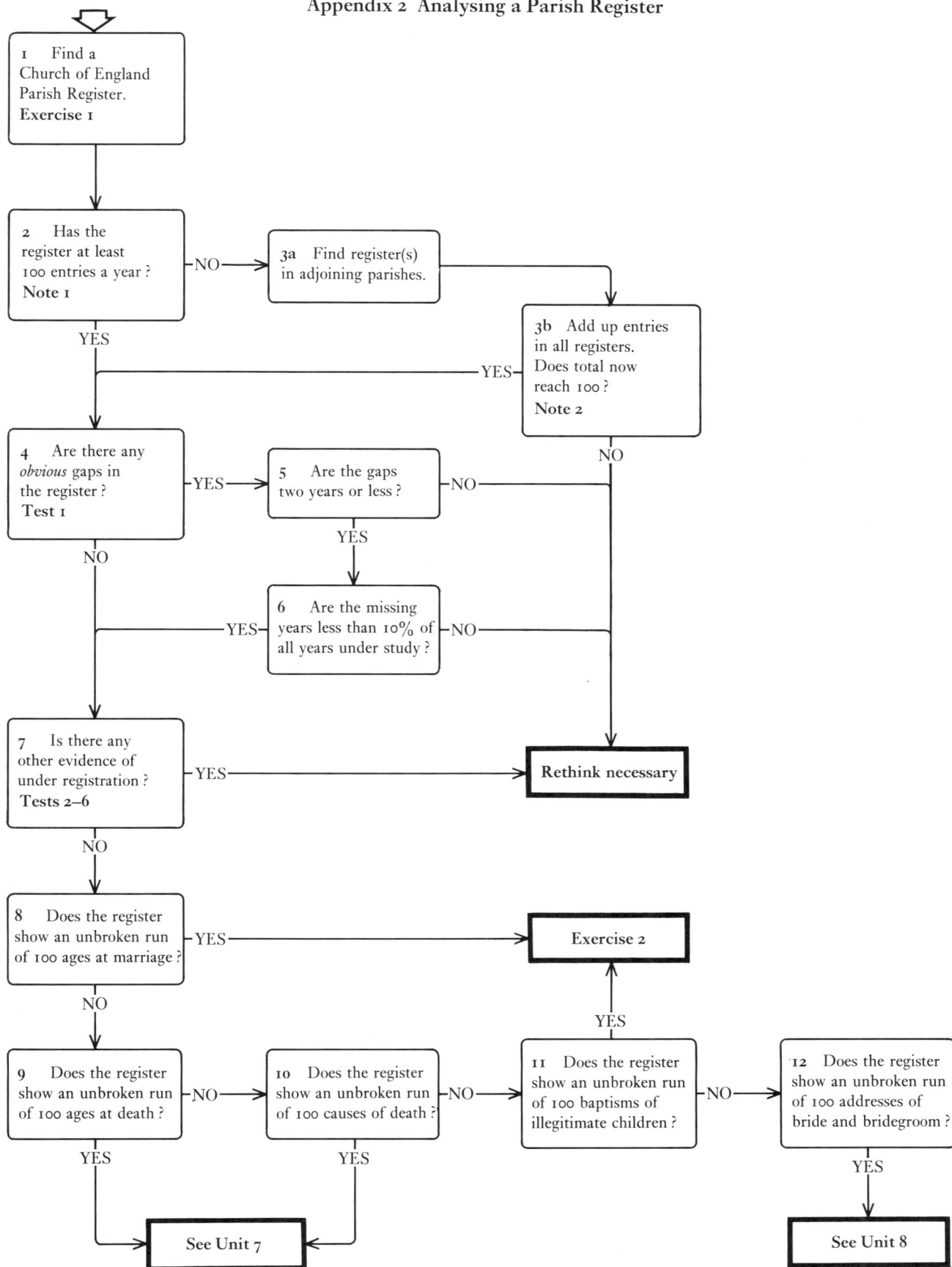

```
        ▽
┌──────────────────┐
│ 1   Find a       │
│ Church of England│
│ Parish Register. │
│ Exercise 1       │
└──────────────────┘
        │
        ▼
┌──────────────────┐                    ┌──────────────────┐
│ 2    Has the     │                    │ 3a   Find        │
│ register at least│───NO──────────────▶│ register(s)      │
│ 100 entries a    │                    │ in adjoining     │
│ year?            │                    │ parishes.        │
│ Note 1           │                    └──────────────────┘
└──────────────────┘
        │                                        ┌──────────────────┐
       YES                                       │ 3b   Add up      │
        │          ───────────────YES───────────│ entries          │
        │          │                             │ in all registers.│
        ▼          │                             │ Does total now   │
┌──────────────────┐│                            │ reach 100?       │
│ 4    Are there   ││  ┌──────────────┐          │ Note 2           │
│ any obvious gaps ││  │ 5   Are the  │          └──────────────────┘
│ in the register? ││─YES│gaps two years│──NO──          │
│ Test 1           │   │or less?      │      │          NO
└──────────────────┘   └──────────────┘      │           │
        │                     │              │
       NO                    YES             │
        │                     ▼              │
        │          ┌──────────────────┐      │
        │          │ 6    Are the     │      │
        │───YES────│ missing years    │─NO───
        │          │ less than 10% of │      │
        │          │ all years under  │      │
        │          │ study?           │      │
        │          └──────────────────┘      │
        ▼                                     ▼
┌──────────────────┐              ┏━━━━━━━━━━━━━━━━━━┓
│ 7    Is there    │              ┃ Rethink necessary┃
│ any other        │───YES───────▶┃                  ┃
│ evidence of under│              ┗━━━━━━━━━━━━━━━━━━┛
│ registration?    │
│ Tests 2–6        │
└──────────────────┘
        │
       NO
        ▼
┌──────────────────┐              ┏━━━━━━━━━━━━━━━━━━┓
│ 8    Does the    │              ┃ Exercise 2       ┃
│ register show an │───YES───────▶┃                  ┃
│ unbroken run of  │              ┗━━━━━━━━━━━━━━━━━━┛
│ 100 ages at      │                        ▲
│ marriage?        │                       YES
└──────────────────┘                        │
        │
       NO
        ▼
┌──────────────┐  ┌──────────────┐  ┌──────────────┐  ┌──────────────┐
│ 9  Does the  │  │ 10 Does the  │  │ 11 Does the  │  │ 12 Does the  │
│ register show│  │ register show│  │ register show│  │ register show│
│ an unbroken  │NO│ an unbroken  │NO│ an unbroken  │NO│ an unbroken  │
│ run of 100   │─▶│ run of 100   │─▶│ run of 100   │─▶│ run of 100   │
│ ages at death│  │ causes of    │  │ baptisms of  │  │ addresses of │
│ ?            │  │ death?       │  │ illegitimate │  │ bride and    │
│              │  │              │  │ children?    │  │ bridegroom?  │
└──────────────┘  └──────────────┘  └──────────────┘  └──────────────┘
      │                 │                                    │
     YES               YES                                  YES
      ▼                 ▼                                    ▼
   ┏━━━━━━━━━━━━━━━━━━━━━━━┓                    ┏━━━━━━━━━━━━━━━━━━┓
   ┃     See Unit 7        ┃                    ┃   See Unit 8     ┃
   ┗━━━━━━━━━━━━━━━━━━━━━━━┛                    ┗━━━━━━━━━━━━━━━━━━┛
```

Note: I would like to acknowledge the help of Michael Macdonald-Ross, Institute of Educational Technology at the Open University, in the design of this algorithm.

Appendix 3 Forms used for 'Aggregative Analysis'

BAPTISMS

PARISH:

County:

YEARS:

YEAR	MONTH OF CONCEPTION												Baptisms by Civil Year (totals)		Concep-tions by Harvest Year (totals)	Bastards	Comments
	Apr.	May	June	July	Aug.	Sept.	Oct.	Nov.	Dec.	Jan.	Feb.	Mar.					
	MONTH OF BAPTISM													Jan.-Apr.	May-Dec.		
	Jan.	Feb.	Mar.	Apr.	May	June	July	Aug.	Sept.	Oct.	Nov.	Dec.					
TOTAL																	

iii 66

MARRIAGES

PARISH:

County:

YEARS:

YEAR	Jan.	Feb.	Mar.	Apr.	May	June	July	Aug.	Sept.	Oct.	Nov.	Dec.	Civil Year (totals)	Jan.-July	Aug.-Dec.	Harvest Year (totals)	Comments
TOTAL																	

iii 66

Appendix 3   The Cambridge Group for the History of Population and Social Structure

Instructions for the use of aggregative analysis forms[1]: Baptisms (PEF1); Burials (PEF11); Marriages (PEF111)

1 Each form should begin with the first year of an even number decade (for example, 1601, 1621, 1681; not 1611, 1671, etc.) If the first entry in the register is in, say, 1596, begin the form with the year 1581, even though this means that only the last five lines on the first form are used. This is important because it makes the comparison of forms from different parishes easy. If there is a gap in the register, leave the corresponding period on the form blank. If the gap is, say, from 1564–71, the entries for 1571 should be seven lines lower than those for 1564.

2 Where possible, carry the analysis down from the earliest date in the register to 1837, the year in which civil registration of births, deaths and marriages began.

3 The modern calendar year begins on 1 January. This is the year used on the forms. Until 1752, however, the year began on 25 March (in the sixteenth century some registers begin a new year on still other days). This means that dates in the early part of the year must be converted to conform with modern practice – thus the baptisms occurring in February 1679 in the register will be recorded on the form in February 1680. The period from 1 January to 24 March is moved forward by one year.

---

1 An abridged version of the instructions issued to volunteers helping the Cambridge Group for the History of Population and Social Structure. Reproduced by permission of the Group.

P.E.F. II

BURIALS

PARISH:

County:

YEARS:

YEAR	Jan.	Feb.	Mar.	Apr.	May	June	July	Aug.	Sept.	Oct.	Nov.	Dec.	Civil Year (totals)	Jan.-July	Aug.-Dec.	Harvest Year (totals)	Wanderers	Comments
TOTAL																		

iii 66

4 In some parishes separate registers of baptisms, burials and marriages were kept. In others all the entries were made in a single register. Where the latter was the case, go through the register three times dealing with each type of entry separately.

5 Note that it is not always the case that one entry in the register deals with only one event. The baptism of twins is usually recorded in a single entry, and sometimes the burial of a mother and young baby is also recorded by a single entry. Check each page in the register, therefore, to make sure you have not missed an event in this way.

6 There is a column on the Baptisms Form for bastards, and on the Burials Form there is a column for wanderers. Not all registers record these sub-classes of event. Where they are recorded only sporadically the column should be left blank. If information about them is given with apparent consistency over a long period (say, fifty years or more), it is desirable to have them listed. The Comments column is provided to make it possible to note unusual entries of importance or changes in the character of the register (eg 'here the register makes it clear that the heavy mortality was due to smallpox'; or 'here the register becomes unusually detailed and records the mother's maiden name at the birth of each child'; or 'here the incumbent began to add notes of the character of some of the deceased'; or 'for several years there are occasional comments on the weather'; and so on).

7 If you are working from the original register and it is still in the parish, you should always approach the incumbent in the first instance to seek permission to make use of the register. He and the churchwardens are jointly responsible for its safety.

8 Calculations. The forms provide for addition by line and column to give totals for the calendar year and the month, and also make it possible to calculate the number of events by harvest year. These calculations yield much of interest, but they are laborious if done without the assistance of a machine.

If you do wish to do the work, the following points should be borne in mind in calculating totals for the harvest year.

(i) The year runs from the beginning of August in any one year to the end of July in the following year.

(ii) On the Marriages and Burials Forms the total for the harvest year is obtained by adding the total for August–December of one year, say 1576, to the total for January–July of the next, 1577.
Thus:

	January / July	August / December	Harvest year (total)
1576	33	(28)	48
1577	(20)	19	

(iii) On the Baptisms Form the procedure is different. We wish to know about the number of conceptions rather than the number of baptisms. The number of conceptions is related to the number of baptisms nine months later. Therefore to derive a figure for conceptions by harvest year one must calculate the number of baptisms nine months later. The number of conceptions in the harvest year August 1576–July 1577 is taken to be equal to the number of baptisms, May 1577–April 1578. Thus:

	January / April	May / December	Harvest year (total)
1576	21	36	56
1577	18	(31)	
1578	(25)	37	

Appendix 4 Forms used for the 'Reconstitution of Families'

Form E.S. III (b)

Married | rank

Wife | surname
name
age
residence .... t.p.
spinster / widow / unknown

father
residence .... t.p.
occupation
mother | maiden name

late husband's name

baptised ....
buried ....
wife / widow / unknown

Husband | surname
name ....

Remarks
....
....
....
....
....

Parish ....

E.S. III (b)   ii 65   No. ....

Form E.S. III (a)

Married | Banns/licence

Husband | surname
name
age
residence .... t.p.
occupation
bachelor / widower / unknown

father
residence .... t.p.
occupation
mother | maiden name

Wife | surname
name
age
residence .... t.p.
spinster / widow / unknown

father
residence .... t.p.
occupation
mother | maiden name

late husband's name

Remarks
....
....

Signatures

	Mark	Signed
husband		
wife		

Parish ....

E.S. III (a)   viii 64   No. ....

Form E.S. I

Baptised | christian name | surname
....
born ....

male / female / unknown
bastard / twin
stillborn / abortion

Father
name ....
residence .... t.p.
occupation ....

Mother | maiden name
name ....
mother's father's name
....
residence .... t.p.
occupation ....

Remarks
....
....
....

Parish ....

E.S. I   viii 64   No. ....

Form E.S. II

Buried | christian name | surname
....
died .... residence .... t.p.
occupation
age ....

bachelor / spinster / widow(er)
bastard

son | of ....
daughter | residence .... t.p.
occupation ....
and .... | maiden name

husband | of .... | maiden name
wife | residence .... t.p.
widow(er) | occupation ....

Remarks
....
....
....

Parish ....

E.S. II   viii 64   No. ....

Notes

Unit 7
La crise démographique

Part cover: Woman begging at Clonakilty, Ireland, 1847, and a victim of the Bengal famine, 1943. Sources: *Illustrated London News* Vol. 11, p 100 and Keystone Press Agency

Contents Unit 7

Objectives

After studying this unit and watching Television Programmes 2 and 3 (*From Time to Time* and *Demographic Crisis*) you should be able to:

1 Define the term 'la crise démographique'.

2 List 5 periods of mortality which would appear to fit the definition in Objective 1, indicating the extent, timing and postulated cause(s) of the rise in mortality.

3 Derive a time series from a data matrix.

4 Calculate the linear trend in a time series using the least-squares method.

5 Calculate the non-cyclical fluctuations in a time series exhibiting cyclical influences and a time series that does not.

6 Describe the main methods of determining whether a rise in mortality is a product of food shortages or of disease operating independently of food supply.

La crise démographique

1 Introduction

Here are accounts of two events separated in time by 232 years.

> Multitudes have perished, and are daily perishing under hedges and ditches, some of fevers, some of fluxes and some through downright cruel want, in the utmost agonies of despair. I have seen the labourer endeavouring to work at his spade, but fainting for want of food and forced to quit it. I have seen the aged father eating grass like a beast, and in the anguish of his soul, wishing for his dissolution. I have seen the helpless orphan exposed on the dunghill, and none to take him in for fear of infection. And I have seen the hungry infant sucking at the breast of the already expired parent. (Publicola 1741 p 3)

> Earlier this month, by chance, I became the first reporter to witness this catastrophe. I have seen children, too weak to stand. I have seen men and women in overcrowded huts, huddled together, lying on sacks, suffering from typhus, cholera, pneumonia and TB, waiting to die. I have seen a mother still trying to suckle her newly dead baby – dead because she was too malnourished to feed it. I have seen infants, dreadfully emaciated, no longer able to take food or water, at the point of death. I have seen dead children and adults piled together on one stretcher. I have seen, too, mass graves. (Dimbleby 1973)

The first of these two quotations purports to describe events in Ireland in 1741; the second in Ethiopia in 1973. I chose to present them here partly because the events they describe are central to the concerns of this unit, and partly because I was struck by the similarities between them. Perhaps the similarities strike you too. If so, you may care to note them down before moving to the next paragraph where I point out what occurred to me.

First, both accounts are those of eye-witnesses. Secondly, the two accounts share a common style, even a common vocabulary – 'I have seen . . .'. Thirdly, both ascribe the distress to two factors; shortage of food and infectious disease. The relationship between the two is not, however, clear – not in these extracts at least. Finally, the distress, so the eye-witnesses believed, had resulted in high mortality: 'multitudes have perished' (Publicola), 'I have seen . . . mass graves' (Dimbleby).

Another interesting element which the events described in the two quotations have in common is that both almost failed to be noted by and for posterity. The Irish

Figure 1a The famine in Ireland – funeral at Skibbereen, 1847. Source: *Illustrated London News*, Vol. 11, p 65

Figure 1b Potato famine – starving peasants at workhouse gate, 1846/7. Source: Mary Evans Picture Library

crisis was much reported at the time (see Drake 1968), but the potato famine of the 1840s appears to have all but erased it from popular memory. The Ethiopian crisis of 1973 might very well not have received the attention it got, had not Dimbleby and his camera crew 'by chance', as he put it, been filming in the area. Accounts of eye-witnesses such as these are, of course, notoriously unreliable, for the reasons we discussed in Unit 1. Either they exaggerate the extent of the crisis, generalizing too broadly from their inevitably limited experience, or alternatively, they fail to see the significance of what appears to be happening before them. Anyone who has read *first* reports of floods, earthquakes, famines or such like disasters in today's press and then compared them with later reports, will recognize that, to begin with, the impact of such events tends to be exaggerated. Nevertheless, one does come across the opposite extreme. For example *The Times* informed its readers on 18 June 1851 that it believed the population of Ireland to be not 'much over 8,000,000'. Yet only about a fortnight later, on 4 July 1851, the same paper had to report the 'painful but authentic communication . . . that the population of Ireland is at this moment very little more than six millions and a half' (Drake 1972 p 9). The first report was written after *The Times* had carried numerous *eye-witness* accounts of the potato famine which struck Ireland in the late 1840s and of the packed emigrant ships which proved to be one means of escape from it. The second report appeared after preliminary reports of the 1851 census had been published.

From what has been written in earlier units, and so far in this, it will be apparent that the study of pre-industrial mortality is unlikely to be easy. There are first the problems of determining the extent of the mortality – from year to year, season to season, area to area, as well as from one age group to another. Secondly there is the problem, already touched on, of causation. Does famine alone produce high mortality or must it be accompanied by disease? Do some diseases operate independently of food supply? In either case, how can one demonstrate the relationships involved? What data does one need? What tests should one carry out? These are some of the questions we shall be tackling in this unit. Answering them is difficult, not least because the crises have all too often either passed unremarked or been exaggerated by contemporary commentators.

2 Topic of interest: mortality in pre-industrial societies

It is a commonplace that the current 'population explosion' is the product of a fall in mortality. With crude death rates dropping in the last thirty years, from, say, 40 to 20 per 1,000, whilst crude birth rates have remained at about 45 per 1,000, the *rate of natural increase* has risen from 5 to 25 per 1,000. The change in rates has meant that populations instead of doubling every 140 years, are now in a position to do so every 28 years. So far as is known, this fall in mortality has been more rapid, has affected more people and is of a greater magnitude than any the world has known before. Not only different in scale, it has also been suggested that the causes of recent falls in mortality are very different from those experienced in earlier centuries, particularly in the west. In fact, two models have been posited. The one, the 'technological-diffusion' model, is believed to cover the recent experience of mortality reduction. It accounts for it through the introduction of *exotic* 'medical, public health and agricultural techniques' into the currently underdeveloped countries, where the fall in mortality has mostly occurred, by western societies. In contrast to this is the 'modernization' model, which associates the earlier falls in western death rates with a general 'social and economic revolution' (Goldscheider

The rate of natural increase is simply the difference between the crude birth rate and the crude death rate, ie it is CBR—CDR.

Figure 2 Victim of the Bengal famine, 1943. Source: Keystone Press Agency

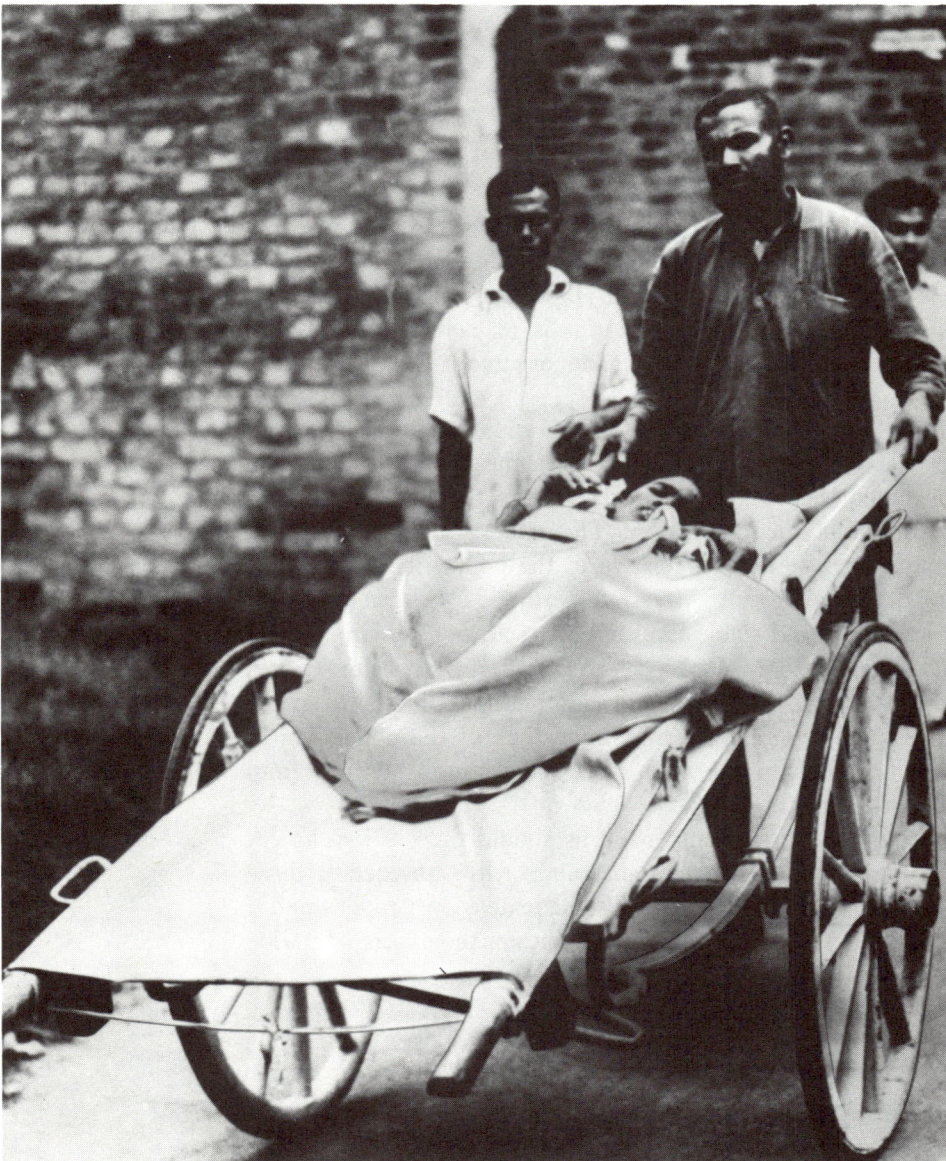

95

1971 pp 122–4). This revolution, often termed the Industrial Revolution, brought rising per capita incomes; better food supplies, as a result of improvements both in agricultural technique and in transport; improvements in sanitation and some, if limited, medical advances.

Whether or not these two experiences of mortality reduction are as starkly different as these two models would suggest is still a matter of dispute. For instance, one might argue that inoculation (and later vaccination) against smallpox played a similar role in eighteenth and nineteenth-century Europe, as DDT sprays against malaria did in India and Africa in recent years. (On the importance of inoculation see Razzell 1965.) Yet the technique of inoculation was exotic to Europe, being introduced from Turkey in the early eighteenth century. Again, to take another illustration, it might be argued that the potato played a similar role in late eighteenth and early nineteenth-century Europe as that the '*green revolution*' is said to have played in parts of the contemporary underdeveloped world (see Drake 1969). And yet the potato too was not native to Europe, being introduced from America in the sixteenth century.

Quite apart from the mechanism of mortality reduction, there is the question of mortality rates before the fall took place. The importance of this for our understanding of economic development has already been touched upon in Unit 5. If the pattern of mortality was similar in the pre-industrial west to what it was in the currently underdeveloped part of the world a generation or so ago, then we have one set of parameters; if, on the other hand, it was different, we have another. It is, then, of some importance to learn what the mortality patterns of the pre-industrial west were. That indeed is the concern of this unit.

The 'green revolution' is the name given to the large increase over the past twenty years in grain yields, resulting from new varieties of wheat, rice etc. Believers in the 'green revolution' are convinced that it is the answer to the world's food problem. Critics say it is little more than a public relations exercise and that recent increases in world output of grain have come from increased acreage rather than increased yields.

3 Articulate problem: how and why did mortality rates fluctuate in pre-industrial western societies?

In trying to answer this question, we must first of all seek to isolate the relevant factors bearing upon it. One way of approaching this is to examine the present mortality pattern in the west, discover the determinants of it and then hypothesize the effect of changes in these on that pattern.

The first characteristic of contemporary western mortality patterns is their stability. From year to year only slight changes occur in the rates. So far as the crude death rate is concerned the bulk of whatever change there is comes from shifts in the age composition of the population. The rate rises when the most mortality-prone age groups increase in size, relative to the population as a whole. It falls when the size of these groups falls. A second feature of western mortality today is that it is kept at its low and stable level by a vast array of environmental and medical services. These range from complex sanitation systems to health services which envelop the population with preventive and curative medical aids from the cradle to the grave. Food, too, is for the overwhelming bulk of the population in abundant supply. Ironically, today in the west more people probably die from over-eating than from under-nourishment!

The examination of pre-industrial mortality patterns should then, if you accept the argument so far, focus on the level of mortality and on the absence of those factors which keep it low and stable today; namely adequate food supplies and a sophisticated battery of measures that reduce, if not eradicate, the effects of a wide variety of diseases.

4 Formulate hypothesis

We will test the Malthusian hypothesis which can be articulated thus: in the pre-industrial west, population growth was checked periodically by *high* mortality, the result of *inadequate* food supplies. Before going on to study the various exercises which, I think, enable us to test this hypothesis, examine it for a moment or two and decide how you might go about testing it. The italicized words will give you some clues.

5 Devise tests

To test this hypothesis we need to examine three sets of relationships. First, there is the relationship between mortality in one year and that in neighbouring years. To what extent is mortality, like today, stable from year to year? To what extent does it fluctuate? And if it fluctuates, to what extent does it do so? Does, for example, the level rise two or three or even more times above its mean level? If so, how often? And does this bring it above the birth rate, so bringing about an actual decline in population? This question of the amplitude of the fluctuations in the death rate is important because it provides a clue to the causes of mortality. For, if the death rate is continuously high (ie stable at a high level), then one might argue that whatever is causing it to be so is endemic, eg disease or food shortages. On the other hand, if the death rate is stable at a low or moderate level for several years, resulting in a considerable natural increase, and then rises sharply, one might argue that one is dealing with an epidemic-type situation. That is to say, the check to population is the result of some factor that is not a permanent feature of the demographic landscape; for example, an outbreak of plague, a smallpox or typhus epidemic, a harvest failure.

Having satisfied ourselves as to the level of mortality we can move on to our two other tests. The first of these involves attempting to measure the relationship between food supplies and mortality. The classic Malthusian position would appear to imply not only that this relationship was the crucial one in determining the rate of population change, but also that it operated in an explosive and cyclical fashion. According to this, the sequence of events would appear to be as follows.

A bad harvest causes widespread food shortages, which lead to starvation, or at least malnutrition. This in turn facilitates the spread of disease. Mortality rises sharply. The population falls, which means the amount of resources (particularly land) per head rises. Farms, businesses, jobs generally, are available earlier than expected. Marriages can take place sooner, the birth rate rises, and since resources are more plentiful per head, mortality falls. Sooner or later, however, the population reaches its former level and begins to press against subsistence. A bad harvest starts the cycle all over again.

An alternative to the Malthusian hypothesis, and one which breaks the link between food supply and mortality, is the third test we must carry out. According to this, disease whether of an endemic or epidemic nature, follows a pattern of its own. This pattern is determined by the nature of the disease, and any connection between its incidence and the advent of food shortages is purely coincidental. If this independent pattern of disease can be shown to be a major determinant of the pre-industrial mortality level, then our explanation of this level becomes a more complex one. For it involves not only the history of man's resistance to particular diseases, but also the history of the diseases themselves; their method of propagation, their virulence, their dissemination, and whether or not they too are subject to external forces affecting each of these aspects.

6 Collect data

Test 1 For this exercise we need to draw on those parish registers which passed the various tests discussed in Unit 5. How long a period we take, or how wide an area we cover, will be dictated partly by our resources and partly by the particular questions we ask. We may also get some *indication* of fluctuations in mortality by counting the number of wills proved in each year of the period in which we are interested (Radio Programme 3, *No Safety in Numbers*).

Test 2 Evidence on food shortages can come from a variety of sources. These include official reports, market prices published in newspapers, food prices paid by institutions such as schools or hospitals and recorded in their accounts, as well as comments by diarists, travellers and letter writers. Indices can be derived from these and then correlated with the records of mortality provided by the parish registers or will counts.

Test 3 Sometimes parish burial registers include marginal comments drawing attention to the supposed cause of death. Usually, however, this only happens in a year of particularly heavy mortality. Valuable as this information is then, one must guard against giving it the prominence it has in the register. One must also examine literary accounts, for though these are fallible (again they tend to highlight the exceptional and their diagnoses are usually those of non-medical men) they do provide some clues.

We must be wary, however, of drawing conclusions from wills proved. Because many people do not make wills they do not provide an unbiased sample.

Table 1 Baptisms, marriages and burials in the Wapentake of Morley from 1540 to 1643

Year	Baptisms	Marriages	Burials	Year	Baptisms	Marriages	Burials	Year	Baptisms	Marriages	Burials
1540	591	152	376	1575	738	201	452	1610	1,050	250	719
1541	578	145	313	1576	759	189	460	1611	1,067	307	774
1542	482	107	387	1577	716	185	452	1612	999	273	724
1543	560	186	404	1578	665	232	409	1613	985	300	1,078
1544	511	129	387	1579	860	240	383	1614	1,065	313	826
1540–44	2,722	719	1,867	1575–79	3,738	1,047	2,156	1610–14	5,166	1,443	4,121
1545	498	148	445	1580	810	277	449	1615	1,136	328	731
1546	478	150	372	1581	820	286	323	1616	1,010	311	799
1547	489	120	351	1582	808	219	450	1617	1,057	294	1,141
1548	567	216	328	1583	798	236	357	1618	1,105	273	782
1549	580	190	342	1584	830	214	463	1619	1,076	321	780
1545–49	2,612	824	1,838	1580–84	4,066	1,232	2,042	1615–19	5,384	1,527	4,233
1550	460	164	308	1585	748	206	473	1620	1,184	302	737
1551	467	118	304	1586	700	192	499	1621	1,197	341	1,021
1552	522	164	255	1587	484	161	1,411	1622	903	222	1,056
1553	593	161	238	1588	696	269	687	1623	800	214	1,660
1554	582	173	266	1589	774	280	487	1624	952	356	992
1550–54	2,624	780	1,371	1585–89	3,402	1,108	3,557	1620–24	5,036	1,435	5,466
1555	551	161	285	1590	600	228	536	1625	1,121	322	734
1556	571	125	389	1591	676	252	639	1626	964	311	672
1557	527	143	615	1592	683	249	512	1627	1,156	313	881
1558	635	204	440	1593	724	260	462	1628	1,095	294	934
1559	564	263	349	1594	890	328	498	1629	1,074	284	909
1555–59	2,848	896	2,078	1590–94	3,573	1,317	2,647	1625–29	5,410	1,524	4,130
1560	721	233	385	1595	866	178	625	1630	1,029	284	865
1561	567	201	370	1596	815	227	892	1631	966	288	1,102
1562	679	228	454	1597	666	190	1,002	1632	1,083	339	1,241
1563	566	146	364	1598	799	253	758	1633	1,194	338	929
1564	595	198	343	1599	919	279	630	1634	1,076	370	903
1560–64	3,128	1,006	1,916	1595–99	4,065	1,127	3,907	1630–34	5,348	1,619	5,040
1565	623	179	394	1600	907	289	632	1635	1,099	334	1,121
1566	614	184	397	1601	848	218	687	1636	1,056	261	1,000
1567	733	175	390	1602	889	269	818	1637	1,055	275	1,021
1568	712	187	364	1603	964	295	765	1638	1,031	333	948
1569	669	164	411	1604	1,017	329	680	1639	1,084	300	842
1565–69	3,351	889	1,956	1600–04	4,625	1,400	3,582	1635–39	5,325	1,503	4,932
1570	700	183	576	1605	1,094	289	663	1640	1,205	394	1,119
1571	648	187	376	1606	1,066	297	673	1641	1,162	372	1,078
1572	750	186	437	1607	1,081	323	709	1642	1,225		963
1573	623	208	434	1608	1,091	261	797	1643			2,453
1574	691	189	388	1609	1,024	290	725	1644			
1570–74	3,412	953	2,211	1605–09	5,356	1,460	3,567	1645			

7 Carry out tests

Test 1 The distribution of deaths

1 Our first task is to use the parish registers to tell us the distribution of burials by year, by season, by age group and by locale. We can also discover the relationship between the number of burials and the number of baptisms. To illustrate these various measures, we will use, for the most part, the data provided by the various Yorkshire parish registers listed in Unit 6.

Table 1 shows the number of baptisms, marriages and burials *derived* from the registers of certain parishes in the Morley Wapentake from 1540 to 1643. In graphical form they appear in Figure 3.

SAQ 1 Examine the graph of burials in Figure 3. What do you think are its most important features?

2 Our next exercise is to find what seasonal variations there were in burials. Since burials can be expected to follow closely on deaths (unlike baptisms on births, see

Actually, the figures appearing in Table 1 are the product of certain extrapolatory exercises. For the details see Appendix 1.

Figure 3 Graph of baptisms, marriages and burials in the Wapentake of Morley from 1540 to 1643

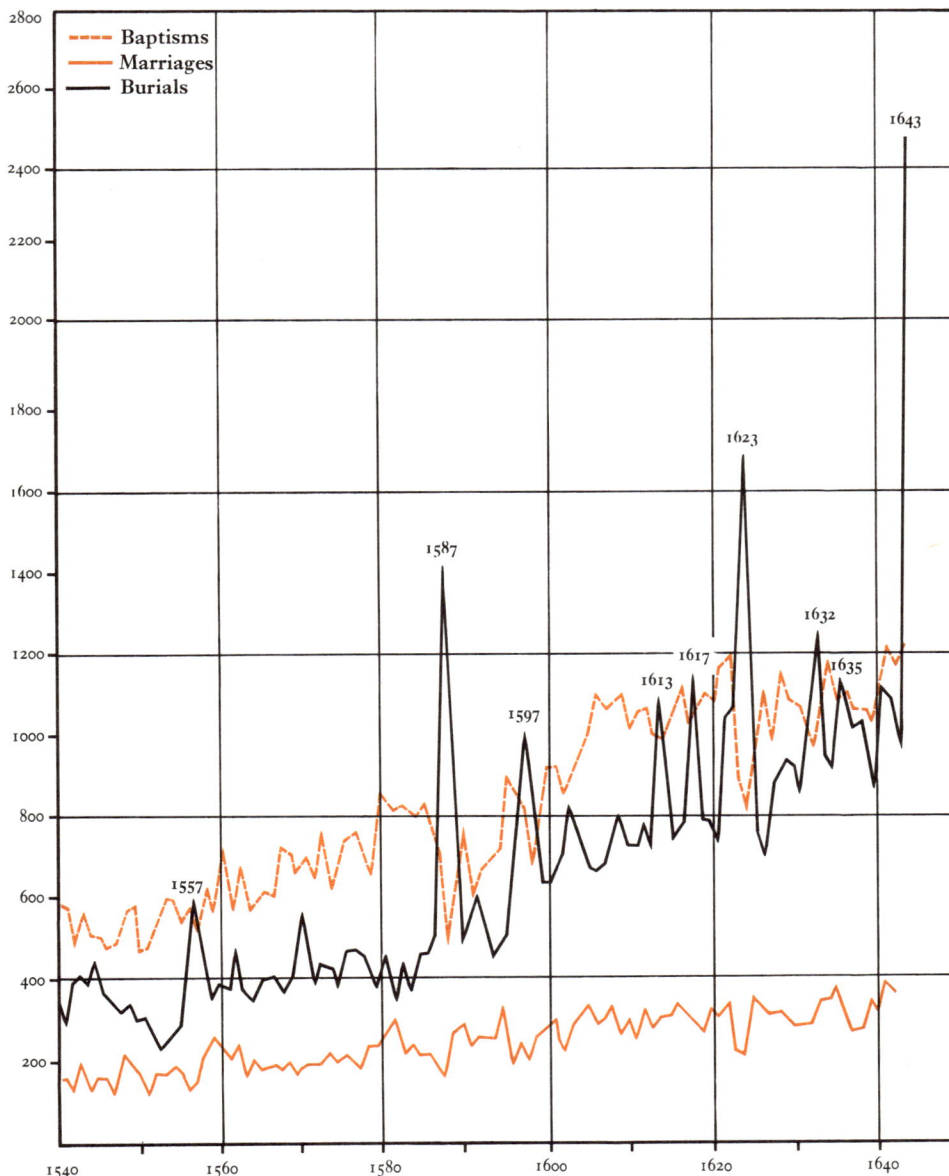

Mills 1973) we can equate the two. Table 2 shows the number of Halifax burials per quarter for each decade from 1540–1639.

SAQ 2 Examine Table 2. What strikes you about the distribution of burials by quarter?

Table 2 Halifax Parish Registers: burials (each quarter expressed as percentage of annual total)

Decade	Jan–March	April–June	July–Sept	Oct–Dec	Number of burials
1540–49	31.0	24.3	20.9	23.7	1742
1550–59	29.4	22.2	23.8	24.5	1622
1560–69	28.7	25.7	19.6	25.9	1479
1570–79	31.5	26.3	20.9	21.2	2102
1580–89	32.6	22.0	18.3	27.0	2384
1590–99	32.5	24.3	18.6	24.6	2949
1600–09	29.5	25.0	21.6	23.8	3394
1610–19	29.7	24.2	22.5	23.5	3965
1620–29	29.4	24.2	21.1	25.3	4334
1630–39	30.0	25.7	20.1	24.2	4485
Total 1540–1639	30.3	24.5	20.8	24.3	28456

3 Getting at the age distribution of burials is more difficult than the seasonal or annual distributions, unless ages are given in the register: an unusual occurrence until the late eighteenth and early nineteenth centuries. There are, however, various indirect methods which can be of value in certain circumstances. For instance, Appleby (1973) noticed that often the burial registers give the family status of the deceased, in the form: 'wife of', 'child of', 'daughter of', 'widow of' and so on. He admits that 'to treat all persons listed as sons and daughters as "children" and all others as "adults" is a rather crude method of determining age.' Nevertheless, he goes on to argue that 'if striking changes appear in the proportion of each group in the burial records, they offer a clue to the cause of mortality under study' (Appleby 1973 p 413). An illustration of the technique appears in Table 3. This shows a very pronounced rise in adult deaths in 1587. Appleby uses this as evidence to support his contention that the sharp rise in burials, which was a feature of this year throughout Cumberland and Westmorland, was due to typhus. His reasons for this were first that 'typhus very rarely kills children' and second that it occurs most commonly in winter, which is when these deaths mostly occurred.

Table 3 Number of burials of adults and children recorded in the Dacre (Cumberland) Parish Register 1582–9

	Year							
	1582	1583	1584	1585	1586	1587	1588	1589
Children	6	8	11	Missing	10	10	16	8
Adults	9	10	13	Missing	12	53	21	9

Source: Appleby (1973) p 413

4 Another distribution pattern that is worth seeking out is that of burials by area, for this too can provide clues as to the cause and extent of mortality in any particular period. To do this particular exercise one can either take a sample of parishes over a fairly wide area, or a number of parishes that are adjacent to each other. Table 4 shows an example of the latter. It was drawn up to see to what extent the rise in burials in 1623 in the Morley Wapentake (see Table 1 and Figure 3) was confined to parts of the Wapentake, or whether it was general throughout the Wapentake, and to what extent it was a feature of neighbouring parishes.

Table 4 Burials in certain Yorkshire parishes 1619–27, (church years)

Number of burials

Year	1619	1620	1621	1622	1623	1624	1625	1626	1627
Bradford	124	133	180	187	334	175	127	146	203
Elland	102	101	126	108	223	146	113	74	108
Wakefield	140	188	173	140	250	163	311*	121	142
Dewsbury	35	49	46	31	68	44	41	27	65
Batley	17	17	25	25	37	31	29	15	30**
Huddersfield	83	71	114	115	173	93	73	64	83
Horbury	16	14	9	13	26	15	11	15	15
Thornhill	25	26	24	30	40***	29	24	27	27
Halifax	387	330	489	482	698††	455	319	314	370
Leeds	263	279	278	253	492	413	325	264	281
Rothwell	53	59	53	27	85	69	54	43	65
Mirfield	18	13	26	19	33	20	18	15	15
Keighley	40	(16)‡	(34)‡‡	46	113	36	27	32	31
Bingley	56	41	40	43	99	58	48	37	52
Methley	16	29	13	19	14	18	12	16	13
Hartshead	18	16	13	13	14	13	15	11	17
Birstall	62	63	63	89	105	71	62	50	61
Swillington	9	10	6	6	21	12	6	6	3
Heptonstall	54	63	105	132	183	89	67	48	84
	1518	1518	1817	1778	3008	1950	1682	1325	1665

*Of which 128 said to have died *de peste* between 8 August and 16 January.
**Bishop's Transcript. Sheard gives only 12.   ***Register ends 25 January 1623.
††31 July Marteris Martin, Vicar's warden, buried, then gap in register of burials till 27 August when Henry Savile, parish clerk, is buried.
‡Register ends 29 September 1620.   ‡‡Register began 3 January 1621.

SAQ 3 Examine Table 4. How widespread was the rise in burials in 1623? Is there any other year which has above average mortality? If so, is there anything special about it?

Figure 4 Morley Wapentake: baptisms per 100 burials, 1542–1640 (five-year moving average)

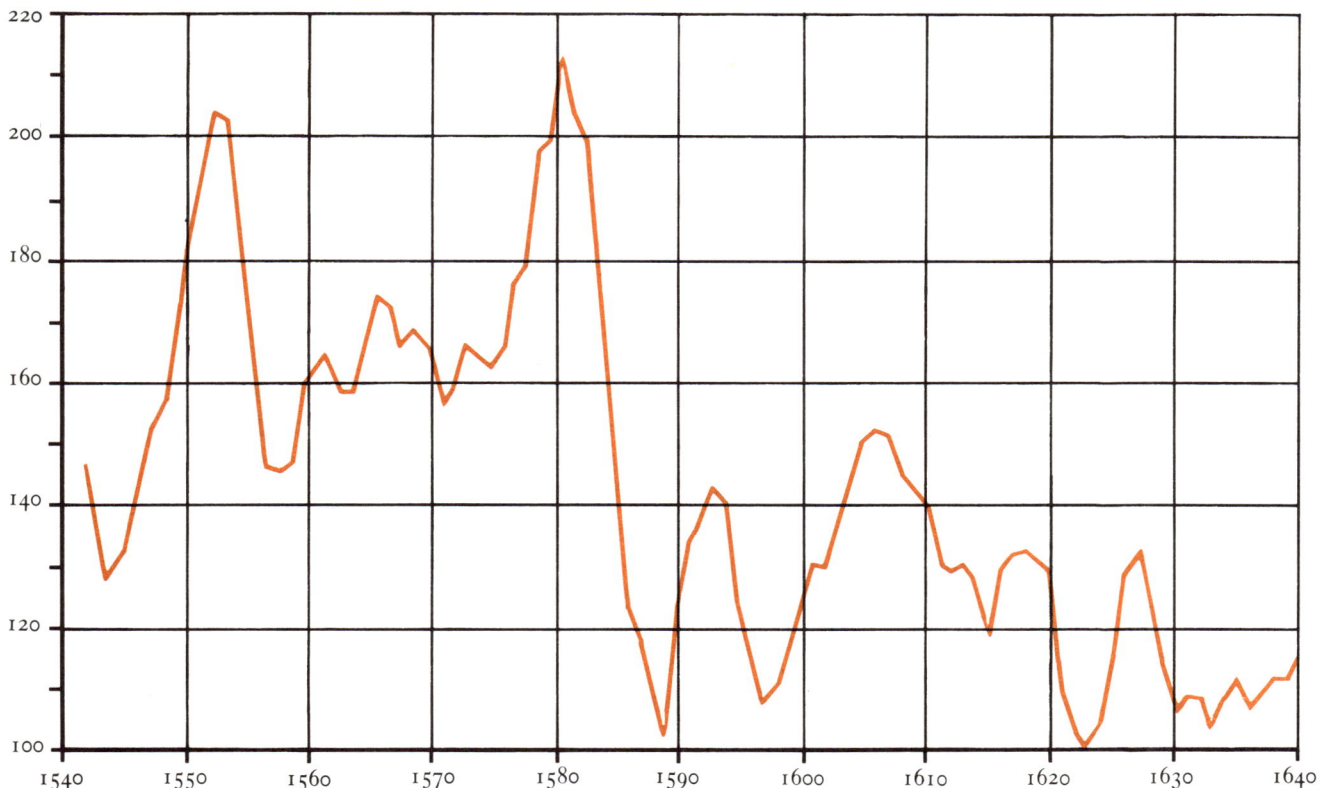

5 The distribution of burials relative to baptisms is another important indicator of the role of mortality in population change. For most places and periods it is, in fact, the only satisfactory surrogate for crude birth and death rates, since various attempts at working these out, on the basis of the information in the registers alone, have not proved satisfactory. For such attempts see Sogner (1963) and Razzell (1965). Figure 4 shows the number of baptisms per 100 burials in the Morley Wapentake parishes from 1542–1640. The series has been 'smoothed' somewhat by taking a *five-year moving average*.

SAQ 4 Examine Figure 4. What two features strike you as being particularly noteworthy?

6 One final measure, indicating the extent of mortality, can be gauged from the length of time it took for a population to recover its numbers, after a period when burials exceeded baptisms, assuming it was doing so by natural increase, unassisted by immigration. The calculation of this measure is an easy one. One merely counts the excess of baptisms over burials in the years after the period in question until their number equals the number lost in that period. An example is given for the Morley Wapentake parishes, in Table 5.

Table 5 Years in which burials exceeded baptisms in the Morley Wapentake (1540–1639) together with the number of years taken, in each instance, for the population to recover its losses, assuming natural increase only

Years in which burials exceeded baptisms	Number of years taken for population to recover
1557	Under 1 year
1587	7 years
1596	4 years
1597	3 years
1613	1 year
1617	1 year
1623	4 years
1624	1 year
1631	3 years
1632	2 years
1635	1 year

A five-year moving average is calculated by averaging the figures for the first five years of a series, and entering the result as the figure for the third year; then averaging the figures for the second to sixth years, entering that result as the figure for the fourth year; and so on, until all years in the series have been included. (This means that the figures for the first two and last two years of the series are 'lost', but that the violent fluctuations in the original figures are attenuated somewhat.) This averaging process can be done for any period that one chooses; in Television Programme 3, an eleven-year moving average is mentioned.

From the various exercises conducted so far on this limited set of data, certain conclusions appear to emerge. They are:
1 Mortality, as measured by the number of burials, could change sharply from year to year. In 1587, for example, burials in the Morley Wapentake were three times as high as the mean figure for the previous five years (Table 1).
2 Although burials could rise sharply, there were periods of up to thirty years when they did not do so (1557–87). During such a period the number of baptisms might rise to twice the number of burials. Translated into crude rates this could mean that a birth rate of 40 per 1,000 went together with a death rate of 20.
3 The oscillations in the number of burials and, therefore, presumably of deaths, are such a striking feature of the mortality picture it would seem proper to focus our attention on them. For it does appear that, as Malthus postulated, populations could be held back by periods of unusually high mortality following on periods of unusually low mortality. Put in numbers it would seem we can have two patterns of mortality, both of which produce the same mean level but by very different routes. For a mean crude death rate of say 35 per 1,000 over a period of ten years could result from a pattern like this:

28   26   24   25   23   21   28   50   75   50

This seems to be rather like the pattern in the Morley Wapentake in the early part of the period 1540–1639. Towards the end, however, one might imagine a situation more akin to this. Again the mean is 35:

30 29 32 50 35 33 36 40 35 30

To conclude this section you might look at Figure 5 which shows these two patterns in one and the same country. The Norwegian diocese of Bergen did not suffer the peaks of mortality experienced by the neighbouring Akershus diocese in the years 1735–1815. During this period the differences between the mean crude death rates was comparatively slight: 27 per 1,000 in Akershus as against 23 per 1,000 in Bergen. As Figure 5 shows, however, the patterns of mortality which produced these two rates were very different.

Figure 5 Deaths per 1,000 mean population in the dioceses of Akershus and Bergen 1735–1865
Source: Drake (1969A) p 39

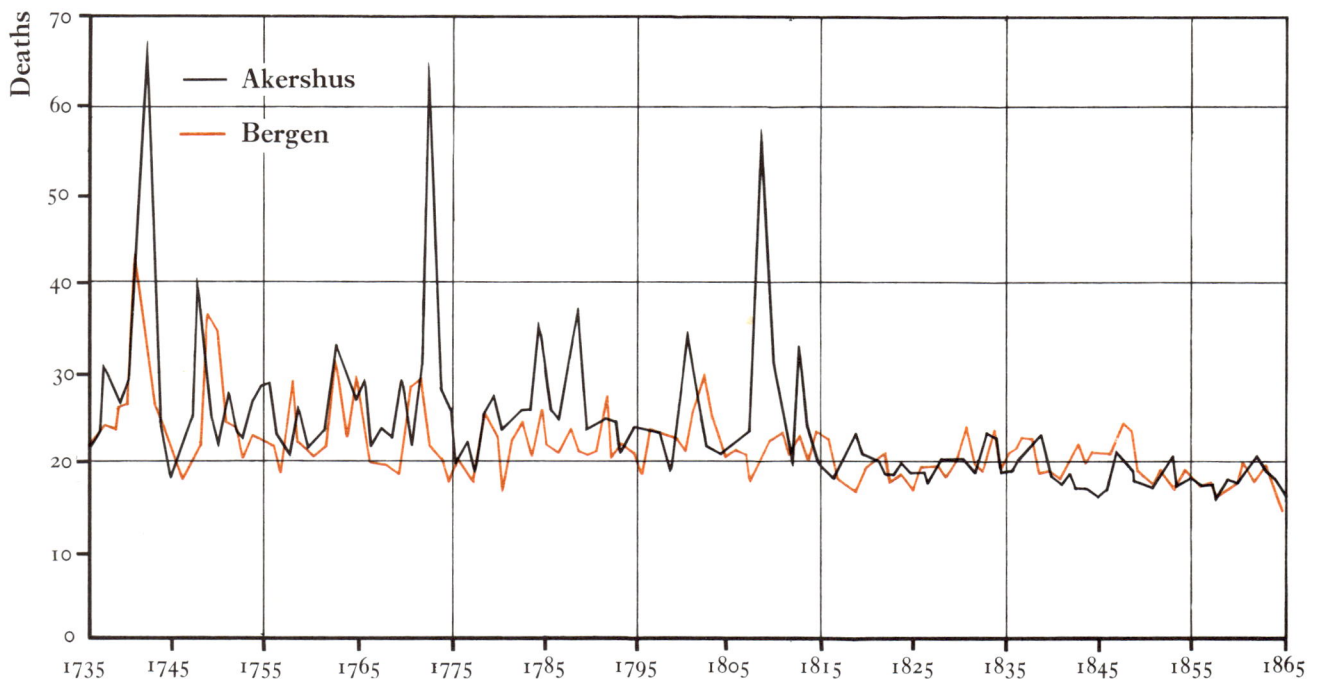

Test 2   Food and mortality

We turn now to examine the relationship between mortality and food supply. This brings us to the title of our unit. For our little affectation in using a French title is in deference to the work of historical demographers of that country who first isolated what might be called the classic demographic crisis. This was closely associated with wheat prices. The anatomy of such a crisis was as follows. First a bad harvest causes food shortages. This induces deficiency diseases, one effect of which is to reduce fecundity and so lower the number of conceptions. If the shortage continues mortality increases. And since in pre-industrial societies high food prices, brought about by crisis conditions, adversely affected the prosperity of the economy, the setting up of new families was delayed, so marriages fell too. Once the crisis had passed, conceptions rose, deaths fell and marriages increased, possibly to higher levels than before the onset of the crisis as there were 'dead men's shoes' to be filled. An example of such a crisis is given in Table 6 and Figure 6. Other examples appear in Television Programme 3 (*Demographic Crisis*).

To illustrate how the calculations are carried out in order to show the existence or not of a crisis caused by food shortages, we will turn to data provided by the Halifax registers. Table 7 shows the number of baptisms in each month from August 1582 to September 1592. These are laid out along the lines of the form designed by the

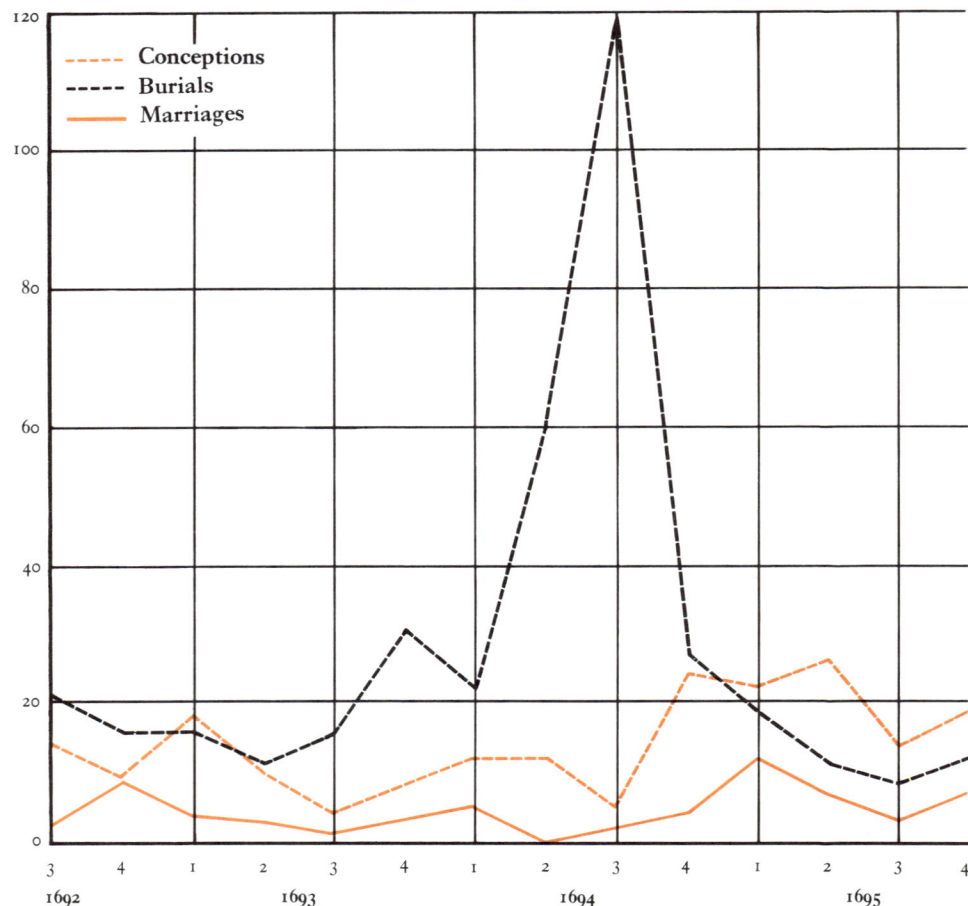

Figure 6 Conceptions, burials and marriages in Breteuil, by quarter, 1692–5

Table 6 The demographic crisis in Breteuil 1693–4

	1692		1693				1694				1695			
Quarters	3	4	1	2	3	4	1	2	3	4	1	2	3	4
Conceptions	14	9	18	10	4	8	12	12	5	24	22	26	14	19
Burials	21	16	16	11	15	31	22	60	120	27	18	11	8	12
Marriages	3	9	4	3	1	4	5	0	2	4	12	7	3	7

Source: Goubert (1960) II pp 56–7

Table 7 Baptisms and conceptions by month in Halifax Parish 1582–92

	Month of conception												Bap-tisms by Civil Years	Concep-tion by Harvest Years		
	Apr	May	June	July	Aug	Sept	Oct	Nov	Dec	Jan	Feb	Mar				
	Month of baptism															
	Jan	Feb	Mar	Apr	May	June	July	Aug	Sept	Oct	Nov	Dec		Jan–Aug	May–Dec	
1582								20	38	20	18	30				317
1583	33	28	30	19	23	27	32	27	26	20	26	36	327	110	217	353
1584	27	26	27	20	32	26	25	36	32	31	22	27	331	100	231	299
1585	31	31	34	26	22	17	(21)*	17	27	35	29	21	311	122	189	289
1586	32	35	20	23	22	24	27	25	20	34	18	30	310	110	200	166
1587	21	19	15	34	20	16	11	18	10	4	10	18	196	89	107	289
1588	17	15	8	19	12	18	15	25	17	16	26	30	218	59	159	319
1589	27	35	37	31	25	36	20	24	25	31	24	30	345	130	215	298
1590	27	24	29	24	23	18	18	21	19**	19**	30	26	278	104	174	329
1591	31	42	25	26	42	19	30	32	23	32	21	21	344	124	220	
1592	25	22	35	27	37	23	21	23	24					109		

*Mean of May, June, August and September totals.
**Mean of July, August, November and December totals.

Source: Crossley (1910)

Cambridge Group for the History of Population and Social Structure. (For a facsimile see Unit 6 Appendix 3.) The assumption underlying this is that baptisms took place just after birth and, therefore, by counting back nine months one is able to locate the date of conception. Table 8 shows the number of monthly burials in

Table 8 Monthly burials in Halifax Parish 1582–92

Year	Jan	Feb	Mar	Apr	May	Jun	Jul	Aug	Sept	Oct	Nov	Dec	Civil year totals	Jan–July	Aug–Dec	Harvest year totals
1582	16	13	19	22	15	11	16	10	19	5	11	19	176	112	64	183
1583	23	24	26	12	13	10	11	8	6	11	12	16	172	119	53	163
1584	10	14	19	15	17	20	15	12	17	16	11	13	179	110	69	201
1585	23	20	25	15	19*	15*	15*	15	12	21	15	18	213	132	81	231
1586	26	28	33	17	21	9	16	13	12	12	15	22	224	150	74	259
1587	21	30	36	37	26	18	17	30	50	71	101	99	536	185	351	784
1588	131	86	66	52	41	37	20	25	18	19	16	25	536	433	103	248
1589	20	27	27	16	22	16	17	18	15	17	15	20	230	145	85	193
1590	17	26	23	14	14	4	10	20	15	20	20	15	198	108	90	279
1591	24	27	44	30	26	21	17	19	23	21	20	35	307	189	118	298
1592	23	39	32	24	19	13	30	13	23	11	9	20	256	180	76	

* Mean of May, June and July totals for years 1580–4 and 1586–90

Source: Crossley (1910)

Halifax for the years 1582–92. By using the layout designed by the Cambridge Group it is also possible to calculate easily the number of burials by harvest year. By comparing Tables 7 and 8 for the years 1586 and 1587 we appear to find the classic demographic crisis. The bad harvest of 1586 leads first to a fall in conceptions and then to a rise in burials.

SAQ 5 Using the material in Tables 7 and 8, produce a seasonal distribution of conceptions and burials as in Table 6 and Figure 6.

We have presented these two illustrations of the classic demographic crisis rather starkly, without qualifications. But you may already have your doubts. After all, there are quite a number of hidden assumptions lurking behind the exposition. For instance, you may recall the discussion of correlation in Unit 4 and of the dangers adverted to there. Ideally, we should know both the quantity and quality of food consumed as well as the exact cause of death – for each individual. In both the illustrations given we have neither. Failing that we are bound to use indirect indicators. For example, we can take food prices. Goubert (1960, I p 404), for instance, did have wheat prices for the Breteuil area. These showed a five-fold increase between 1690–91 and 1693–4. No such figures are available for Halifax in the 1580s. However, Phelps Brown and Hopkins (1956 p 311) have demonstrated that in *southern* England 'prices of consumables' rose sharply in 1587. Their index (1451–75 = 100) for the years 1585 to 1589 was 388, 352, 491, 346, 354. In the northern cloth-producing areas like Halifax living standards may have been reduced further by the 'undoubted depression of 1586–7' in the woollen industry (Stone 1947 p 106).

Admittedly, it seems reasonable to assume that when food prices rise some portion of the population will be forced to reduce its purchases. This may bring about deficiency diseases, or at least reduce resistance to other diseases, resulting in sickness and possibly death for some. Plausible though such a line of reasoning is, in any particular situation the relationship is subject to a variety of other, so called, intervening variables. A 'rich' society, for instance, is cushioned against rising food prices because it can divert spending power away from non-food items. In some societies too the proportion of the population buying its food, as opposed to growing it, will be smaller than in others. Market prices will then be less of an indicator of the *general* food supply position. Another factor that has to be borne in mind is

whether or not the society in question has experienced high mortality, from whatever cause, not many years before the onset of high food prices. If it has, the effect
of high prices may be muted because the weaker members of the community will
probably have died during the earlier crisis.

I have spelled out some of these complications, rather laboriously perhaps, because
it is important to recognize that a one-to-one relationship between food supplies
and mortality does not exist. That said, it would be silly not to try to find out the

Figure 7 Famine in Siena (fifteenth-century miniature from *Il Biadajolo*). Source: Biblioteca Medicea-
Laurenziana, Florence

Table 9 Mean price of wheat per quarter (40 stones) in Dublin at the beginning of each month 1740–3*

Year	Jan	Feb	Mar	Apr	May	June	July	Aug	Sept	Oct	Nov	Dec
	s. d.	s. d.	s. d.	s. d.	s. d.	s. d.	s. d.	s. d.	s. d.	s. d.	s. d.	s. d.
1740	31 6	34 0	37 6	39 6	43 0	60 6	62 0	68 6	56 0	52 6	56 6	63 6
1741	62 6	61 6	60 0	69 0	66 0	66 0	52 6	37 6	32 0	34 6	34 0	37 6
1742	39 9	37 0	37 0	34 6	32 6	31 0	32 0	31 0	25 6	24 0	23 0	24 6
1743	24 0	21 6	21 6	18 0	20 0	18 0	18 6	20 6	19 0	18 6	18 0	19 0

* The assize of wheat, regulating the price of bread, was published in *Faulkner's Dublin Journal*. It was based on the average of the highest and the lowest priced wheat sold on the Dublin market. The figures in this table are those that were published during the first week of each month.

Source: Drake (1968) p 113

food supply position, as indicated by price changes, for as Malthus said 'food is necessary to the existence of man'. Table 9 shows one set of food prices during a period of allegedly high mortality in Ireland (1740–1). I say 'allegedly' because although there is plenty of literary evidence of distress, the statistical evidence is slight (Drake 1968). These prices were taken from newspaper reports. Floud (1973, p 110) shows another series of prices for wheat for the years 1713–18. In his case they came from Winchester College Accounts. Yet another source is illustrated in Table 10 for Denmark. These are average prices of rye for the years 1695–1789.

We have already noted that the link between high food prices and mortality may be affected by a number of factors. This is also true of the link between poor harvests and high prices. One might well assume that high prices *result* from a deficient harvest. But this is not the only relationship. For instance, you will note that in Dublin (Table 9) wheat prices rose slowly through the early months of 1740 and then jumped sharply (by about 50%) between the beginning of May and the beginning of June. This was, of course, well before the harvest had been gathered. It was caused by the *expectation* of a bad harvest consequent upon the late spring and cold summer (Drake 1968 p 112). A further factor was the extremely cold winter. A severe frost set in on 27 December 1739 and continued for seven weeks. This period of severe weather was general throughout northern and western Europe. Indeed, in central England from 1698 to 1957 there were no two consecutive months with lower average readings than January and February 1740 (Drake 1968 pp 104–5). This cold, according to contemporaries, caused extreme distress and an increase in mortality. It also led to less land being put under crops in 1740 (due to labour shortages) – and so further reduced the harvest of that year.

Another reason for rising food prices is given by Lassen (1965 pp 281–2). He says that, in eighteenth-century Denmark, food prices rose as a result of army purchases *prior* to a military campaign rather than *after* a bad harvest. In a society the bulk of whose population bought their food a rise in food prices resulting from army purchases could have just the same effect on mortality as one resulting from a bad harvest. But if we are dealing with a society the majority of whose population grew their own food, or a substantial portion of it, then this would not be the case. For in this latter situation, as we have noted already, food prices would not be an index of food supplies for the population as a whole.

As we may be led astray by food prices, it is necessary to look for other indicators which may help us to determine the nature of the link between food supply and mortality. One such link is the geographical extent of mortality. We have already touched on this in Table 4. There, we see, mortality rose very widely in 1623. This might indicate that food shortages played a part. Appleby (1973 p 413), for instance, argued, in the case of the rise in mortality in Cumberland and Westmorland in 1587, that the geographical extent of the rise suggested famine, since it was unusual to have an outbreak of typhus (the other major contender) in so widespread a rural area.

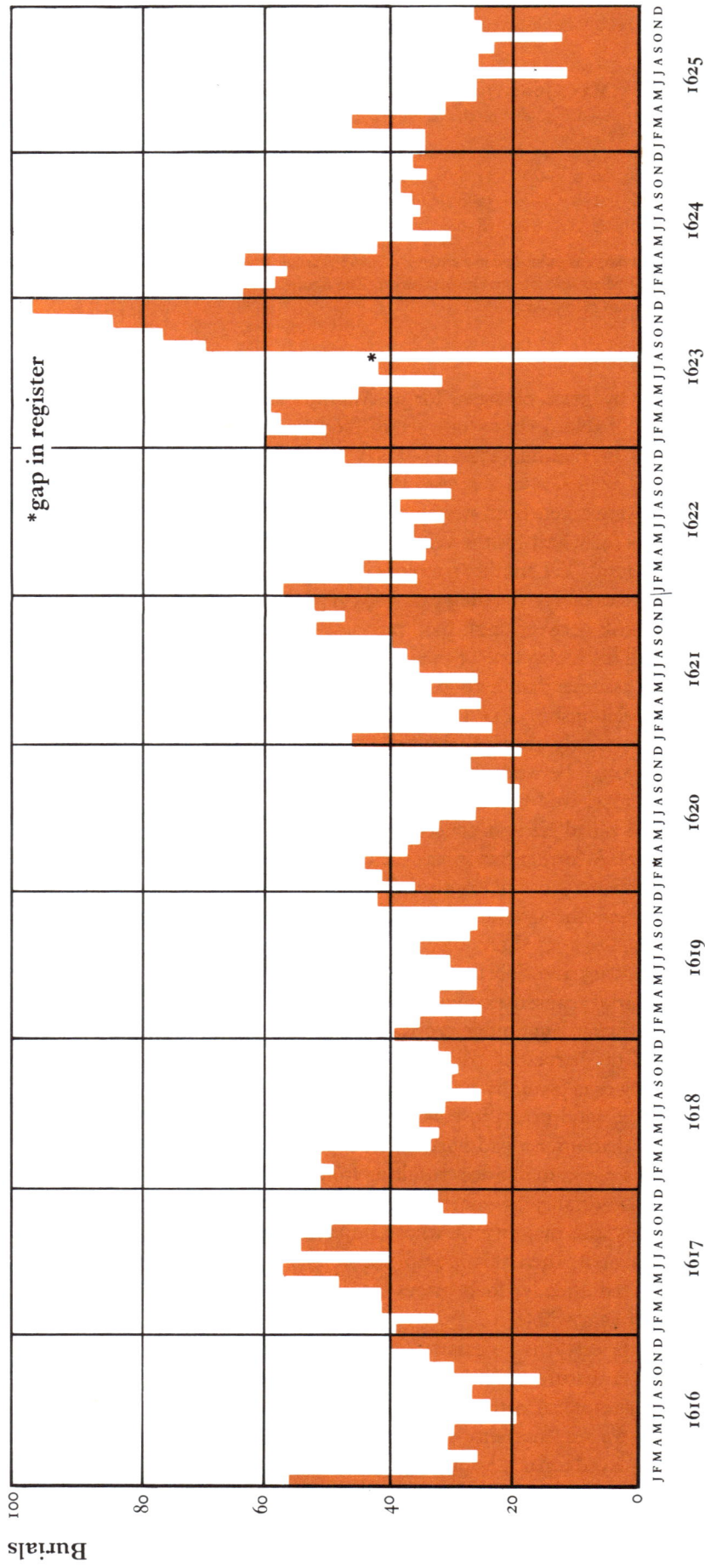

Figure 8 Monthly burials recorded in the Halifax Parish Register 1616–25. Source: Register of Burials, Halifax Parish Church

*gap in register

Burials

108

The timing of the rise in mortality may also provide an important clue to its cause. Deaths resulting from food shortages might be expected to occur in the winter and spring following the rise in food prices, expecially if that rise is the product of a harvest failure. If then one is dealing with a crisis it is worthwhile plotting the burials month by month, as in Figure 8. This shows monthly burials from 1616 to 1625. These years embrace two years of above average mortality. That of 1617 was probably caused by plague, or some other epidemic unassociated with food; that of 1623 by food shortages, caused both by a decline in food supply *and* a decline in purchasing power resulting from a slump in the cloth trade, the main non-agricultural employer in the district (Drake 1962 p 432). You will notice the differences in the seasonal pattern of mortality.

Summing up our discussion so far, it would seem that food shortages may be the cause of mortality rising, but are not the only cause. They are, to use an expression well beloved of social scientists, a sufficient but not a necessary cause. We have also suggested that a rise in food prices need not necessarily be a product of harvest failure and could have widely differing effects on mortality, depending on the society in which it occurred and on its timing and duration. Finally, it has been remarked that factors other than food shortages could raise mortality sharply. Plague, for instance, in Wakefield in 1625 appears to have done so (see Table 4), and may also have done so in the summer months of 1617 in Halifax and again there in 1643 and 1645 (Figure 9). So we turn now to these causes of high mortality which have nothing to do with food supplies.

A *necessary* condition is a condition which must be present to guarantee a certain outcome or result, but which will not do so itself. A *sufficient* condition is a condition which need not be present to guarantee a certain outcome or result but which, if it is present, will guarantee that outcome or result.

Figure 9 Monthly burials recorded in the Halifax Parish Register 1640–45
Source: see Figure 8

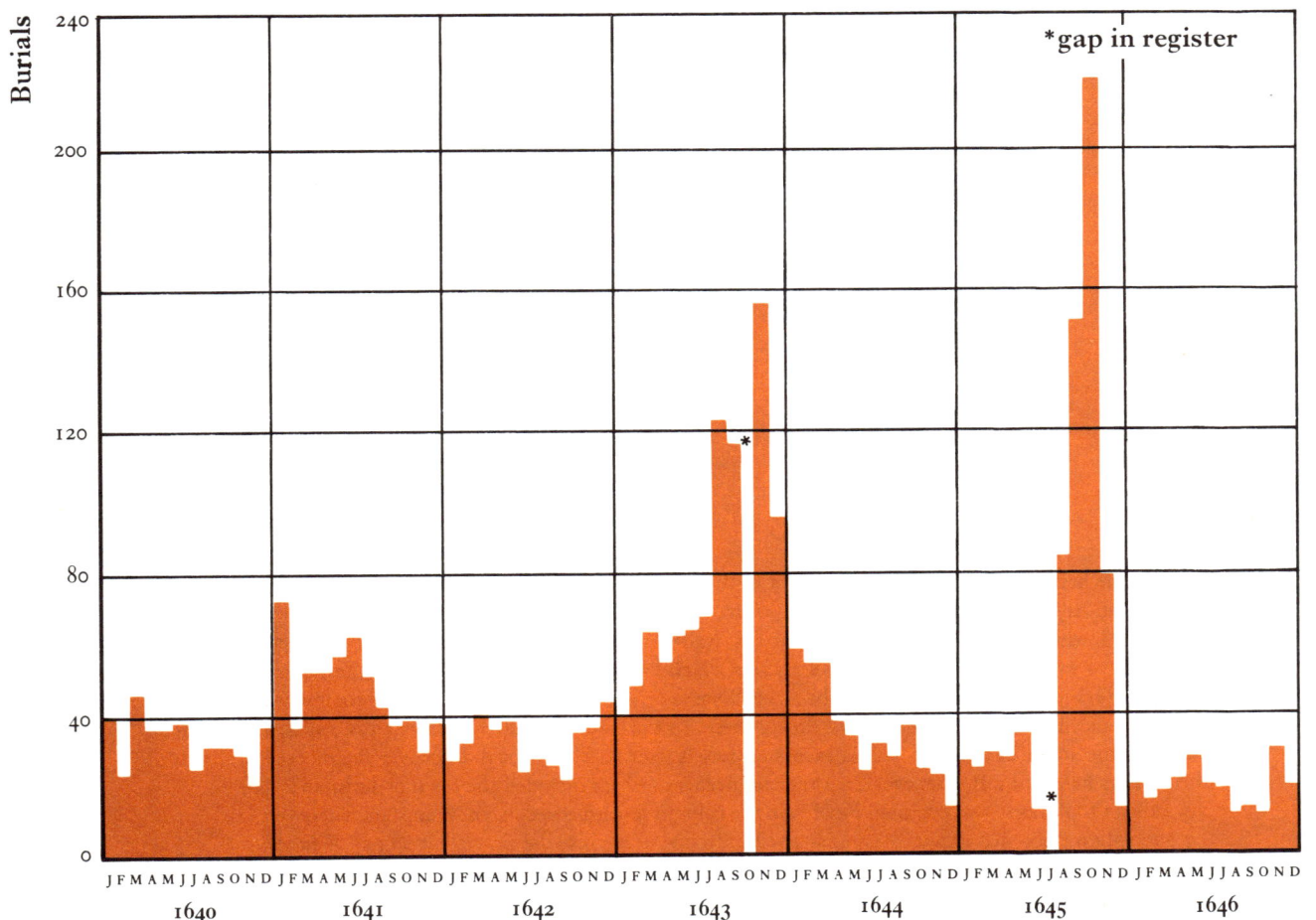

Table 10 Mortality and food price indices in Scandinavia 1695–1799

Year		Århus Diocese		Norway	Sweden
1695		1	1–32		
1696		4H	2–16		
1697	K	3	3–00		
1698		8H	4–00		M
1699	A	22H	3–80		M
1700	KÅ	21H	1–64		
1701	Å	21H	1–40		
1702		2	1–40		
1703	K	2H	1–32		
1704		5H	2–00		
1705	? Å	???	1–64		M
1706		2	1–72		M
1707		0	1–48		M
1708	K	7	2–24		M
1709	K	4H	4–00		M
1710	KÅ	23H	2–08		M
1711	D	1	1–32		M
1712		4H	1–32		
1713		2	1–32		
1714		0	1–80		
1715		0	1–32		
1716		2	1–48		
1717		4	2–32		
1718		6	3–32		
1719		1	2–48		
1720		?	1–72		
1721		0	1–32		
1722		2	1–32		
1723		0	1–32		
1724	KÅ	?	2–16		
1725		3	1–80		
1726	KÅ	20H	3–00		
1727	K	4	1–88		
1728	K	6	1–80		
1729	K	8H	1–80		
1730	K	10	1–24		
1731	KÅ	13H	1–24	B	
1732		2H	1–16		
1733	K	0	1–32		
1734		4H	1–32		
1735		0	1–68		
1736	K	1	2–32		
1737	D	4H	2–00	B	MF
1738	K	18H	1–36		
1739		9H	1–56	B	M
1740	D	1	2–88		F
1741	DÅ	13H	2–84	NAB	F
1742	DÅ	22H	2–08	NAB	MF
1743	KÅ	13H	1–72	NAB	MF
1744	K	0	1–32		M
1745	K	1	2–00		
1746	K	1	2–32		
1747	K	7H	2–08		
1748	DÅ	16H	2–36	NAB	U
1749	Å	19H	2–32		U
1750	K	7	1–24		
1751	K	4H	1–38		
1752		3	1–20		
1753		4H	1–24		
1754		4	1–72	B	
1755	K	7H	2–40	B	
1756	DÅ	26H	2–64		U
1757	K	1	3–00	B	U
1758	DÅ	5	2–80		
1759	K	8H	1–64	B	M
1760	K	6	1–32		
1761		2H	1–80		U
1762	K	4H	3–00		U
1763	DÅ	23H	2–20	NAB	U
1764	DÅ	22	2–72	B	U
1765	K	2H	4–00	B	
1766	K	2	2–12		
1767	K	3	2–32		
1768		6H	3–32		
1769	K	7	2–64		M
1770	K	7H	3–40	B	M
1771	DÅ	22H	4–40		MUF
1772	DÅ	18H	3–80	B	MFU
1773	DÅ	24H	2–08	NAB	MF
1774		0	2–42	AB	M
1775	K	2	3–64		M
1776		1	1–64		
1777	Å	15H	2–00		
1778	K	5	2–80		
1779	DÅ	25H	1–80	B	
1780		1			U
1781	K	3	2–48		U
1782	K	4	4–00	B	U
1783	K	3	4–16	B	U
1784		12H	2–82	B	M
1785	Å	17H	4–16	NB	M
1786	DÅ	20H	4–48		
1787	D	9H	2–64		
1788		5	3–88	B	
1789		5H	4–00		F
1790		3			
1791		2			
1792		2			
1793		7			
1794	A	13			
1795		2			
1796		4			
1797		3			
1798		6			
1799		11			

Key: In the first column of letters to the right of the dates, K appears against those years in which Copenhagen had an excess of burials over baptisms, D whenever this applies to the whole of Denmark, and A whenever there is an excess of burials in the Århus Diocese. Under the column headed *Århus Diocese* are given the number of communes which had an excess of burials in any particular year. (Note there were 26 communes in the Århus Diocese.) The letter H means that Hasle commune, which embraced the town of Århus, was among these. In the column headed *Norway* an N appears whenever the whole of Norway had an excess of burials over baptisms, an A whenever the diocese of Akershus had, and a B whenever the Bragnaes deanery (which included the town of Kristiania – now called Oslo) was in this position. Finally, in the column headed Sweden, an M appears whenever the population (recorded annually here) showed a decline as against the previous year; an F (after 1721) signifies an excess of burials over baptisms and a U that the harvest 'failed'. The numbers in the *Århus Diocese* column give the mean price of rye in *rigsdaler* and *skilling*.

Source: Lassen 1965 pp 527–8

Test 3 Disease and mortality

Aksel Lassen's figures in Table 10 show that burials exceeded baptisms in many of the areas he studied even when food prices were low. This may, of course, have been because the index of prices that he used was not a good indicator of food shortages. But it also appears likely that factors other than food could bring about a sharp rise in mortality. The late Professor Chambers, whose pioneering study of the historical demography of the Vale of Trent we have already referred to, put it this way:

> The comparison of the two examples of 1736 and 1708–10 is sufficient to suggest that epidemics were a more important and food supply a less important factor in demographic change than has hitherto been realized. It is clear that an epidemic, without the assistance of food shortage, was an effective cause of change; it is not certain that the same can be said of food shortage. (Chambers 1957 p 28)

Figure 10 Poster published in Banbury during the cholera outbreak, 1831
Source: Banbury Public Reference Library, Potts Collection

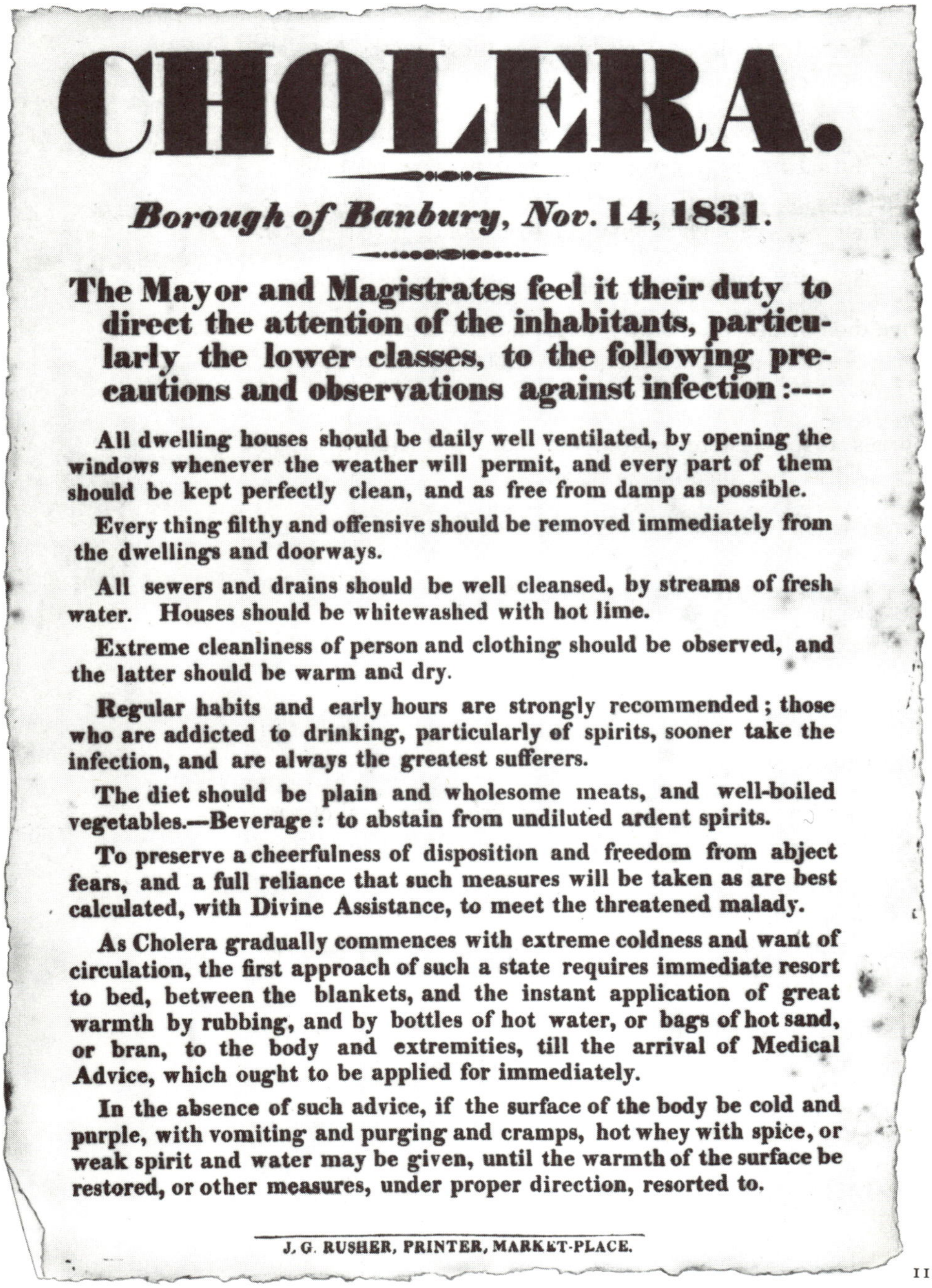

CHOLERA.

Borough of Banbury, Nov. 14, 1831.

The Mayor and Magistrates feel it their duty to direct the attention of the inhabitants, particularly the lower classes, to the following precautions and observations against infection:----

All dwelling houses should be daily well ventilated, by opening the windows whenever the weather will permit, and every part of them should be kept perfectly clean, and as free from damp as possible.

Every thing filthy and offensive should be removed immediately from the dwellings and doorways.

All sewers and drains should be well cleansed, by streams of fresh water. Houses should be whitewashed with hot lime.

Extreme cleanliness of person and clothing should be observed, and the latter should be warm and dry.

Regular habits and early hours are strongly recommended; those who are addicted to drinking, particularly of spirits, sooner take the infection, and are always the greatest sufferers.

The diet should be plain and wholesome meats, and well-boiled vegetables.—Beverage: to abstain from undiluted ardent spirits.

To preserve a cheerfulness of disposition and freedom from abject fears, and a full reliance that such measures will be taken as are best calculated, with Divine Assistance, to meet the threatened malady.

As Cholera gradually commences with extreme coldness and want of circulation, the first approach of such a state requires immediate resort to bed, between the blankets, and the instant application of great warmth by rubbing, and by bottles of hot water, or bags of hot sand, or bran, to the body and extremities, till the arrival of Medical Advice, which ought to be applied for immediately.

In the absence of such advice, if the surface of the body be cold and purple, with vomiting and purging and cramps, hot whey with spice, or weak spirit and water may be given, until the warmth of the surface be restored, or other measures, under proper direction, resorted to.

J. G. RUSHER, PRINTER, MARKET-PLACE.

Here Chambers was referring to a sharp rise in burials in Nottingham and neighbouring villages in the summer of 1736 'during a period of low prices (and) ample food supplies' (Chambers 1959 p 25). By contrast the years 1708–10 witnessed the highest grain prices until the 1790s, 'the Michaelmas price of wheat rising from 24s a quarter in 1707 to 39s in 1708 and to 80s in 1709 after which it sank to 60s then in 1711 to 47s' (Chambers 1957 p 25). Yet during these years burials rose but slightly. You may note, if you turn to Table 10, that the years 1708–10 were also marked by high price rises in Denmark. But, here, by contrast with the Vale of Trent, there were more burials than baptisms in 23 of the 26 parishes of the Århus diocese in 1710.

In seeking out rises in mortality caused by diseases, not associated with food shortages, one could well begin with the parish registers. For they frequently remark upon such diseases – if they turn out to be sufficiently destructive. There are many such references in the Yorkshire registers we have used before.

Bingley. Annual burials 1629–33 were 34, 50, 72, 47 and 45. Included in the 1631 total of 72 were 25 people who 'died of the infection of the plague in the P'ish of Bingley July 6 1631 and not buried in the church yarde'.

Dewsbury. Annual burials 1591–5 were 37, 28, 58, 18, 30. Included in the 1593 figure were 20 said to have died of the plague; first burial of these on 18 July, last on 20 December. Eight of the victims had the name Denton.

Halifax. Annual burials 1549–53 were 161, 145, 146, 120, 112. Included in the 1551 total of 146 were 43 buried in August who were said to have died of the 'sweating sickness'. Another one succumbed in September. The total number of burials in August was 49. This was the highest total for that month between 1540 and 1617.

Annual burials 1629–33 were 434, 404, 530, 633, 411. Included in the 1631 total of 530 were 61 said to have died of the 'pestilence'. These burials began on 7 July. Monthly totals were July, 6; August, 36; September, 11; October, 4; November, 2; December, 2.

Heptonstall. Annual burials 1629–33 were 71, 82, 117, 62, 59. Included in the 1631 total of 117 were 107 said to have died of the plague.

Keighley. An entry in 1645 reads 'All yt dyed this month of October was of the Plague'.

Kirkburton. The phrase 'plague time' set against entries in the burial register for July, August and September 1558. In the 1645 register 4 people are specifically said to have died of plague.

Methley. Annual burials 1603–7 were 20, 15, 51, 12 and 18. Of the 1605 total of 51 many are said to have been caused by plague.

Mirfield. Annual burials 1629–33 were 23, 23, 139, 13, 20. Of the 1631 total of 139, an entry in the register dated 25 April 1631 notes: 'A poor woman being a stranger named Elizabeth Prince was suspected to bring playge to town'. An entry of 13 May reads 'Jenet Fraunces Widdow the xiii day, beinge the first pson after the foresayd stranger wch died of playge. The number of those yt. died of the fearefull visitacion from which good Lord deliv' us is Centr' et Triginta'.

Wakefield. Annual burials from 1623–7 were 250, 163, 311, 121, 142. Of the 311 buried in 1625 there were 128 said to have died 'de peste' between 8 August and 16 January.

Annual burials 1643–7 were 357, 268, 345, 234, 151. Of the 1645 figure of 345, some 177 said to have died 'de peste', the first being buried on 2 August. Of the

234 registered burials in 1646 there were 62 said to have died 'de peste'. The last of these was buried on 31 August.

SAQ 6 What, if any, generalizations can you make about these plague deaths?

Plague was not the only disease to be mentioned specifically in the registers. During the eighteenth century smallpox appears frequently. How widespread this disease was, how many people died from it and what effect inoculation had on bringing it under control, are questions which have given rise to a lively debate in recent years (see Razzell 1965, and 1973; Bradley 1973; Boorman 1968). Like plague, the incidence of smallpox seems to bear no relationship to food supplies. In some places it appears to be endemic; in others epidemic. Sometimes its incidence and spread across a parish can be traced with considerable precision. For example, in 1778, there were 182 burials recorded in the Yorkshire parish of Birstall. The cause of death was given in the case of 140. Of these 140, some 53 were said to have died of smallpox. Age and supposed cause of death were given for 132 of those buried including 40 of the smallpox victims. The latter were heavily weighted in the youngest age groups (Table 11). This suggests smallpox was *endemic* in the area. Otherwise

Figure 11 Smallpox deaths in Birstall (Yorks) Parish, 1778, by month of burial and locale. Source: Register of Burials, Birstall Parish Church

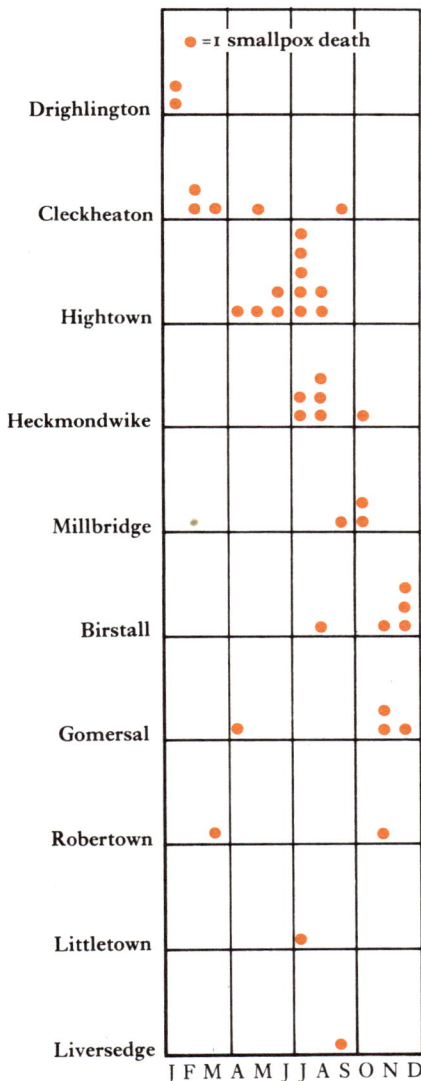

Smallpox: total deaths 2 2 2 2 2 2 8 6 3 3 4 4 =40

Table 11 Ages of those buried in Birstall, 1 January–30 December 1778, where cause of death stated

Age in years	Smallpox deaths	All other causes	Total deaths
Under 1	4	11	15
1–4	34	15	49
5–9	2	3	5
10–14	—	1	1
15–19	—	8	8
20–24	—	7	7
25–29	—	5	5
30–34	—	6	6
35–39	—	5	5
40–44	—	2	2
45–49		3	3
50–54	—	4	4
55–59	—	4	4
60+	—	18	18
Total	40	92	132

Source: Register of Burials, Birstall Parish Church

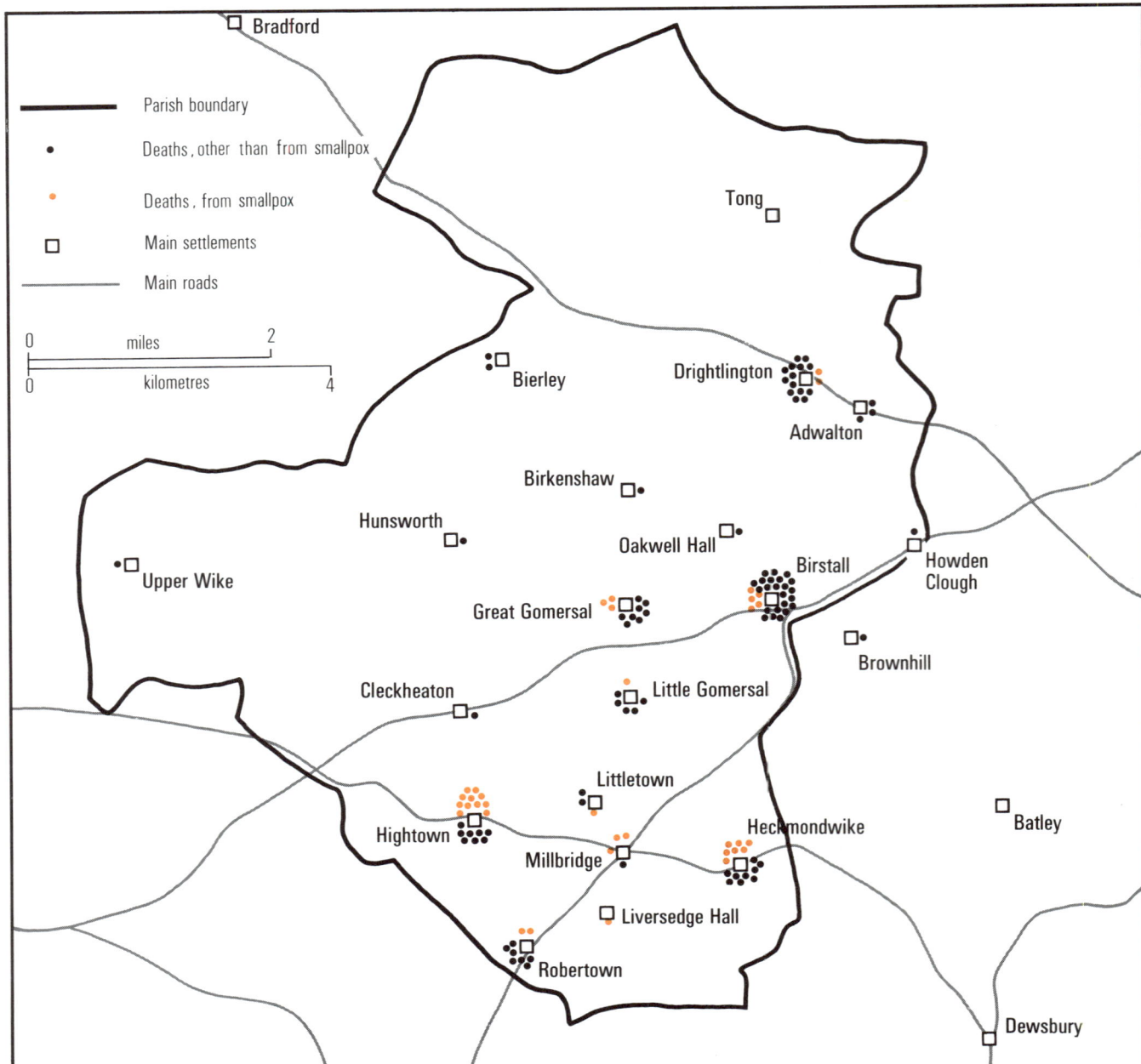

Figure 12 Distribution of deaths, distinguishing those attributed to smallpox, in the parish of Birstall, Yorkshire, 1778. Source: Birstall Parish Register

some adults, having missed contracting the disease in childhood, would have succumbed on this occasion.

The geographical spread of the smallpox deaths is given in Figure 12. This shows that, like plague, but unlike those diseases which appear to be associated with food shortages, smallpox was strongly local. It also appears, in the Birstall parish cases of 1778 at least, to have been of short duration in those parts of the parish where it caused death. This can be seen in Figure 11. Again, this would suggest the disease was endemic so that the pool of potential victims was small in any one area. It is of interest to speculate why Hightown was the main centre of smallpox mortality on this occasion. Was it pure chance? Was it because the area was a little more isolated than other parts of the parish and had a somewhat larger number of potential victims?

8 Conclusion

We have now subjected to a variety of tests the hypothesis that, in the pre-industrial west, population growth was checked periodically by *high* mortality, the result of *inadequate* food supplies. On the basis of the evidence we have used, fragmentary and scattered though it is, it would appear we can draw the following conclusions.

1 Sharp rises in mortality were characteristic of a number of areas in western Europe from the sixteenth century to the eighteenth. These we have called demographic crises. Their three outstanding characteristics are their suddenness, their intensity and their short duration (Meuvret 1963 p 93). Whether we define a demographic crisis as a period when burials just exceed baptisms, or when burials are 50% above the mean (in the neighbouring five or ten years) or two, three or more times is, and must remain, an arbitrary decision. Obviously the higher the mortality one 'requires', the fewer crises one will find.

2 There is some evidence to suggest that particularly severe crises come after periods of relatively high natural increase, periods that is of twenty to thirty years. Areas with relatively low natural increase experienced more crises, but these were of a more moderate variety. In terms of the spectrum we discussed above these crises are more likely to consist of periods when burials just exceeded baptisms rather than when burials are five or six times above their mean.

3 Our tests have shown that food shortages resulting from harvest failure, exceptional demand (eg in time of war), or depleted purchasing power resulting from trade depression, could *on occasion* raise mortality and reduce fertility. If deaths rose over a relatively wide area, especially if this were a rural area where the spread of epidemics was inherently difficult, and across all age groups, food shortages were a likely cause. If, too, conceptions fell and, subsequently, deaths rose in the winter and spring, this was further evidence of food shortage.

4 Sometimes demographic crises occurred when there was no statistical or literary evidence of food shortages. If, in such cases, certain age groups suffered greater mortality than others, then this could indicate the prevalence of particular diseases. For example, typhus seems to have struck adults more severely than children. On the other hand where smallpox was endemic, children between the ages of one and five years were the main victims. The seasonality of mortality also appears to have been related to its causes. Plague deaths appear to have occurred mostly in the summer and early autumn, particularly August and September. Finally diseases like plague, typhus and smallpox were relatively confined, in a geographical sense. Sometimes only one town or village was struck. If, however, such diseases occurred at a time of distress brought on by trade depression or harvest failure, the movement of people, especially poor people, in search of food and work, could spread these diseases more widely. (Drake 1962 pp 435–6)

It would seem then that our hypothesis is partly confirmed. Population growth was checked particularly by high mortality and, *on occasion*, food shortages seem to have caused this. The key phrase is *on occasion*. For it appears that diseases operating independently of food supply could produce equally sharp rises in mortality.

Appendix 1

Table 1 purports to show the totals of baptisms, marriages and burials in the parishes of the Morley Wapentake. In fact, a goodly proportion of these are estimates since, as was pointed out in Unit 6, not all the registers began in 1538. In fact, they are complete only from 1611. For the years before that I have assumed that the totals of baptisms, marriages and burials in the missing registers accounted for the *same* proportion of the totals for the Wapentake as a whole as they did after 1611. I was encouraged to make this assumption because from 1611–40 the shares of the different parishes remained very stable. So to take burials from 1611–40, the figures in Table 1 represent 100% of the entries in the Wapentake's registers; from 1597–1611, they represent 98% (the Hartshead register being missing); from 1594–6, they represent 77% of the entries (the Hartshead, Bradford and Calverley registers being missing); from 1561–94, they represent 70% (in addition to the others, the Heptonstall register no longer exists). Finally, for the years 1540–1560 I assume my total to be only 47% of the Wapentake's as I have only the Halifax register. In each of these stages, I grossed up the figure to 100%. Similar calculations were then made for the baptisms and marriages.

A second piece of estimating had to be carried out before Table 1 could emerge. This arose because of the need to fill the gaps of from a few weeks to a few years which appeared in all the registers. Various criteria were adopted to complete this task. If the gap was under six months, it was assumed the missing entries accounted for the same proportion of the annual total, as the missing months did to the year, eg if six months' entries were missing, I doubled the total for the six months that were recorded. Gaps of up to two years were filled by averaging the entries for the four years either side of the gap. Where entries were missing for more than two years an estimate was made on the basis of what was happening in the other parishes.

I have dwelt on these rather tedious matters not because I wish to commend my solutions to the problems I faced, but to emphasize the point I mentioned earlier about making quite explicit whatever procedures one follows.

Answers to SAQs

Answer SAQ 1 To my mind the most important features are:

1 The sharp rise in burials in certain years, eg 1557, 1587, 1597 etc.
2 The relative increase in the number of years in which burials rise sharply as one approaches the end of the period.
3 The fact that up to 1587 the gap between burials and baptisms was comparatively wide. After that the gap between the two series narrowed appreciably, reaching its smallest extent in the 1630s.

Answer SAQ 2 First, the January–March quarter shows the highest mortality in every decade. The lowest mortality in each decade, apart from that of 1550–9, is in the July–September quarter. A second point to notice is that burials in the January–March quarter exceed those of the July–September quarter by about 50%.

Answer SAQ 3 Of the 19 places listed in Table 4, as many as 18 had a greater number of recorded burials in 1623 than in 1622. In 16 of them the total of burials was the highest for any year from 1619–27. Overall there were about 70% more burials in

1623 than in 1622, and 66% more than the mean number for the years 1619–27. The other year and place that stands out is Wakefield in 1625. There, of the 311 deaths 128 were said to have been due to the plague (*de peste*). The first of these burials was on 8 August, the last on 16 January. Note that I am here using the church year which ran from 25 March to 24 March. If these deaths were due to plague it is interesting to note how circumscribed was its incidence. There is no evidence at all of it having spread to neighbouring parishes. This is an important point to note when trying to determine the cause of a rise in mortality in any particular year or place.

Answer SAQ 4 The first feature to strike me about Figure 4 is that overall there is quite a considerable degree of oscillation from one year to the next, despite the averaging process which reduces it to some degree. This quite violent fluctuation from year to year is, of course, even more noticeable in Figure 3. The second point is that before 1584 the excess of baptisms was considerably higher than in the period after it. Indeed, if one uses the figures in Table 1 to calculate the difference, one finds that in the years 1540–84, there were 164 baptisms for every 100 burials whilst in the years 1585–1639, there were only 118. The difference between the beginning and end of the period is particularly marked in this regard.

Answer SAQ 5

The demographic crisis in Halifax 1585–8

Quarters	1585		1586				1587				1588			
	3	4	1	2	3	4	1	2	3	4	1	2	3	4
Conceptions	69	72	82	55	70	39	32	40	49	57	72	99	92	69
Burials	42	54	87	47	41	49	87	81	97	271	283	130	63	60

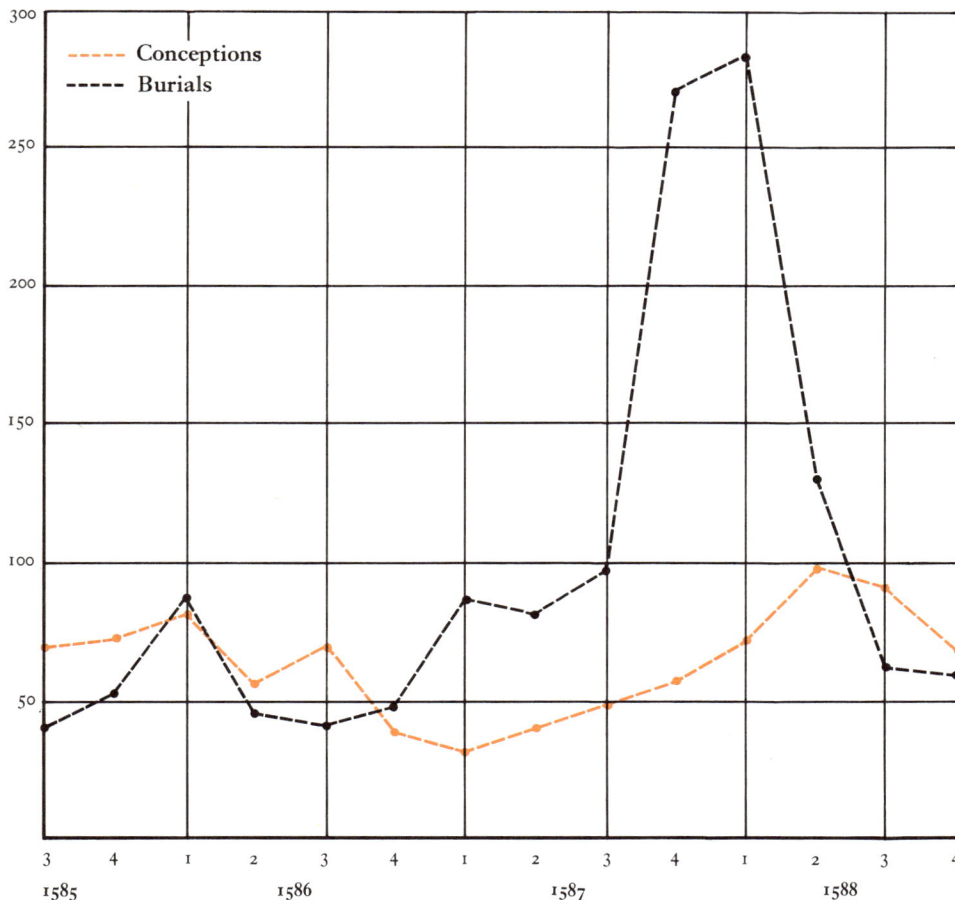

Answer SAQ 6 The following points struck me:

1 In a year when plague is specifically said to be present, burials are usually above those of the two years either side of the 'plague year'.

2 In a year when plague is said to be present, a substantial proportion of the deaths are ascribed to it.

3 Plague burials appear to begin in the summer months and fall off towards the end of the year. It has been suggested by Shrewsbury (1970 pp 463, 476) that:

When a parish register shows an excessive number of burials in a year and a monthly analysis shows that more than 50% of these is contributed by three successive months of the plague season, June to October inclusive, the record is suggestive of an outbreak of plague. When more than 66% of the total annual burials occur in the three months July to September inclusive, this almost certainly indicates plague.

Unit 8 Migration

Part cover: A view of Preston, Lancashire (1862). Source: *The Illustrated London News*, Vol. 41, part 2

Contents Unit 8

Objectives

After completing the study of this unit and the associated television programme, *The Urban Migrant*, you should be able to:

1 Give a brief summary of contemporary knowledge on migration.

2 List five types of historical source material of use in migration studies.

3 Explain why the topic of migration is especially suited to Applied Historical Studies.

4 State the Redford and the Deane and Cole explanations of the mechanics of migration from rural to industrial areas in nineteenth-century Britain.

5 Describe the difficulties encountered by Michael Anderson in testing these explanations.

Migration

1 Introduction

This unit is different in format from Units 6 and 7, but the underlying strategy remains the same. It consists of two articles. Between them they encompass the various stages of research we introduced first in Unit 1 and have exemplified in Units 6 and 7. That is to say, they cover the initial exploration of a topic (in this case migration) through the formulation of a hypothesis, the collection of data and the testing of the hypothesis. As with our earlier illustrations, the conclusion is that 'further research is necessary'!

In going through the two articles you may like to keep the following question in mind:

What points do Hollingsworth and Anderson make which suggest that enquiries into the problems of migration fit the objectives of Applied Historical Studies?

Historical studies of migration

by T. H. Hollingsworth[*]
University of Glasgow, Department of Social and Economic Research

Introduction

Few of the historians who have studied migration have had much demographic knowledge, either of techniques of measurement and analysis or of the results of contemporary demographic studies. There must be many scholars who have excellent material that they do not know how best to use, and many instances where some idea of the improbability of a result in terms of current knowledge would be extremely useful. In this paper we hope to help those who are interested in the problems of historical migration but are uncertain how to set about studying it.

After a brief review of contemporary knowledge of the phenomena of migration, depending almost entirely upon studies made with twentieth century data, we consider five types of source-material in turn. Some of the more interesting studies are mentioned, but there is undoubtedly a much larger number that we have not been able to notice. We then suggest how one might tackle the problem of making a synthesis of the available data for a certain period or problem, using three examples to do so. Finally, the importance of migration in modern demographic study is stressed.

Contemporary knowledge[1]

Distance has a very great influence upon the decision to migrate, but no very clear law relating the distance moved to the frequency of movement has emerged. However, one can usually say that almost all the volume of migration into or out of an area is short-distance. This has the corollary that the size of the area considered is itself important, because for a fairly large area much of the movement will be inside it and not be counted as migration. Thus people change house much more often than they change the district in which they live; and they change the region, or country, or continent that they live in much less often still.

[*]*Annales de Démographie Historique 1970*, Paris Mouton and Co. 1971 pp 87–96

1. This section is based mainly on a book of mine now in the press. Its title will probably be *Migration. A study based on Scottish experience*, and it is to be published by Oliver and Boyd (Edinburgh) during 1970.

Here Hollingsworth is referring to two kinds of scales on which migration can be measured – spatial scales and temporal scales. The problem of the spatial scale of study raises the question of the selection of areal units and of defining migration boundaries. Geographers distinguish in this context between adjacent and non-adjacent areas – see Friedlander and Roshier (1966) and Lawton (1958). The problem of the temporal scale of study raises the question of the selection of time periods, both for study by the investigator, as

Time has a similar effect to distance. Migrants go to a town but often do not stay there very long. When they move again, quite often they go back to where they first came from. This means that measuring migration rates over ten years gives us much lower rates than if we measured them over five years. Taking just a single year would give a still higher annual migration rate. All the multiple movers can only be counted once, and those who arrived and returned home within the period of observation cannot be counted at all !

Some people are habitual migrants, others move rarely or never. A soldier or a waiter or an international expert may move very often, while a farmer or a lawyer or a landowner may have the same permanent residence for a very long time. Education and intelligence have been found to be statistically associated with migration, but this is really the same as the old idea that the ambitious young man goes away to seek his fortune. Usually he migrates to a city or town, but in modern times migration has become more complex than it was in the past.[2] Migrants in an advanced country are just as likely nowadays to go from city to city or even from city to semi-rural suburb. In the developing countries, however, matters are still much more like the past.[3]

The ordinary demographic variables, age and sex, have only slight influences upon migration. The likelihood of moving declines in the early years of life, but not nearly as steeply as the chance of dying declines at the same ages. The minimum is reached at about age 15 in a modern country. There is then a very steep increase in the likelihood of moving until about age 25, which is followed by a slow decline. After about age 60, the decline flattens out into a low, constant, rate. The first fifteen years are a reflection of the years 25 to 40, for children migrate with their parents. The steep rise between 15 and 25 corresponds to getting more or higher education, finding a job and getting married, all of which tend to happen in rapid succession. A sequence of jobs produces more migration, but home life becomes more static as one settles down. Migration comes back into some prominence at the age of retirement, but this is only a slight effect.

The sexes migrate together for the most part. Little difference can be discerned between their migration rates, age for age, except that women reach their peak rate of migration a little younger than men because they also marry a little younger. Marriage, indeed, accounts for a very large share of the total migration at present, although marriage moves are mostly over quite short distances.

The motivation for migration tends to be more economic and less social the longer the distance moved. The costs in migrating a long distance must be recouped, which discourages long-distance movements that would not show a pecuniary profit. Migrants normally go from areas of low wages to areas of high wages, but the relationship with unemployment is less clear-cut. Migrants sometimes go to areas of high wages in such numbers as to oversupply the vacancies and produce unemployment ; this is particularty true of migrants to the cities in a developing country.

Many other variables have been studied, but the difficulties of getting migration data and of comparing the levels of migration in different places are substantial. A comprehensive theory, therefore, does not yet exist, and perhaps never will exist.

Hollingsworth points out here, and in defining migration on this scale. (For example, the upper extreme limit is the lifetime migration; the investigator must select his own lower limit, below which a move is not included as a migratory one.)

2. See, for instance, W. ADAMS, « Talent that won't stay put », *Population Bulletin*, XXV, 3 (June 1969), p. 59-87, on the brain drain to the United States.
3. A. BOSE, « Migration Streams in India », *Population Review*, 11, 2 (july-december 1967), p. 39-45.

Historical sources and studies

1. *Nominative lists that give place of origin*. Censuses sometimes provide full data on place of origin, and some old census material can still be reworked.[4] Many other historical lists also tell us the place of origin, however, at least by implication. For instance, at the time surnames were introduced in Europe many of the names were place-names. This means that any list of names that dates from that time will gave us information on gross inward migration.[5] Lists of serfs[6] or tenants, of persons buried or married, of taxes paid or promised will all suffice. Even *grafitti* can sometimes give us clues to the origins of people.[7] The main drawback to the method is that it can only be used for a brief period of time. It also gives us no data on age and occupation of migrants as a rule. But it does refer to a remote period when any sources are scarce.

Marriage licenses or contracts, where preserved, usually tell us the places of birth or residence of the two parties.[8] The higher social classes, however, may well have migrated more than the rest (if only because they could afford it), and also have been disproportionately often represented in the marriage contracts. This would lead to overestimation of migration, although the evidence that the rich migrated most is far from conclusive.[9]

The admission of burgesses to a town's guilds in the mediaeval period provides data with similar shortcomings, although we can get an idea of the areas from which the town was drawing its inmigrants from a list of citizens.[10] Apprenticeship records are rather more valuable, although probably rarer than burgess records. The age and social origins of apprentices make them rather more typical of the population.[11]

Death or burial registers often show whether the deceased was a stranger or not, and sometimes give the place of origin as well. The result is merely the gross volume of recent in-migration, however, which is only likely to be interesting if there are some special circumstances such as a very long series of figures or an outbreak

4. For sixteenth century Geneva, see R. MANDROU, « Les Français hors de France aux XVIe et XVIIe siècles », *Annales E.S.C.*, 14, 4 (1959), p. 662-675. An interesting study is D. FRIEDLANDER and R.J. ROSHIER, « A Study of Internal Migration in England and Wales. Part. 1 : Geographical Patterns of Internal Migration 1851-1951 », *Population Studies*, XIX, 3 (march 1966), p. 239-278. According to *Population Literature*, 2, 3-4 (20 october 1936), n° 1559, there is a complete nominative analysis of American censuses from 1860 to 1930 in James C. MALIN, « The turn-over of farm population in Kansas », *The Kansas Historical Quarterly*, 4, 4 (november 1935), p. 339-372.

5. The pioneers are : Charles HIGOUNET, « Le peuplement de Toulouse au XIIe siècle », *Annales du Midi*, 55, 219-220 (july-october 1943), p. 489-498, and « Mouvements de populations dans le Midi de la France, du XIe au XVe siècles, d'après les noms de personne et de lieu », *Annales E.S.C.*, 8, 1 (january-march 1953), p. 1-24 ; and J. LESTOCQUOY, « Tonlieu et peuplement urbain à Arras aux XIIe et XIIIe siècles », *ibid.*, 10, 3 (july-september 1955), p. 391-395.

6. See I. SZABO, *l'gocsa megye*, Budapest, 1937, p. 604. (This is in his French summary).

7. See C.B. WELLES. « The population of Roman Dura », in *Studies in Roman economic and social history* in honor of Allan Chester Johnson (1951), edited by P.R. Coleman-Norton, p. 251-274, especially p. 265-266.

8. An example is in G.H. KENYON, « Kirdford Inventories, 1611 to 1776 », *Sussex Archaeological Collections*, 93 (1955), p. 78-156, but especially p. 154.

9. See T.H. HOLLINGSWORTH, *Historical Demography*, London, 1969, p. 49-52. Dr. R.S. Schofield tells me that he has similar doubts.

10. See J.C. RUSSELL, « Medieval Midland and Northern Migrants to London, 1100-1365 », *Speculum*, 34 4 (1959), p. 641-645, which is based on B.O.E. EKWALL, *Studies on the Population of Medieval London*, Stockholm, 1956.

11. Apprentice data has been used by E.J. BUCKATZSCH in his « Places of Origin of a group of immigrants into Sheffield 1624-1799 », *Economic History Review*, (2nd Series) 2, (1950), p. 303-306.

of plague. Marriage registers have been used widely for long-period studies of in-migration in a similar way. [12]

Foreigners were sometimes listed, usually when they were to be taxed. The sources of foreign immigration are then validly represented in such a list. The rate of immigration, however, is only deducible as a rough estimate from the total number resident.

2. *Two lists compiled at different dates*. Although neither of two lists may explicitly give the origins of the population, the combination of them can sometimes provide a good deal of information about migration. The rates of gross in- and out- migration, in particular, can often be deduced from a double listing. The interval between the compiling of the two lists should not be too long, but even a decade does not always spoil the chances of measuring migration from the double listings. [13] Deaths may affect the calculations if the the area is large, but three or four years is still short enough for deaths in most towns and villages to be almost negligible compared with migration. [14] If there is further information about the people, for instance about their social position, we can calculate differential rates of migration.

A situation that is somewhat similar arises from certain records of law courts in which a witness had to give a brief autobiography before giving evidence. We may then find how long he spent at each place where he had ever lived, as well as the distances migrated. [15]

Another example is the comparison between a catechetical list at some date and the list of local baptisms over the preceding years. Any child baptised some 10 to 15 years earlier and not on the catechetical list or in the burial register might be assumed an out-migrant, provided that the religious cohesion of the community is likely to have been strong. Communicants' lists can be used similarly, of course. [16]

3. *Lists of actual population movements*. Such lists might be regarded as ideal for the study of migration, but in practice they are usually somewhat limited in scope. Most of them refer to movements that were controlled in some way, often compulsory evictions of a segment of the population. England has numerous « Settlement Cer-

12. In England, the chief studies are : R.F. PEEL, « Local Intermarriage and the Stability of Rural Population in the English Midlands », *Geography*, XXVII, 1 (march 1942), p. 22-30 ; A. CONSTANT, « A Geographical Background of Inter-Village Population Movements in Northamptonshire and Huntingdonshire, 1754-1943 », *ibid.* XXXIII, 2 (june 1948), p. 78-88 ; and A.J. BOYCE, C.F. KUCHEMANN and G.A. HARRISON, « Neighbourhood knowledge and the distribution of marriage distances », *Annals of Human Genetics*, 30, 4 (may 1967), p. 335-338. The Barcelona marriage registers are mentioned in J. NADAL and E. GIRALT, *La population catalane de 1553 à 1717. L'immigration française et les autres facteurs de son développement*, Paris 1960, as a source for migration data. In Sweden, too, geneticists have made studies of marriage distances : L. BECKMAN, « Breeding patterns of a North Swedish Parish », *Hereditas*, 47, 1 (25 may 1961), p. 72-80.

13. In G. PRAT, « Albi et la peste noire », *Annales du Midi*, 64, 1 (january 1952), p. 15-25, the gap is 14 years (1343-1357). Mortality and migration are here inextricably confused, for a gross out-migration of 10 % per year would imply *no* deaths, but is not impossibly high.

14. A sampling scheme to study migration in England by this method was urged nearly 20 years ago by E.J. BUCKATZSCH, « The Constancy of Local Populations and Migration in England before 1800 », *Population Studies*, V, 1 (1951), p. 62-69.

15. An example is given by J. CORNWALL, « Evidence of Population Mobility in the Seventeenth Century », *Bulletin of the Institute of Historical Research*, XL (1967), p. 143-152.

16. Suitable data were found by J. RUWET, « La population de Saint-Trond en 1635 », *Bulletin de la Société d'Art et d'Histoire du Diocèse de Liège*, 40 (1957), p. 151-193.

tificates » dating mainly from the eighteenth century, [17] for example, and there are also data of expulsions of people from Spain, [18] Ireland, [19] Hungary, [20] and Russia [21] at various dates. The emigrants from La Rochelle to the West Indies and Canada at the time of Louis XIV are a rather similar example, for they were sent on the basis of labour contracts to be sold on arrival. [22]

Not all such historical data, however, has quite such a strong element of compulsion about it. An occasional listing of inhabitants of a village may also give the addresses of out-migrants, which obviously enables one to analyse outward movements for once. [23] In Finland, the nineteenth century migration certificates, with some supplementation from other sources, give the opportunity for a very complete study of migration at a time when most other parts of the world (except Sweden) were still only collecting place of birth data at the census or nothing at all. [24]

4. *Indirect estimation of migration volume.* There are many studies in which assorted pieces of data have led to the conclusion that substantial migration must have taken place. However, few of these are quantitative, and we leave their consideration to the next section. Among the quantitative studies, the London Bills of Mortality have been the source of several attempts to calculate the net rate of migration into London during the 17th and 18th centuries. [25] We should get very good estimates of gross migration for a parish from the parish registers if families are reconstituted. [26] Assuming that the registers really include all the baptisms, burials, and marriages that took place and that there were no people who did not receive these rites, we can say that all the baptized who cannot be traced as eventual burials must have been out-migrants, and all the burials who cannot be traced as previous baptisms must be in-migrants. Marriage data, as well as providing an extra source for finding people, give some guide to the ages at which migration may have taken place. However, omissions are indistinguishable from migrants, and may lead to grave mistakes in estimation.

17. See R. MELVILLE, « Records of Apprenticeship and Settlement in a Berkshire Village in the Eighteenth Century », *Transactions of the Newbury and District Field Club*, X, 2 (1954), p. 32-43, and R. BRETTON, « Settlement certificates and removal orders », *Halifax Antiquarian Society*, 6th january 1959, p. 9-26.

18. H. LAPEYRE, *Géographie de l'Espagne morisque*, Paris, S.E.V.P.E.N., 1959. See p. 232-239.

19. W.H. HARDINGE, « On Circumstances attending the outbreak of the Civil War in Ireland on 23rd october, 1641, and its continuance to the 12th may, 1652 (etc.) », *Transactions of the Royal Irish Academy*, 24, Part 3 (Antiquities), (1874), p. 379-420.

20. Szabo, *op. cit.*, refers to the Turkish conquest of 1717.

21. Fr.-X. COQUIN, « Faim et migrations paysannes en Russie au XIXe siècle », *Revue d'histoire moderne et contemporaine*, XI, 2 (april-june 1964), p. 127-144.

22. MANDROU, *loc. cit.* (note 4).

23. A good example is given by N.L. TRANTER, « Population and Social Structure in a Bedfordshire Parish : The Cardington Listing of Inhabitants, 1782 », *Population Studies*, XXI, 3 (november 1967), p. 261-282.

24. A. ROSENBERG, « Mobility of Population in the Finnish County of Usimaa (Nyland) 1821-1880 », *Scandinavian Economic History Review*, XIV, 1-2 (1966), p. 39-59.

25. The best-known are : J. GRAUNT, *Natural and political observations upon the Bills of Mortality*, London, 1662, reprinted from the 1665 edition in *Journal of the Institute of Actuaries*, 90, 384 (1964), p. 4-61 ; and R. PRICE, « Observations on the expectations of lives, the increase of mankind, the influence of great towns on population, and particularly the state of London with respect to the healthfulness and number of inhabitants », *Philosophical Transactions of the Royal Society*, 59 (1769), p. 89-125.

26. Presumably this was what was done by O.K. ROLLER, *Die Einwohnerschaft der Stadt Durlach im 18. Jahrhundert in ihren wirtschaftlichen und kulturgeschichtlichen Verhältnissen dargestellt aus ihren Stammtafeln*, Karlsruhe, 1907.

A typical fraction of families that can be reconstituted in a parish is 15 %. If we assume that only 15 % of the children born in a parish are still there 25 years later, does this mean that out-migration was at an impossibly high rate ? Not at all. A steady loss of 8,32 % per year of the existing population means that 15 % are left after 25 years, and this is not an incredible rate of gross loss of population for a small parish. Nevertheless, lower rates of loss would lead to higher proportions remaining, and the question of omissions cannot well be settled by such considerations.

A special case arises in a parish where the ages at death are given. If there are a sufficient number of deaths of children under 10 or 15, as during a plague period, better estimates of migration can be made. There are a few parishes in London for which this can be done for 16th and 17th century plagues. [27]

The sex-composition by age of the population has sometimes been thought to be evidence of recent migration. However, we also need some background knowledge of a society before we can say with confidence whether young men or young women migrate more. At least over short distances in modern India, the women are the main migrators, whereas in Africa today the men migrate the more. [28]

5. *General considerations*. It is probably fair to assume that the recovery of certain European towns from the Black Death was rapid because of heavy net migration to them from the surrounding countryside, [29] for that is the only way they could have regained their populations quickly. Similarly, detailed study of German populations during and after the Thirty Years' War can show that the urban populations fled to neighbouring villages and settled in them, for this is the most rational explanation of the strange pattern of population change observed. [30] A slightly less detailed example is provided by the population statistics of Cornwall for 1672, 1744 and 1779. [31]

In earlier times, the desertion of fields in Egypt [32] or Syria was very probably caused by a flight from the land, influenced no doubt by high taxation. Similarly, one can well assume that much of the mediaeval desertion of fields was caused by migration, to towns or to more prosperous rural areas. But the role of mortality cannot be overlooked in causing population decline, and even fecundity may have been lowered in certain cases. [33] Where there is insufficient data to tell whether migration is the main cause of population change, we should be ready to admit this. An example would be the depopulation of Greece in the 3rd century B.C., which may have been partly because of heavy migration to the lands newly conquered by Alexander, [34] but could as well have been from natural decrease.

27. My sister and I have written a paper on this subject that we hope to publish soon. (See *Population Studies* for March 1971).

28. See Bose, *loc. cit.*, S.M. Ominde, *Land and Population Movements in Kenya*, London (Heinemann) 1968.

29. H. Reincke, « Bevölkerungsprobleme der Hansestädte », *Hansische Geschichtsblätter*, 70 (1951), p. 1-33 ; R. Bridbury, *Economic Growth ; England in the Later Middle Ages*, London (Allen and Unwin), 1962, p. 54 *et seq.*

30. M. Kuhlmann, *Bevölkerungsgeographie des Landes Lippe*, Remagen, 1954, p. 38 *et seq.*

31. N.J.G. Pounds, « Population movement in Cornwall and the rise of mining in the Eighteenth Century », *Geography*, 28, 2 (1943), p. 37-46.

32. See D.C. Dennett, *Conversion and the Poll Tax in Early Islam*, Cambridge, Mass., (Harvard University Press), 1950, p. 110-115.

33. See R.F.R. Scragg, *Depopulation in New Ireland. A Study of Demography and Fertility*, Port Moresby (lithographed), november 1957, p. 117-118.

34. See G. Glotz (translated by M.R. Dobie), *Ancient Greece at Work. An economic history of Greece from the Homeric period to the Roman conquest*, London and New York, 1926, p. 318.

Syntheses

The most difficult task of the historical demographer is putting his sources and studies together to from a consistent whole. As a rule, he has an assorted set of date, of different degrees of reliability and referring to slightly different dates and slightly different populations. There is rarely enough similarity between two situations to allow him to use the same synthesis that he has used before. Yet all depends upon his skill in blending his sources into a reasonable demographic description of the people he has studied. Since no two problems are the same, we can only cite illustrations here.

1. The data on ancient Egypt are very sparse, especially on migration. Yet the laws that were passed, the prices that were paid, a fragment of a tax list here, and the names that soldiers scratched on a wall there, when put together [35] seem to show that Egyptian population was in some decline up to the fourth century A.D., and that migration to the towns to avoid taxes meant that the countryside was becoming depopulated. [36] A similar thing seems to have recurred in Arab times. [37]

2. Mediaeval towns in Europe seem to have arisen through in-migration rather than through a low death-rate. [38] (In twentieth century terms, they were not Costa Ricas, but Israels.) The migrants come from far and wide, [39] but were especially people for whom there was a financial inducement to migrate. There was no social enthusiasm for migration to a town, as far as one can tell, of the kind that is supposed to explain much of the nineteenth and twentieth century rural-urban migration. Taxation avoidance and the opportunities for indulging in profitable trade seem to have been the main reasons for mediaeval urban growth.

After the mediaeval period, when more statistics of mortality are available, it is certain that the large towns generally had much higher mortality levels than the rural areas. If this were also true at the very beginning of European urbanization, the ambivalent attitude towards migration to a town would not be difficult to understand.

3. The role of migration in the early stages of the Industrial Revolution is still not clearly understood. Migration became so much easier after the spread of railways that rapid urban growth in Europe and North America after 1850 hardly needs further explanation. [40] But we really know very little about migration before 1850, at least in England, although industrialism and urban growth were already well under way by 1750. Possibly, the gross volume of English internal migration did not change much before 1850, although turnpike roads and canals probably accelerated it a little. [41] Yet, while London

35. See the comprehensive study by H. BRAUNERT, *Die Binnenwanderung : Studien zur Sozialgeschichte Agyptens in der Ptolemäer- und Kaiserzeit*, Bonn (Historical Inquiries, 26), 1964.

36. C. PRÉAUX, « La stabilité de l'Egypte aux deux premiers siècles de notre ère », *Chronique d'Egypte*, 31, 62 (july 1956), p. 311-331.

37. DENNETT, *loc. cit.*

38. A general summary of the subject is given by J.F. BENTON (editor), *Town Origins. The Evidence from Medieval England*, Boston (D.C. Heath and Company), 1968.

39. See HIGOUNET, *loc. cit.* ; LESTOCQUOY, *loc. cit.* ; K. BUCHER, *Die Bevölkerung von Frankfurt am Main im XIV und XV Jahrhundert*, Vol. 1, Tübingen, 1886, p. 454.

40. For the spread of railways and the increase in migration, see CONSTANT, *loc. cit.*

41. BUCKATZSCH, *loc. cit.* (1950), provides data on the constancy of migration patterns before 1800.

was probably the goal of most English migrants around 1700, the provincial cities must have become the main destinations by 1800. Could this disinclination to go to London have arisen through the spread of the knowledge that London was very unhealthy ? The worst mortality in London of the eighteenth century seems to have occured in the 1740's, when gin was being drunk in very large per capita amounts. The new industries might have been lucky to be growing at just the time when a certain fear of London life would be spreading. [42]

Conclusions

Migration is becoming the most important branch of demography, just as fertility has dominated the scene for the past 80 years or so and mortality did before that. It will take some time yet before migration's primacy is everywhere recognized, but for so many problems of modern planning migration is the most important contributor to population change that much more study of migration seems certain to be required in the coming years.

This change in demographers' interests has its consequences also for history. We always tend to study those aspects of the past that interest us in the present. In particular, we shall need to learn something of the long-term causes and consequences of migration. Only history can show what these ever were, but thus far the sources of migration data have been little searched for and only sporadically studied. One hopes that this paper will suggest many new pieces of work to those who are interested in this growing subject.

42. A fourth illustration, that draws upon numerous sources, is A. Lopez Toro, « Migraciòn y cambio social en Antioquia durante el siglo XIX », *Demografia y Economia*, II, 3 (1968), p. 351-403. We mention it for its unusual geographical setting. It seems that population growth in Colombia was very rapid after 1778.

Urban migration in nineteenth-century Lancashire: some insights into two competing hypotheses

by Michael Anderson
University of Edinburgh, Scotland

Two different interpretations have been offered of the processes involved in migration from rural areas to the industrial towns of nineteenth century England, though all observers agree that most migration involved only short distance moves.

One thesis, which finds its clearest expression in Redford's *Labour migration in England, 1800-1850* [1], published in 1926, sees most migration as consisting not of a simple and direct movement of individuals from country to town, but instead as following a wave-like motion, with migrants from country areas concentrating first in smaller towns, from which, in turn, men and women moved to the industrial areas.

See Appendix p 144 for extracts from Redford setting out this thesis.

Deane and Cole [2], while agreeing that some kind of wave-like movement may have occurred among migrants to London [3], argue that in the case of other urban areas such as Lancashire, the towns stimulated a growth of population in the surrounding areas, and that part of this population increase was then siphoned off into the nearby towns.

Either of these interpretations, if fully verified, would be of more general sociological and demographic interest. That a two-step process involving the same people was normal elsewhere in Europe was, however, firmly denied by Weber, though he did point out that considerable numbers of the migrants found in major European towns had been born in another town [4]. This tendency for migrants to come from other towns has also been observed in many currently developing nations particularly in Africa, where, however, some kind of two-step process has also been shown to occur [5]. This is normally associated with the learning of skills which can later find a ready market in industrial centres, while at the same time easing the culture shock that a direct move from small farming communities to large and busy industrial towns would otherwise involve.

Deane and Cole's interpretation, if verified, also has obvious and important implications, notably for theories of population growth in industrialising societies, though they make no suggestions as to the precise mechanisms by which such rise in the rate of natural increase of population might occur.

Both these interpretations are, however, based almost entirely on aggregated data from published census returns (supplemented in Redford's case by some limited descriptive material). This kind of data is, unfortunately, easily biased by such chance factors as the nearness of town to county boundaries, and can be seriously misleading in situations, as was the case in Lancashire at least, where the

---

* *Annales de Démographie Historique 1971*, Paris Mouton and Co. 1972 pp 13-26

1. A. REDFORD, *Labour migration in England, 1800-1850*, Manchester, 1926, p. 54 *sq.*

2. P. DEANE et W. A. COLE, *British economic growth 1688-1959*, Cambridge, 1962, p. 116 *sq.*

3. An idea originally suggested by C. BOOTH, *Life and labour of the people in London*, tome III, p. 68, though he believed that it was the *same* individuals who were migrating in this two-step manner (see below).

4. A. F. WEBER, *The growth of cities in the nineteenth century*, New York, 1899, chap. 4.

5. See specially, UNESCO, *Social implications of industrialisation and urbanisation in Africa south of the Sahara*, London, 1956, p. 255 ; UNESCO, *Urbanisation in Latin America*, Paris, 1961, p. 214.

Figure 1 Simple stepwise migration. Source: devised by W. T. R. Pryce

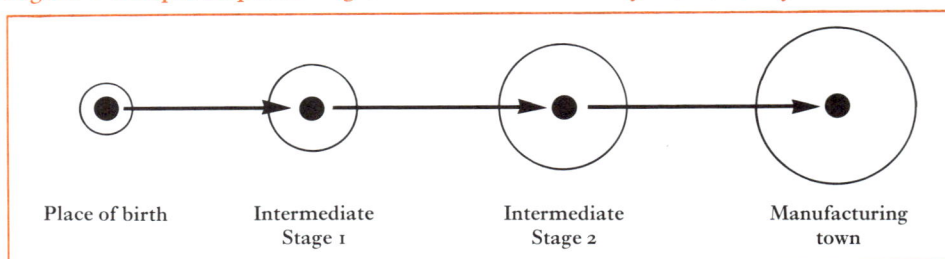

| Place of birth | Intermediate Stage 1 | Intermediate Stage 2 | Manufacturing town |

Figure 2 Stepwise migration with replacement. Source: devised by W. T. R. Pryce

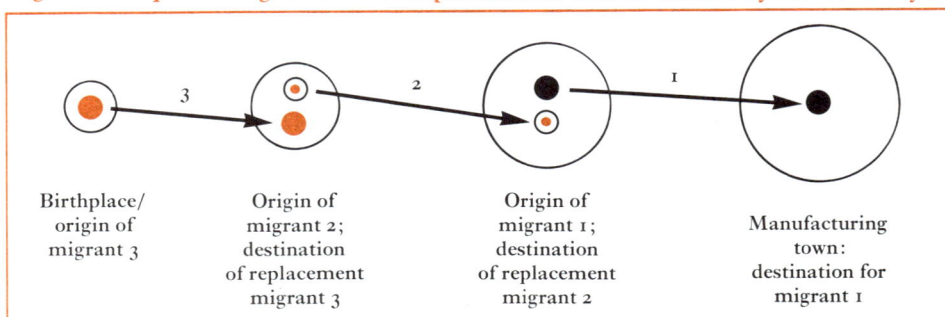

| Birthplace/ origin of migrant 3 | Origin of migrant 2; destination of replacement migrant 3 | Origin of migrant 1; destination of replacement migrant 2 | Manufacturing town: destination for migrant 1 |

population, in addition to substantial rural-urban migration, was also highly mobile between neighbouring industrial towns and between neighbouring villages of all kinds. It is thus perhaps surprising that, in spite of the recent upsurge of interest in the use of the original census enumerators' books among English social historians, few attempts have been made to use their data to investigate further these hypotheses [6].

This paper reports some work which arose as a bye-product of a study of family structure in nineteenth century Lancashire towns [7]. As part of this enquiry a ten per cent sample was taken from the census enumerators' books for 1851 of the occupants of houses in the town of Preston. The census enumerators' books give not merely data on names, relationships, ages, and occupations, but also give the parish of birth of every person born in England and Wales, and the country of birth of the remainder of the population [8]. All these data were abstracted for analysis.

Preston had in 1851 a population of about 69,500. About one third of its adult population were directly employed in the cotton industry and many of the remainder had at some time been dependent upon it or now had children working in it. The town was set at the north-eastern corner of the main Lancashire cotton manufacturing area. To the north and north-west, and immediately to the south, lay relatively prosperous farming areas, many of whose inhabitants had, nevertheless, traditionally depended for a substantial part of their incomes on hand-loom weaving. This trade was, however, by 1851, on the verge of extinction as a result of competition from factory based power-looms.

6. Among the few papers which have come to my notice, the most interesting and relevant is R. LAWTON, « The population of Liverpool in the mid-nineteenth century », *Transactions of the Historical Society of Lancashire and Cheshire*, 107, 1955, p. 89-120.

7. M. ANDERSON, *Family structure in nineteenth century Lancashire*, Cambridge University Press, forthcoming.

8. For detailed description of these documents see W. A. ARMSTRONG, « Social Structure from the early census returns », in E.A. WRIGLEY, *An introduction to English historical demography*, London, 1966, p. 209-237.

To the east and south-east lay the other major manufacturing towns, spread over an area some 25 km. from east to west, and some 50 km. from north to south. To the south, beyond the farming area, lay the port of Liverpool, a major immigration point for the masses who were still being driven forth from Ireland following the disastrous potato famine.

As part of the analysis of the enumerators' book data, attempts were made to locate the birthplace of every member of the sample on a map of Britain. It proved possible to do this for 98 % of the population. The migrant group consisted of 3345 persons, who had been born in some 425 different places. For each person in the sample who had been born in England and Wales the following pieces of information were then recorded :

1. The distance of the birthplace from Preston, measured in a straight line ;

2. The size of the community. All communities with over 5 000 inhabitants were classified as towns, the rest as villages. Most of these towns had some industry ; many were as industrialised as Preston, and some, Manchester, for example, were considerably larger ;

3. All villages situated at less than 30 miles (48 km) from Preston were then classified by their economic type in 1831, the only year for which adequate published data can be obtained. The categories used were as follows. (All figures refer to adult males only) :

Figure 3 Preston district, 1841. Source: The Royal Geographical Society.

a) Agricultural ; over 50 % of the population engaged in agriculture ;

b) Manufacturing ; over 50 % of the population engaged in manufacture. This includes, in some ways unfortunately, both hand-loom and factory cotton manufacture ;

c) Mixed ; over 25 % of the population engaged in agriculture, and over 25 % in manufacturing ;

d) Miscellaneous ; villages not falling into *a*), *b*), or *c*).

Data from the subsamples taken of the populations of these villages in 1851 (which are described below) suggested that this classification had some real significance, though it failed to distinguish very adequately between different levels of factory industry ; both the industrial and mixed types had about the same proportions (14 %) engaged in factory industry. This should be borne in mind when interpreting the results given below. Table I shows the occupational structure of these villages in 1851.

TABLE I. — OCCUPATIONS OF THE MALE POPULATION AGED 12 AND OVER, BY COMMUNITY TYPE, VILLAGE SUBSAMPLE, 1851, PER CENT.

Type of Community	Occupations as per cent of all					
	Agricultural	Manufacturing	Artisan and trade	Other	All %	N
Agricultural	78	4	6	12	100	126
Mixed	35	29	22	14	100	78
Manufacture	29	35	16	20	100	89
Miscellaneous	48	9	29	14	100	130

Birthplaces of migrants to Preston, 1851

In most of the cotton towns, among the adult population, migrants from elsewhere outnumbered those born in the town. In Preston, 70 % of the adult population had not been born there.

Table II shows how far the Preston sample had migrated from their place of birth, and confirms the suggestion of earlier workers that most migration was short distance only.

TABLE II. — BIRTHPLACES OF THE RESIDENT, NON-INSTITUTIONALISED, POPULATION OF PRESTON [a]. PRESTON SAMPLE, 1851 [b].

Birthplace		Of population	Of inmigrants [c]	Of 1831 population of such communities [d]
		%	%	%
In Preston		48	..	105.0
At 1-4.9 miles (1-8 km)		8	15	22.0
At 5-9.9 miles (8-16 km)		13	27	9.8
At 10-29.9 miles (16-48 km)		14	28	0.1
At over 30 miles (48.3 km) (other than Ireland)		8	16	0.0
In Ireland		7	14	0.0
Not traceable		2	..	..
Total population	%	100	100	..
	N	6741	3345	..

a) (..) = not applicable.
b) Visitors and those in institutions are excluded.
c) Excluding not traceable.

d) $\dfrac{\text{Sample population} \times 10}{\text{1831 population}}$ of all villages at this distance.

Here Anderson has 'grossed up' the sample values by 10 (the size of the sample fraction) to give 'point estimates' of the 1851 Preston population in each category of origin – ie he has estimated the 1851 population in each category by multiplying the numbers in the 1 in 10 sample by 10.

Over 40 % of the migrants had come less than ten miles (16 km), and only about 30 % were more than 30 miles (48 km) from their places of birth. Only some 2 % of the sample had been born more than 100 miles (160 km) from their birthplaces, but within England Wales or Scotland. Table 2 also gives some idea of the local nature of migration from the point of view of the sending community. The number of migrants from within five miles (8 km) living in Preston in 1851 was the equivalent of 22 % of the 1831 population of the communities falling within this arc. As one moves further away the proportion falls rapidly. This seems to confirm that it was above all the nearest town that was providing the impetus for migration. This 22 % figure is all the more astonishing because, taken as a whole, the population of the area in question increased by nearly 9 % between 1831 and 1851 ; on average, moreover outmigrants made up as large a proportion of the population of communities whose population was expanding as of those which were declining. It was, of course, partly on the basis of data such as these that Redford proposed the two step migration hypothesis, though, of course the Deane and Cole hypothesis is equally compatible with these figures.

Table III shows the type of community of birth of the sample population.

TABLE III. — BIRTHPLACES OF THE NON-INSTITUTIONALISED RESIDENT MIGRANTS TO PRESTON, BY COMMUNITY TYPE, PRESTON SAMPLE, 1851.

% born in :			
Within 30 miles			
Towns	24		
Manufacturing villages	9		
Mixed villages	8		
Farming villages	13		
Miscellaneous villages	16		
Over 30 miles		All % N	100 3345
Towns	6		
Villages	7		
Uncertain (including e.g. "Scotland")	3		
Ireland	14		

There are two notable features in this table :

1. The rather small proportion of the migrants coming from mainly agricultural communities. It should be noted, however, that Lancashire may have been somewhat unique in this respect because of the collapse of the economic base of the surrounding villages with the decline in hand-loom weaving, and because there just were not many purely farming villages in the immediate environs. Further research on other communities is necessary to substantiate this point[9] ; some data presented later are also of relevance.

2. The very large proportion born in other towns, particularly other cotton towns. This was almost certainly only a small part of the total migration between towns. This kind of migration was particularly the result of the periodic depressions during which thousands of men left their homes to search for work in other industrial areas.

Because of the great effect of distance on migration patterns, and because different types of community are not equally distributed at

9. More generally, it must also be stressed that Lancashire's peculiarities in this and other respects mean that the conclusions of this paper must not be generalised in any way outside their immediate geographical context. Each area of England must be studied separately, for the nature of the surrounding communities, their population density, and the skills required of those who moved to the towns all varied widely from region to region.

the different distances from Preston, it is meaningless to calculate the aggregated proportions that migrants comprised of the total 1831 populations of the different types of communities. Table IV presents instead these data for two subgroups, those born at less than five, and between five and nine miles from Preston. (Figures in brackets show that the data are based on fewer than 30 migrants in the sample. The symbol... indicates that no cases fell into this area and so no percentages could be calculated.)

TABLE IV. — MIGRANTS FROM ELSEWHERE LIVING IN PRESTON IN 1851 AS PERCENTAGES OF THE POPULATION OF THEIR HOME COMMUNITIES IN 1831, AGGREGATED BY COMMUNITY TYPES.

% born	Type of community				
	Agricultural	Manufacturing	Mixed	Miscellaneous	Towns
0-4 miles distant					
To north & west	35	38	(21)	34	..
To south & east	(31)	23	17	..	15
All	34	31	17	34	15
5-9 miles distant					
To north & west	18	20	27	22	..
To south & east	(20)	7	7	(6)	7
All	18	11	9	20	7

A glance at the 'All' rows of table 4 suggests that migrants made up a larger proportion of the population of farming areas than they did of industrial villages or towns at the same distance. The remaining rows, however, show the figures to be an artifact. Industrial villages and towns were particularly situated to the south and east of a line drawn through Preston from north east to south west, while farming villages were predominantly to the north and west of such a line. The areas to the south and east were also nearer to other industrial areas, while Preston, situated on the north-west corner of the Lancashire cotton areas was presumably attracting most of the migrants from the north and west. When location of village of birth is thus controlled, differences of this kind more or less disappear, the only slight variations being probably attributable to sampling error. This finding thus strengthens the notion that migrants were being drawn to the nearest manufacturing town. In Lancashire, at least, they seem to have been drawn almost equally from all community types.

The process of migration

This section considers some aspects of one of the two hypotheses discussed earlier in the paper, the two-step migration hypothesis. It is necessary first, however, to specify the hypothesis in a somewhat clearer form as the process involved could take one or more of four forms :

1 a. A person born in a country area migrates first some distance from his home to another community nearer to the manufacturing districts, and later moves to a large manufacturing town.

1 b. A person born in a country area migrates first to a nearby small town, or village with a more 'developed' economy, and later moves on to a large manufacturing town.

2 a. People from country areas migrate to communities nearer to the manufacturing districts, and replace the indigenous population who are migrating to large manufacturing towns.

2 b. People from country areas migrate to small towns or more 'developed' villages, where they replace the indigenous population who are migrating to large manufacturing towns.

Figure 4 Redford's stepwise migration model. Source: devised by W. T. R. Pryce from Redford (1926) pp 158–61

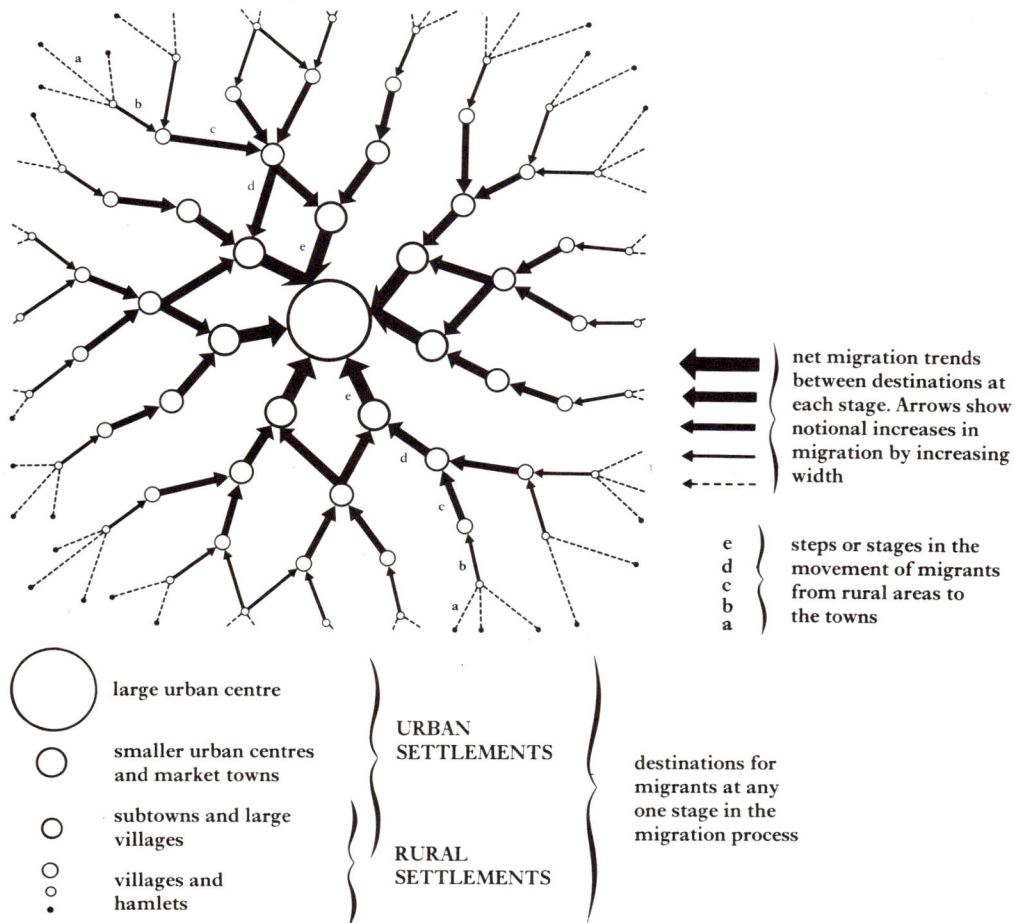

net migration trends between destinations at each stage. Arrows show notional increases in migration by increasing width

e
d
c
b
a
} steps or stages in the movement of migrants from rural areas to the towns

large urban centre

smaller urban centres and market towns

subtowns and large villages

villages and hamlets

URBAN SETTLEMENTS

RURAL SETTLEMENTS

} destinations for migrants at any one stage in the migration process

Any of these versions of the two-step migration hypothesis are compatible with Redford's statements on the topic, which are of a very imprecise kind. Hypothesis 2 *a* appears to correspond most closely to the notion of the two-step migration which Deane and Cole suggest was occurring around London. Hypotheses 1 *a* and 1 *b* correspond most closely to Booth's views on the topic. All are obviously compatible with the data on substantial migration associated with growth of population in the sending areas revealed above, though obviously hypotheses 2 *a* and 2 *b* fit this situation better.

In order to investigate these hypotheses, data are required on the birthplaces of those who were living in 1851 in the villages where the Preston migrants had been born. This requires an investigation of the 1851 population of these villages.

If hypothesis 2 *a* were correct, one would expect to find that a considerable part of the population of these villages had been born in places situated at a greater distance from Preston than the village where they were living in 1851. It would also be necessary to establish that this migration to villages nearer to Preston was not being counterbalanced by a heavy reverse migration. If heavy reverse migration was found to occur, this would simply suggest a large turnover of the country population, and would give no support to the two-step migration hypothesis.

If hypothesis 1 *a* were correct, one would also expect to find some tendency of this kind, but, since, migrants on their way to Preston would probably only be staying in these villages for a few years before moving on to Preston, the tendency would not be so marked.

If hypothesis 2 *b* were correct, one would expect to find that a considerable proportion of the population of the small towns and manufacturing villages which were supplying migrants to Preston had been born in farming areas, and that no substantial reverse migration was occurring from these towns and manufacturing villages to the farming areas.

If hypothesis 1 *b* were correct, some slight tendency of this kind would be expected, but it would not necessarily be so marked.

Some of the data relevant to the investigation of these hypotheses have been collected for other purposes, using sampling fractions for each village which were proportional to the number of heads of households and wives born in that village who fell into the Preston sample. These data have unfortunately only been partly analysed as yet for the work involved is somewhat time-consuming. Also, information on relevant town populations and on places situated at more than 30 miles from Preston have not yet been collected. The conclusions that follow are thus based on a subsample of some 350 households taken from villages situated within 30 miles from Preston. These conclusions must, therefore be considered tentative, but they should be enough to establish whether any of these hypotheses merit further investigation.

In the analysis of data relevant to hypotheses 1 *a* and 2 *a* it has once again proved fruitful to divide the birthplaces of the Preston migrants between those in a north-westerly arc centred on Preston and those to the south-east. For those in the nord-westerly arc, Preston was in the main the nearest industrial town. In this area any net migration that can be detected into places which sent population to Preston and which has come from places further away from Preston to the north west, can be seen as giving support to the two-step migration hypothesis. The communities to the south east, by contrast, are in the main almost equidistant from several different towns. Thus a first move away from Preston might well be a move nearer to another town. A definitive test in the case of this area would apparently require a different and more sophisticated approach.

It is thus not unexpected that analysis of the relevant villages in this area to the south-east showed that inhabitants who had moved away from their birth places were as likely to be living further from Preston as they were to be living nearer to it, and that there was no evidence of a net population movement into these villages from further away. But this finding, when taken together with the fact that 88 % of the population of these villages had moved less than ten miles and that only 3 % had been born somewhere outside the immediate cotton manufacturing area, does suggest that any two-step migration that was occurring was comparatively insignificant and that the Deane and Cole natural increase hypothesis may be more plausible for this area.

By contrast, however, among those living in villages to the north west, some definite evidence did emerge that would tend to support the two-step migration hypothesis. Attention was turned in particular to those villages within this area which were situated within five miles of Preston. This group of villages were represented in Preston in 1851 by numbers equivalent to 35 % of their 1831 population. Sample figures were used to estimate the total population numbers involved; this of course introduces the possibility of substantial inaccuracies due to sampling error, but should nevertheless allow one to establish whether the hypothesis is worth pursuing further.

On this rough basis, it was found that some 25 % of the 1851 population of these villages (somewhere in the region of 2100 persons) had come from communities to the north-west, but situated more than five miles from Preston. This figure is the equivalent of some 80 % of the estimated number of migrants from these villages living in Preston in 1851 (2560). This is not, however, the complete picture. Firstly, a considerable number of persons were found while sampling

Note the explicit use here of variable sample fractions, selected according to the material.

other areas of Lancashire who had been born in these villages near to Preston but were living in 1851 more than five miles to the north or west of Preston. Because not quite all villages were sampled (sampling being limited to villages which had sent migrants to Preston who had fallen into the Preston sample), the resulting figure is not a complete tally of those involved in the reverse migration process; even so they are estimated as the equivalent of 875 persons. If these are subtracted from the imigrant group, net imigration to these villages falls to about 1200, or about half the total numbers migrating to Preston.

There remains, however, the probability that some of the people born in these villages were living in 1851 elsewhere within the manufacturing area, so that simply measuring the outflow from these villages to Preston would underestimate their true population loss to the industrial areas due to migration. The population equivalent of some 400 persons was indeed located by chance in villages in the area sampled, and, if one assumes on the basis of the figures discussed for Preston in the first section of this paper, that some five per cent of the 1831 population of these villages were living in 1851 in other manufacturing towns (which were not sampled) this adds about another 400 to the total, making some 800 in all. This figure, which is probably still an underestimate, is 200 more than the number of persons (about 600) who had migrated from these industrial areas into the villages under study.

Two other figures are also relevant. An estimated 600 persons who had been born in Preston were living in these villages in 1851. And, the population of these villages was growing slowly. If for analytical purposes one treats as the relevant period of time the 20 years between 1831 and 1851 the population of these villages rose by some 300 persons. (Between 1841 and 1851 the growth was about 240).

In sum, taking all these considerations into account the following picture emerges:

Net migration to Preston	1 960
Net migration to other manufacturing areas :	200
Population growth, 1831-1851	300
	2 460
Net two-step type immigration	1 200

This suggests that two-step type migration might well have accounted for about one half of the relevant population changes in this sector of rural Lancashire. The rest must presumably be attributed to natural increase of some kind.

It must once again be stressed, however, that the conclusions of this section of this paper are of a very provisional nature. The data so far collected are not complete and the figures are based on estimates from samples which are themselves rather small. In addition, the procedure used has made a number of assumptions which may or may not be valid, and which themselves need further research. Nevertheless, it would seem that further research on both the two step and natural increase hypotheses is warranted by these results.

If attention is turned very briefly to hypotheses 1b and 2b there is little evidence to suggest any important migration from agricultural to manufacturing villages within the country areas. Of the population of the manufacturing villages, 16 % had been born in other manufacturing villages, 10 % in mixed villages, and only 2 % in farming villages. 5 % had been born in towns and 12 % elsewhere including the miscellaneous category. Conversely, of the population of farming villages, 23 % had been born in other farming villages, 9 % in mixed villages, and 4 % in manufacturing villages and 15 % elsewhere. This suggests that most of the very considerable movements within the country areas were confined to villages of a similar economic type.

Figure 5 Deane and Cole's 'natural increase' hypothesis. Source: devised by W. T. R. Pryce from Deane and Cole (1967) pp 111–21

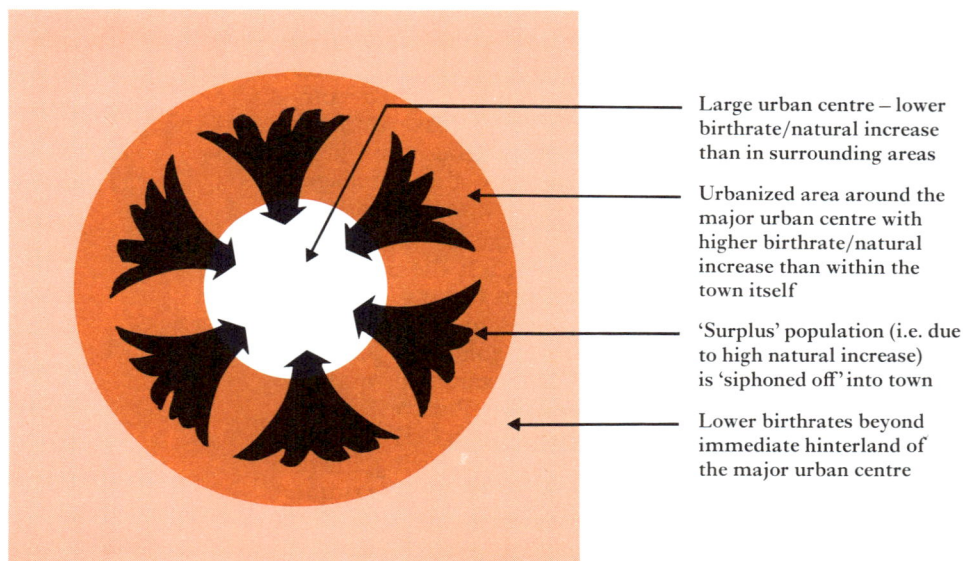

Large urban centre – lower birthrate/natural increase than in surrounding areas

Urbanized area around the major urban centre with higher birthrate/natural increase than within the town itself

'Surplus' population (i.e. due to high natural increase) is 'siphoned off' into town

Lower birthrates beyond immediate hinterland of the major urban centre

Before hypotheses 1b and 2b can be completely rejected, however, evidence must be gathered and analysed on the smaller manufacturing towns which were providing a substantial migration to Preston. It will also be necessary to look at the small number of thriving industrial manufacturing villages in more detail, since one might not necessarily expect to locate much migration to a group of villages which included a substantial declining hand-loom weaving element in their population.

The analysis so far has only considered migration within the country areas, and thus has been unable to differentiate between the first pair of hypotheses, those where the *same* person moves first to other country areas and then to the towns, and the second pair of hypotheses which simply suggest that when the population of one community move to the nearby towns, they are replaced by other people migrating from further away, or from areas with less developed economies.

Further investigation of hypotheses 1a and 1b on their own can be undertaken in some detail on the basis of data from the Preston sample. If hypothesis 1a were correct one would expect to find that a large proportion of the migrant population had some children born neither in the village of their birth nor in Preston, but in some other community nearer to Preston than their birthplace. This would be the case unless all migrants were single when they migrated, which is known not to have been the case.

Analysis of data relevant to this hypothesis showed some interesting results. The procedure used was to compare, for all nuclear families having both parents and at least one child at home, the birthplace of the father with that of the eldest co-residing child. This showed where the family was living at the time that the child was born.

In all, in 28 % of all families where the father had been born neither in Preston nor in Ireland or elsewhere overseas, the eldest co-residing child had been born in a different community from that of the father but not in Preston. In very few cases was this child born instead in the mother's birthplace. Of course, the total number of families who had migrated via an intermediate community was certainly considerably higher than this figure of 28 %. Some of the adults would have migrated to Preston before marriage or before the birth of their first child, but nevertheless have stopped off in

The movement of the *same* person, in steps, is referred to in the fourth television programme *(The Urban Migrant)* as *simple stepwise migration*: stepwise movement involving *different* people is referred to in that programme as *stepwise migration with replacement*. (See Figures 1 and 2, p 132.)

NB: There is the problem, however, that young mothers may have returned home to their own mothers' residence to have the first child. For comments on this, see Bryant (1971).

another community on the way, some would have children born in an intervening community, but all such children had since left home or died, while some may well have migrated via such a community after the end of their child-bearing period. In only 6 % of cases did families who had migrated during the period when their children were being born have no children born elsewhere than in Preston or in the father's community of birth.

Even more interesting, however, are the results presented in Table V. The figures in columns D and E suggest very strongly (as might perhaps have been expected)[10] that direct movement to Preston was most likely to occur among those born near to Preston, while intermediary stops in other communities were most likely among those born at a distance. There is no apparent difference in this case between those who were born to the south east and those born to the north-west of Preston.

TABLE V. — PARISH OF RESIDENCE OF FAMILY AT TIME OF BIRTH OF ELDEST CO-RESIDING CHILD, BY DISTANCE TO FATHER'S BIRTHPLACE, PRESTON SAMPLE, 1851.

Father born at	In Preston	In father's birthplace Family moved		In intermediate community (% of such cities nearer Preston)		All	
		After birth of last child	During child-bearing period				
A	% (B)	% (C)	% (D)	% (E)	% (F)	% (G)	% (H)
0-4 miles	60	6	8	26	(31)	100	99
5-9 miles	62	8	7	23	(42)	100	174
10-19 miles	60	8	9	24	(53)	99	80
20-29 miles	57	4	3	36	(54)	100	67
Over 29 miles	58	4	1	36	(85)	99	91
All	60	6	6	28	(54)	100	511

Also of interest is a consideration of the direction of the moves made. These data are given in column F of table V. Only among those coming from a great distance was there any tendency for the first move to be to somewhere markedly nearer to Preston. Among the short distance migrants in particular, the move was more likely to be away from Preston than nearer to it. Such a finding is compatible with a notion that first moves were largely random with respect to any given town, though, among those coming from a distance, they were generally oriented in the direction of the manufacturing areas as a whole.

Finally, attention may be turned briefly to hypothesis 1 b. Here too some interesting results were obtained. Although almost equal proportions of all groups had spent an intervening period of time living in a third community, the type of community was not random. This is clear from Table VI.

The principal conclusions to be drawn from this table seem to be :

1. Where the father had been born in a more 'advanced' community, the family seldom moved to a less advanced one. Indeed it is probable that many would not have moved again at all had not a move been forced on the family by the need to obtain employment elsewhere during depression periods.

10. A similar findings is reported by PONS for Stanleyville in UNESCO, *Social implications..., op. cit.*, p. 255.

TABLE VI. — PARISH OF RESIDENCE OF FAMILY AT TIME OF BIRTH OF ELDEST CHILD BORN NEITHER IN PRESTON NOR IN THE FATHER'S BIRTHPLACE, BY COMMUNITY TYPE OF FATHER'S BIRTHPLACE AND CHILD'S BIRTHPLACE, PRESTON SAMPLE, 1851.

Father born in	Of all families		Of all living in intermediate community			% living	
	% with child born in intermediate community	All (100%)	In towns	In manufact. villages	In agr. or mixed villages	Elsewhere	All
	%	N	%	%	%	%	%
Town over 30 miles away	33	36	75	–	17	8	100
Town within 30 miles	27	133	67	8	8	16	99
Manufacturing village	28	72	50	20	20	10	100
Mixed village	32	44	36	36	21	7	100
Farming village	26	88	17	4	43	35	99

2. That migrants from less 'advanced' communities had some tendency to move to 'more advanced' communities, where they could often probably obtain some training relevant to urban life. Such a process was, however, by no means universal, and many almost certainly migrated direct from farming areas to the towns. It is not perhaps irrelevant to note at this point that migrants born in 'more advanced' communities were definitely more likely to enter the more secure and better paid jobs in the town [11]. There is also some limited evidence to suggest that, of those born in less advanced communities, the only ones who managed to get the better jobs were those who had either migrated via some more advanced community, or who had kinsmen in the town who were able to help them get good jobs. The rest seem to have ended up either in domestic service of some kind or in the lowest labouring jobs. This hypothesis needs further investigation before it can be considered fully verified, and this will require a much larger sample than that at present collected.

Conclusions

The tentative conclusions of this analysis which seem to point the way for further research appear to be:

1. That, as most previous investigators have suggested, migration only rarely took place over distances of more than a few miles.

2. That a large proportion of the migrants who were living in Preston in 1851 had lived in one or more other communities in addition to their place of birth.

3. That most of the short distance movement was not clearly directed towards any one community, though it did involve some slight tendency to drift into communities where skills more relevant to urban life could be learned.

4. That deliberate two-step migration by the same individuals was only clearly apparent among migrants from a distance who made up a fairly small proportion of the total.

5. That there is some evidence that two-step migration involving different individuals was occurring, particularly from areas right outside the cotton manufacturing areas proper. This migration was, however, probably not on a large enough scale to have made possible both migration to the towns on the scale that was occurring, and the gradual increase in population in the sending communities. Migration on the scale

11. The relevant data are reported *in* M. ANDERSON, *op. cit.*

Here Anderson is looking at the *social* implications of migration (as opposed to the simply *spatial* ones). The migrant often crosses social distances, perhaps from a rural to an urban culture, or from one social class to another, as he moves over geographical distances.

that was occuring probably also required some steady natural increase of the rural population. Deane and Cole have suggested a mechanism of this kind, and have argued that the growth of the towns must have stimulated population growth in the surrounding areas. By this they presumably mean to imply that some increase in fertility took place. First impressions, however, lead me to suggest that this is improbable, because in the area to the north and west of Preston at least there was a later age of marriage than in most other areas of rural England, and the proportion of the population ultimately marrying was if anything also lower [12]. If the rate of natural increase of population in these areas was higher than elsewhere in rural England, it seems more likely that it resulted from their lower rates of infant and child mortality, for which no adequate explanation seems at present to exist. The extent to which these areas did in fact have a rate of natural population increase so much higher than that elsewhere in rural England is anyway very difficult to establish, in view of the massive migrations which were taking place. Further research is obviously necessary on these points.

12. For some preliminary data on this point see M. ANDERSON, « Sources and techniques for the study of family structure in nineteenth century Britain », in E. A. WRIGLEY, *The study of nineteenth century society*, London, Weidenfeld and Nicholson, 1970.

4 Conclusion

My answer to the question posed in the introduction to this unit would include the following points:

1 Hollingsworth stresses 'the importance of migration in modern demographic study'. He believes it 'is becoming the most important branch of demography, just as fertility had dominated the scene for the past eighty years or so and mortality before that'. Migration is then, if Hollingsworth is to be believed, a key problem area of one of the most central of the social sciences – demography. It follows, if one accepts the ideology of Applied Historical Studies, that it is too important to be left for analysis in a purely contemporary context. Hollingsworth indeed asserts as much. Anderson in turn urges the relevance of his enquiry as being of 'general sociological and demographic interest'.

2 The actual exposition by both Hollingsworth and Anderson exemplify the research strategy we have recommended. Hollingsworth's article can be seen as the first stage of that strategy – namely the exploration of a *topic of interest*. He does this by first looking at contemporary interpretations of the phenomenon, then discusses the various types of historical data which might be drawn upon to test those interpretations. And, from the point of view of the substantive theme of this block of units (ie population and industrialization), we observe him noting that 'the role of migration in the early stages of the Industrial Revolution is still not clearly understood'.

We have already noted that Anderson first places his proposed exercises in a more general context, again underlining their importance for 'theories of population growth in industrializing societies'. He then uses a data source hitherto neglected for this purpose, namely the census enumerators' books. Note too that Anderson structures his study around the testing of two apparently mutually contradictory hypotheses: Redford's on the one hand, Deane and Cole's on the other. Again, an important point, he finds it necessary to specify Redford's hypothesis 'in a somewhat clearer form': a salutary reminder that hypotheses can mislead unless they are specified with absolute clarity.

3 Anderson demonstrates the importance of quantitative measures. Those he uses are by no means sophisticated (sampling excepted), but without them it is difficult to see how his study could even have been started.

Appendix[1]

'. . . All the rising centres of industry and commerce were attracting workers by a process of short-distance migration from the surrounding country; where the attractive force of a large town was exerted over a wide area the inward movement took place usually by stages. The majority of the migrants to the towns came from the immediately surrounding counties, their places in turn being taken by migrants from places further away . . . There was a fairly uniform lessening in the intensity of migration as the distance from the absorbing centre increased . . . The characteristic features of this process, up to the middle of the century, are very clearly seen in the statistics of migration collected at the 1851 census.

. . . The migration into London had been affected in some measure by special migrations from all the great manufacturing and commercial centres . . . [and] . . . the attractive force of the capital city was felt in every part of the United Kingdom.

. . . The movement out of any county was practically the reverse of the process already traced: the outward migration lessened in intensity as the distance from the home county increased, at any rate until some active centre of attraction was reached.

. . . These two processes of migration, opposite in tendency but similar in form, may be traced in all parts of the Kingdom. In each case the area affected was roughly circular; the process of absorption was centripetal, the process of dispersion centrifugal. The great majority of the migrants went only a short distance, and migration into any centre of attraction having a wide sphere of influence was not a simple transference of people from the circumference of a circle to its centre, but an exceedingly complex wave-like motion . . . The migration was by stages, in a wave-like motion; the movement of population persisted over a wide area, even though most of the migrants did not make any long journey.'

---

1 From A. Redford (1926) *Labour migration in England, 1800-1850*, Manchester University Press pp 158-61.

Units 5–8 Annotated bibliography

The items selected for brief comment here cover the subjects discussed in Units 5–8.

BOURGEOIS-PICHAT, J. (1973) *Main Trends in Demography*, London, Allen and Unwin. This brief, eighty-page booklet provides an up-to-date summary of the main interests of demographers today. The author hopes for closer collaboration between demographers and the other sciences and to that end discusses the relevance of demographic research for students of biology, economic development, human ecology and sociology.

BRADLEY, L. (1971) *A Glossary for Local Population Studies*, University of Nottingham Adult Education Department. Supplement to *Local Population Studies*. (Available from Subscription Secretary, *Local Population Studies*, 9 Lisburne Square, Torquay, Devon).

An extremely useful guide to the main terms and techniques used by students of historical demography. The author has very much in mind the interests and needs of beginners in the field. The work is divided into three parts: *demographic terms* (eg age-specific, aggregation-aggregative analysis; age-structure etc); *statistical terms* (eg an excellent discussion of the meaning of *variable* and of the main features of a *distribution* followed by arithmetic progression, chi-squared test, confidence intervals etc); *sources and names* (eg bills of mortality, Bishop's transcripts, census etc).

CHAMBERS, J. D. (1972) *Population, Economy and Society in Pre-Industrial England*, Oxford University Press.

The late Professor Chambers was a pioneer of historical demography in Britain. This book summarizes most of his work and is especially useful for his discussion of the independent role of disease (independent, that is, of food shortages) as a cause of mortality in pre-industrial societies. Professor Chambers also examines the main features of the recent controversy over the determinants of the rise in the rate of population growth in mid eighteenth-century England. Can be recommended as a comprehensive and readable introduction to the main concerns of British historical demographers over the last twenty years.

DRAKE, MICHAEL (ed) (1969) *Population in Industrialization*, London, Methuen.

An early exercise in Applied Historical Studies, this collection of articles traces the various steps in the controversy surrounding the relationship between population growth and economic growth during the period of England's Industrial Revolution. The relevance of this to the current discussion of the population problems of today's pre-industrial societies is a key feature of the book. Contributors include A. J. Coale and E. M. Hoover, K. H. Connell, T. McKeown and R. G. Brown, T. H. Hollingsworth, J. T. Krause, P. E. Razzell and E. A. Wrigley.

FLINN, M. W. (1970) *British Population Growth 1700–1850*, London, Macmillan.

This pamphlet provides an excellent summary of the controversy considered in greater depth in the volumes by Chambers (q.v.) and Drake (q.v.). It reveals the many problems involved in researching the causes of population growth in this period. Flinn's cautious conclusions show there is much work still to be done. Contains an excellent annotated bibliography.

GLASS, D. V. and EVERSLEY, D. E. C. (eds) (1965) *Population in History*, London, Arnold.

This very large book (over 700 pages, it tips my scales at 2 lbs 13½ ozs!) contains 27 key contributions from leading historical demographers. The work is divided into three parts; a general section, one dealing with Great Britain, and a final one covering Europe and the United States. Contributors demonstrate a wide range of interests and between them cover the main issues of the relationship between 'population, economy and society' (Eversley), the 'vital revolution' (Helleiner), 'European marriage patterns' (Hajnal), England's population during the Industrial Revolution (Glass,

Marshall, Habakkuk, Chambers, McKeown and Brown, Hollingsworth, Krause and Eversley), developments in the population of France from the sixteenth century to the present (Henry, Goubert, Bourgeois-Pichat, Meuvret), eighteenth-century Scandinavia (Utterström and Jutikkala), Italy 1500–1950 (Cipolla), Ireland 1780–1845 (Connell), Barmen – an old industrial town in western Germany – during the Industrial Revolution (Koellmann), Flanders in the eighteenth century (Deprez) and America 1700–1860 (Potter).

GLASS, D. V. and REVELLE, ROGER (eds) (1972) *Population and Social Change*, London, Arnold.
An important collection of articles showing the wide-ranging interests of historical demographers today, this volume is an excellent guide to current discussions. Ranging from Tristan da Cunha to Japan, the book covers many different societies. It also includes some general essays on such matters as 'the treatment of population in history textbooks' (David Landes) and 'historical sociology and the study of population' (J. A. Banks).

GOUBERT, P. (1960) *Beauvais et le Beauvaisis de 1600 à 1730* 2 vols, Paris, Sevpen.
This is a classic account of demographic change in a pre-industrial western community and perhaps the most famous historical demographic monograph to appear in the last twenty-five years. French populations seem to have lived much closer to subsistence than those of northern Europe and England, hence the appearance of many demographic crises. The latter are discussed in detail and are one of the most important features of the work.

HABAKKUK, H. J. (1971) *Population Growth and Economic Development*, Leicester University Press.
Over the last twenty years, Professor Habakkuk has played an important role in historical demography by summarizing the 'state of play', as it were, at various times and pointing the way to fruitful lines of enquiry. He did this in 1953 (*Economic History Review*, 2nd series, vi, pp. 117–33); in 1958 (*Journal of Economic History*, xviii, pp. 486–501); in 1963 (*The American Economic Review*, LIII, 2, pp 607–18) and in this volume. The four chapter headings indicate the scope of the book; 'pre-industrial population change', 'the demographic revolution', 'the decline in fertility' and 'western population patterns and the under-developed areas'. Based on lectures delivered at the University of Leicester, this is a very readable introduction.

HARSIN, PAUL and HELEN, ETIENNE (eds) (no date) *Actes du Colloque International de Démographie Historique, Liège 1963*, Paris, Genin.
This collection of papers appears mostly in English or French, though there are also contributions in German and Spanish. The volume is divided into two parts, the first on sources and methods covering France, Belgium, the Netherlands, Norway, Sweden, Switzerland, Czechoslovakia, Hungary, Romania, Turkey, Bolivia, the USA and the USSR. The second part of the book focuses on the study of mortality, with a particular emphasis on demographic crises in France, Belgium and Italy. There is also an important article by D. E. C. Eversley, 'Mortality in Britain in the eighteenth century: problems and prospects'.

HAWTHORN, GEOFFREY (1970) *The Sociology of Fertility*, London, Collier-Macmillan.
The author admits to having 'chosen to interpret "the sociology of fertility" as the study of the social determinants of human fertility' not 'the consequences of particular fertility patterns'. Summarizes very succinctly the major work in the field which appeared during the 1960s. Ends with an extremely useful twenty-two page annotated bibliography.

HOLLINGSWORTH, T. H. (1969) *Historical Demography*, London, Hodder and Stoughton.
Without exaggeration this book can be described as a 'mine of information'. Dr Hollingsworth reviews at a breathless pace virtually every conceivable source that has been used or could be used by historical demographers. There is an important cautionary chapter on 'the limits of demographic research in history', a good bibliography and excellent index.

SOCIAL SCIENCE RESEARCH COUNCIL (1971) *Research in Economic and Social History*, London, Heinemann.
Covers a much wider range of subjects than historical demography, but as demography is important to so many of these the volume is more relevant than might, at first sight, be supposed. The five chapters are 'economic and social history: some main themes in modernization'; 'methodological problems'; 'some areas of current research'; 'selected periods and problems' and a concluding chapter, 'research resources and development in economic and social history'.

TRANTER, N. L. (1973) *Population since the Industrial Revolution: The Case of England and Wales*, London, Croom-Helm.
This is a good introduction to the population history of the last two hundred years. Despite its subtitle, the author sets the English 'case' within the context of western Europe. Being the most recent of the general surveys considered in this bibliography it has the advantage of being the most up-to-date. It is also more comprehensive in time and subject matter as it examines population problems down to the present day.

WRIGLEY, E. A. (ed) (1966) *An Introduction to English Historical Demography*, London, Weidenfeld and Nicolson.
Although this book considers some of the main substantive issues that have concerned English historical demographers, its primary task is to review the promise and pitfalls of the sources and to teach the main techniques of historical demography. Chapters are 'the numerical study of English society' (Laslett); 'population history and local history' (Eversley); 'exploitation of Anglican parish registers by aggregative analysis' (Eversley); 'family reconstitution' (Wrigley); 'the study of social structure from listings of inhabitants' (Laslett); 'social structure from the early census returns' (Armstrong). Although much work has been done since this book appeared, and advances made in some of the techniques, it is still essential reading for students beginning historical demography.

WRIGLEY, E. A. (1969) *Population and History*, London, Weidenfeld and Nicolson.
This book provides a very good synthesis of work done in historical demography throughout the world in a relatively small compass (about 250 pages). Though the subject matter it covers is the same as in a number of the other books referred to in this bibliography (eg Chambers, Drake, Flinn, Habakkuk, Tranter) it has the edge on them by being illustrated with diagrams, maps, graphs and well-displayed tables, some of which are in colour.

Other references

This section includes full bibliographical details of works cited in the texts of Units 5–7, unless they have already been covered in the annotated bibliography above. There are also references of other works related to the subject matter of Units 5–7.

ALLISON, K. J. (ed) (1969) *Victoria History of the Counties of England: York East Riding*, Vol. 1, Oxford University Press.

ANDERSON, MICHAEL (1971) *Family Structure in Nineteenth-Century Lancashire*, Cambridge University Press.

ANDERSON, MICHAEL (1972) 'Urban migration in nineteenth-century Lancashire: some insights into two competing hypotheses', *Annales de Démographie Historique 1971*, Paris, Mouton, pp 13–26.

ANDERSON, MICHAEL (1972) 'Household structure and the industrial revolution: mid-nineteenth-century Preston in comparative perspective' in LASLETT 1972.

APPLEBY, ANDREW, B. (1973) 'Disease or famine? Mortality in Cumberland and Westmorland 1580–1640', *Economic History Review*, Second Series, Vol. 26, No. 3, pp 403–32.

ARKELL, V. T. J. (1972) 'An enquiry into the frequency of the parochial registration of Catholics in a seventeenth-century Warwickshire parish', *Local Population Studies* No. 9, pp 23–32.

BARNETT, HAROLD, J. (1970–71) 'Population problems – myths and realities', *Economic Development and Cultural Change*, Vol. 19, pp 545–59.

BENJAMIN, BERNARD (1968) *Demographic Analysis*, London, George Allen and Unwin.

BARCLAY, GEORGE, W. (1958) *Techniques of Population Analysis*, New York, John Wiley.

BANKS, J. A. (1954) *Prosperity and Parenthood*, London, Routledge and Kegan Paul.

BENJAMIN, BERNARD; COX, PETER R. and PEEL, JOHN (eds) (1973) *Resources and Population*, London and New York, Academic Press.

BERESFORD, M. W. and JONES, G. R. J. (1967) *Leeds and its Region*, Leeds, British Association.

BLAGG, T. M. and WADSWORTH, E. A. (1930) *Abstracts of Nottinghamshire Marriage Licenses*, 2 vols, London, British Record Society.

BOND, DAVID (1973) 'The Compton Census – Peterborough', *Local Population Studies*, No. 10, pp 71–4.

BOORMAN, WILLIAM, H. (1968) 'Smallpox in eighteenth-century Winchester', *Local Population Studies*, No. 1 pp 35–39.

BOSERUP, ESTER (1965) *The Conditions of Agricultural Growth*, London, Allen and Unwin.

BOSWELL, DAVID (1973) 'Labour migration and commitment to urban residence' in Drake, Michael *et al*, *The Process of Urbanization*, Milton Keynes, Open University Press.

BOULDING, KENNETH, E. (ed) (1959) *Thomas Robert Malthus, Population: The First Essay*, Ann Arbor, University of Michigan Press. See also MALTHUS, 1970.

BOYNTON, L. (1967) *The Elizabethan Militia, 1558–1638*. London, David and Co.

BRADLEY, L. (1973) 'Smallpox: a difference of opinion', *Local Population Studies*, No. 10, pp 67–9.

BRITISH MUSEUM ADDITIONAL MANUSCRIPTS 6896 AND 6897 (1811). Transcripts of 'the answers given to questions addressed to the officiating ministers and overseers in England and Wales and the schoolmasters in Scotland, preparatory to the Population Act of 1811 relative to the non-entry of baptisms, burials and marriages in the parish registers and decrease of the population'.

BRYANT, DAVID (1971) 'Demographic trends in South Devon in the mid-nineteenth century' in K. J. GREGORY and W. C. D. RAVENHILL (eds) *Exeter Essays in Geography*, Exeter University Press, pp 125–42.

BUCKATZSCH, E. J. (1951) 'The constancy of local population and migration in England and Wales before 1800', *Population Studies*, Vol. 5, pp 62–9.

BULL, EDVARD (1966) 'Handverksvenner og arbeiderklasse i Kristiania Sosialhistoriske problemer', *Historisk Tidsskrift*, 45, Oslo, pp 88–114 (English summary).

CARLSSON, GÖSTA (1966) 'The decline of fertility: innovation or adjustment process', *Population Studies*, Vol. 20, pp 149–74.

CARTWRIGHT, R. A. (1973) 'The structure of population living on Holy Island, Northumberland' in D. F. ROBERTS and E. SUNDERLAND (eds) *Genetic Variation in Britain,* Vol. 12 of Symposia of the Society for the Study of Human Biology, London, Taylor and Francis.

CHALKIN, C. W. (1960) 'The Compton Census of 1676: the dioceses of Canterbury and Rochester', *Kent Records*, Vol. 17, pp 173–83.

CHAMBERS, J. D. (1957) 'The Vale of Trent, 1670–1800, A regional study of economic change', *The Economic History Review, Supplement 3*, London, Economic History Society.

CIPOLLA, CARLO (1962) *The Economic History of World Population*, Harmondsworth, Penguin Books.

CLARK, COLIN (1967) *Population Growth and Land Use*, London, Macmillan.

CONSTANT, A. (1948) 'The geographical background of inter-village population movements in Northamptonshire and Huntingdonshire, 1754–1943', *Geography*, Vol. 33, pp 78–88.

CORNWALL, J. E. (1959) 'An Elizabethan Census', *The Records of Buckinghamshire*, Vol. 16, No. 4, pp 258–73.

CORNWALL, J. E. (1970) 'English population in the early sixteenth century', *Economic History Review*, Second Series, Vol. 23, No. 1, pp 32–44.

COX, J. C. (1910) *The Parish Registers of England*, London, Methuen.

CROSSLEY, E. W. (ed) (1910) *The Parish Register of Halifax 1540–1593*, Yorkshire Parish Register Society, Vol. 37.

DALRYMPLE, SIR JOHN (1771–3) *Memoirs of Great Britain and Ireland. From the Dissolution of the Last Parliament of Charles II until the Sea-Battle off La Hague*, Edinburgh and London, Vol. II, pp 11–15.

DARBY, H. C. (1943) 'The movement of population to and from Cambridgeshire between 1851 and 1861' *Geographical Journal*, Vol. 101, pp 118–25.

DAVIS, KINGSLEY (1945) 'The world demographic transition', *The Annals of the American Academy of Political and Social Science*, Vol. 237, January, pp 1–11.

DEANE, P. and COLE, W. A. (1962) *British Economic Growth, 1688–1959*, Cambridge University Press.

DIMBLEBY, JONATHAN (1973) 'Emergency Appeal: Ethiopian and African Drought' BBC Radio 4, 31 October 1973, 5.45 pm.

DRAKE, MICHAEL (1962) 'An elementary exercise in parish register demography', *Economic History Review*, Second Series, Vol. 14, No. 3, pp 427–45.

DRAKE, MICHAEL (1963) 'Marriage and population growth in Ireland, 1750–1845', *Economic History Review*, Second Series, Vol. 16, pp 301–13.

DRAKE, MICHAEL (1966) 'Malthus on Norway', *Population Studies*, Vol. 20, pp 175–96.

DRAKE, MICHAEL (1968) 'The Irish demographic crisis of 1740–41', in T. W. Moody (ed) *Historical Studies VI*, London, Routledge and Kegan Paul, pp 101–24.

DRAKE, MICHAEL (1969A) *Population and Society in Norway*, Cambridge University Press.

DRAKE, MICHAEL (1972) 'The census 1801–1891' in E. A. WRIGLEY (ed) (1972).

DRAKE, MICHAEL (ed) (1973) *Applied Historical Studies: An Introductory Reader*, London, Methuen.

EMMISON, F. G. (1967) *How to read local archives, 1550–1700*, London, The Historical Association.

EMMISON, F. G. and SMITH, W. J. (1973) *Material for Theses in Some Local Record Offices*, Chichester, Phillimore.

EVERSLEY, D. E. C. (ed) (1972) 'Demography and economy', *Contribution to the Third International Conference of Economic History, Munich 1965*, Section 7, Paris, Mouton.

FISHER, F. J. (1965) 'Influenza and inflation in Tudor England', *Economic History Review*, Second Series, Vol. 18, No. 1, pp 120–9.

FLETCHER, T. W. and SINHA, R. P. (1965) 'Population growth in a developing economy', *Journal of Development Studies*, Vol. 2, pp 2–18.

FLEURY, M. and HENRY, L. (1965) *Nouveau manuel de dépouillement et d'exploitation de l'état civil ancien*, Paris, Institut National d'Etudes Démographiques.

FLOUD, R. (1973) *An Introduction to Quantitative Methods for Historians*, London, Methuen.

FORSTER, G. C. C. (1961) 'York in the seventeenth century', in TILLOT (ed) (1961) pp 162–5.

FORSTER, G. C. C. (1967) in BERESFORD and JONES.

FORSTER, G. C. C. (1969) 'Hull in the sixteenth and seventeenth century' in ALLISON (ed) (1969).

FRIEDLANDER, D. and ROSHIER, D. J. (1966) 'A study of internal migration in England and Wales', *Population Studies*, Vol. 19, No. 3, pp 239–79 and Vol. 20, No. 1, pp 45–59.

GALLAWAY, L. E. and VEDDER, R. K. (1971) 'Mobility of native Americans', *Journal of Economic History*, Vol. 31, No. 3, pp 613–49.

GAUTIER, E. and HENRY, L. (1958) *La Population de Crulai*, Paris, Institut National d'Etudes Démographiques, Cahier 33.

GLASS, D. V. (ed) (1953) *Introduction to Malthus*, London, Watts.

GLASS, D. V. (1965) 'Two papers on Gregory King' in GLASS and EVERSLEY (1965).

GLASS, D. V. (1973) *Numbering the People*, Farnborough, Saxon Press.

GOLDSCHEIDER, CALVIN (1971) *Population, Modernization and Social Structure*, Boston, Little, Brown and Co.

GOLDTHORPE, JOHN, H.; LOCKWOOD, DAVID; BECHHOFER, FRANK and PLATT, JENNIFER (1969) *The Affluent Worker in the Class Structure*, Cambridge University Press.

GOODER, A. (1972) 'The population crisis of 1727–30 in Warwickshire', *Midland History*, Vol. 1, No. 4.

GOUBERT, P. (1970) 'Historical demography and the reinterpretation of early modern French history: a research review', *Journal of Interdisciplinary History*, Vol. 1, No. 1, pp 37–48.

GUILFORD, E. L. (1924) 'Nottinghamshire in 1676', *Transactions of the Thoroton Society*, Vol. 28, pp 106–13.

HAIR, P. E. H. (1966) 'Bridal pregnancy in rural England in earlier centuries', *Population Studies*, Vol. 20, No. 2, pp 233–43.

HAIR, P. E. H. (1970) 'Bridal pregnancy in earlier rural England further examined', *Population Studies*, Vol. 24, No. 1, pp 59–70.

HAJNAL, J. (1965) 'European marriage patterns in perspective' in GLASS and EVERSLEY (eds) pp 101–43.

HARDIN, GARRETT (1964) *Population, Evolution, Birth Control*, London, W. H. Freeman.

HARLEY, J. B. (1964) *The Historian's Guide to Ordnance Survey Maps*, London, National Council of Social Service.

HARLEY, J. B. (1972) *Maps for the Local Historian, A Guide to British Sources*, London, National Council of Social Service.

HARRISON, G. A. and BOYCE, A. J. (1972) 'Migration exchange and the genetic structure of populations' in HARRISON, G. A. and BOYCE, A. J. (eds) *The Structure of Human Populations*, Oxford, Clarendon Press, pp 128–45.

HEATON, HERBERT (1920) *The Yorkshire Woollen and Worsted Industries*, Oxford, Historical and Literary Studies.

HENRY, L. (1956) *Anciennes Familles Genevoises*, Paris, Institut National d'Etudes Démographiques, Cahier 26.

HOLLINGSWORTH, T. H. (1964) 'The demography of the British Peerage', *Supplement to Population Studies*, Vol. 18, No. 2.

HOLLINGSWORTH, T. H. (1970) *Migration: A Study Based on Scottish Experience between 1939 and 1964*, Edinburgh, Oliver & Boyd.

HOLLINGSWORTH, M. F. and T. H. (1971) 'Plague mortality rates by age and sex in the Parish of St Botolph's Without, Bishopsgate, London 1603', *Population Studies*, Vol. 25, pp 131–46.

HOLLINGSWORTH, T. H. (1971) 'Historical studies of migration', *Annales de Démographie Historique 1970*, Paris, Mouton, pp 87–96.

HOLLINGSWORTH, T. H. (1973) 'Population crises in the past' in BENJAMIN, B.; COX, PETER R. and PEEL, JOHN (eds) *loc cit*, pp 99–108.

HUZEL, J. (1969) 'Malthus, the Poor Law, and Population in early nineteenth-century England', *Economic History Review*, Second Series, Vol. 22.

HUBERT, J. (1965) 'Kinship and geographical mobility in a sample from a London middle-class area', *International Journal of Comparative Sociology*, Vol. 6, pp 61–80.

INSTITUTE OF HERALDIC AND GENEALOGICAL STUDIES (nd) *Parish Maps of the Counties of England and Wales*, Northgate, Canterbury, Kent.

JAMES, F. G. (1952) 'The population of the diocese of Carlisle in 1676', *Transactions of the Cumberland and Westmorland Antiquarian Society*, Vol. 52, pp 137–41.

JAMES, PATRICIA (ed) (1966) *The Travel Diaries of T. R. Malthus*, Cambridge University Press.

JOHNSON, J. H. (1967) 'Harvest migration from nineteenth-century Ireland', *Transactions of the Institute of British Geographers*, No. 41, pp 97–112.

KNIGHTS, PETER, R. (1969) 'Population turnover, persistence and residential mobility in Boston 1830–60' in THERNSTROM and SENNETT (eds) pp 258–74.

KNODAL, J. (1967) 'Law, marriage and illegitimacy in nineteenth-century Germany', *Population Studies*, Vol. 20, No. 3, pp 279–94.

KNODAL, J. (1970) 'Two and a half centuries of demographic history in a Bavarian village', *Population Studies*, Vol. 24, No. 3, pp 353–76.

KRAUSE, J. T. (1958) 'Changes in English fertility and mortality, 1781–1850', *Economic History Review*, Second Series, Vol. 11, No. 1, pp 52–70.

KRAUSE, J. T. (1963) 'English population movements between 1701 and 1850', *International Population Conference*, London. Reprinted in DRAKE (ed) 1969.

KÜCHEMANN, C. F., BOYCE, A. J. and HARRISON, G. A. (1967) 'A demographic and genetic study of a group of Oxfordshire villages', *Human Biology*, Vol. 39, pp 251–76. Reprinted in DRAKE (1973) pp 195–219.

KUHLICKE, F. W. and EMMISON, F. G. (1969) *English Local History Handlist: A Select Bibliography and List of Sources for the Study of Local History and Antiquities*, London, The Historical Association, Fourth Edition.

KYD, J. G. (1952) *Scottish Population Statistics Including Webster's Analysis of Population 1755*, Edinburgh, Scottish History Society, Third Series, Vol. 43.

LANDRY, A. (1934) *La Révolution Démographique*, Paris, Libraire au Recueil Sirey.

LASLETT, PETER (1965) *The World We Have Lost*, London, Methuen.

LASLETT, P. (1969) 'The household in England over three centuries', *Population Studies*, Vol. 23, pp 199–223.

LASLETT, PETER (1972) *Household and Family in Past Time: Comparative Studies in the Size and Structure of the Domestic Group over Time*, Cambridge University Press.

LASLETT, PETER and OOSTERVEEN, KARLA (1973) 'Long-term trends in bastardy in England: a study of the illegitimacy figures in the reports of the Registrar General, 1561–1960', *Population Studies*, Vol. 27, No. 2, pp 255–84.

LASSEN, AKSEL (1965) *Fald og Fremgang: Traek af Befolkningsudviklingen i Danmark 1645–1960*, Aarhus, Universitetsforlaget.

LAW, C. M. (1967) 'The growth of urban population in England and Wales 1801–1911', *Transactions of the Institute of British Geographers*, No. 41, pp 125–43.

LAW, C. M. (1969) 'Local censuses in the eighteenth century', *Population Studies*, Vol. 23, pp 87–100.

LAWTON, R. (1955) 'The population of Liverpool in the mid-nineteenth century', *Transactions of the Historical Society of Lancashire and Cheshire*, Vol. 57, pp 89–120.

LAWTON, R. (1958) 'Population movements in the West Midlands 1841–1861', *Geography*, Vol. 43, pp 164–77.

LAWTON, R. (1967) 'Rural depopulation in nineteenth-century England' in STEEL and LAWTON (eds).

LAWTON, R. (1972) 'An age of great cities', *Town Planning Review*, Vol. 43, No. 3, pp 199–24.

MALTHUS, T. R. (1970 edition) *An Essay on the Principle of Population* edited by Anthony Flew, Harmondsworth, Penguin.

MARSHALL, L. M. (1934) *The Rural Population of Bedfordshire, 1671–1921*, Aspley Guise, Bedfordshire Historical Record Society, Vol. 16.

MARSHALL, L. M. (1936) 'The levying of the hearth tax, 1662–88', *English Historical Review*, Vol. 51, pp 628–46.

MCKEOWN, THOMAS and BROWN, R. G. (1955) 'Medical evidence related to English population changes in the eighteenth century', *Population Studies*, Vol. 9, pp 119–41. Reprinted in DRAKE (ed) (1969).

MCKEOWN, THOMAS and RECORD, R. G. (1962) 'Reasons for the decline of mortality in England and Wales during the nineteenth century', *Population Studies*, Vol. 16, pp 94–122.

MCKEOWN, THOMAS; BROWN, R. G. and RECORD, R. G. (1972) 'An interpretation of the modern rise of population in Europe', *Population Studies*, Vol. 26, pp 345–82.

MEEKINGS, C. A. F. (ed) (1940) *Surrey Hearth Tax 1664*, London, Surrey Record Society, Vol. 17.

MEUVRET, JEAN (1963) 'Réflexions d'un historien sur les crises démographiques aiguës avant le dix-huitième siècle' in HARSIN and HELEN (1963) pp 93–97.

MILLS, D. R. (1973) 'The christening custom at Melbourn, Cambs.', *Local Population Studies*, No. 11, pp 11–22.

OLLARD, S. L. and WALKER, P. C. (eds) (1928–31) *Archbishop Herring's Visitation Returns 1743*, Yorkshire Archaeological Society Record Series, Vols. 71, 72, 75, 77, 79.

OWEN, L. (1959) 'The population of Wales in the sixteenth and seventeenth centuries', *Transactions of the Honourable Society of Cymmrodorion*, pp 99–113.

OXFORDSHIRE RECORD SOCIETY (1955) XXXVI, *Oxfordshire Protestation Returns*.

PATTEN, J. (1971) 'The hearth taxes 1662–89', *Local Population Studies*, pp 14–27.

PEACOCK, ALAN T. (1953) 'Malthus in the twentieth century' in GLASS, D. V. (1953) pp 55–78.

PERCIVAL, T. (1774–76) 'Observations on the state of population in Manchester and other adjacent places', *Philosophical Transactions of the Royal Society*, Vol. 64 (1774) pp 54–66; Vol. 65 (1775) pp 322–35; Vol. 66 (1776) pp 160–7.

PERRY, P. J. (1969) 'Working-class isolation and mobility in rural Dorset 1837–1936: a study in marriage distances', *Transactions of the Institute of British Geographers*, No. 46, pp 121–41.

PETERSON, WILLIAM (1965) *The Politics of Population*, New York, Anchor Books.

PHELPS BROWN, E. H. and HOPKINS, SHEILA V. (1956) 'Seven centuries of the prices of consumables compared with builders' wage-rates', *Economica*, New Series, Vol. 23.

POWELL, W. R. (1962) *Local History from Blue Books: a Select List of the Sessional Papers of the House of Commons*, London, The Historical Association.

PRIOR, R. J. (1969) 'Laws of migration: the experience of Malaysia and other countries', *Geographica*, Vol. 5, pp 65–76.

PRYCE, W. T. R. (1973) 'Parish registers and visitation returns as primary sources for the population geography of the eighteenth century', *The Transactions of the Honourable Society of Cymmrodorion*, Session 1971, Part II, pp 271–93.

PRYCE, W. T. R. (1973) 'Manuscript census records for Denbighshire', *Transactions of the Denbighshire Historical Society*, Volume 22, pp 166–98.

PUBLICOLA (1741) *A Letter From a Country Gentleman in the Province of Munster to his Grace the Lord Primate of all Ireland*, Cashel 25 May.

RAVENSTEIN, ERNST GEORG (1885 and 1889) 'The laws of migration', *Journal of the Royal Statistical Society*, Vols. 48, pp 167–227 and 52 pp 241–301.

RAZZELL, P. E. (1965) 'Population change in eighteenth-century England: a re-appraisal', *The Economic History Review*, Second Series, Vol. 18.

RAZZELL, P. E. (1972) 'The evaluation of baptism as a form of birth registration through cross-matching census and parish register data', *Population Studies*, Vol. 26.

RAZZELL, P. E. (1973) 'Smallpox: a difference of opinion', *Local Population Studies*, No. 10 pp 65–6.

REDFORD, A. (1926) *Labour Migration in England 1800–1850*, Manchester University Press.

Reports of the Commissioners for Inquiring into the Conditions of the Poorer Classes in Ireland, Reports from Commissioners (1836) Parliamentary Papers, London, Vols. 30–34.

RICH, E. E. (1950) 'The population of Elizabethan England', *Economic History Review*, Second Series, Vol. 2, pp 247–65.

SCHOFIELD, R. S. and BERRY, B. M. (1971) 'Age at baptism in pre-industrial England' *Population Studies*, Vol. 25.

SCHOFIELD, R. S. (1971) 'Age-specific mobility in an eighteenth-century rural English, parish', *Annales de Démographie Historique 1970*, Paris, Mouton.

SCHOFIELD, R. S. (1971) 'Historical demography: some possibilities and some limitations', *Transactions of the Royal Historical Society*, Fifth Series, Vol. 21.

SCHOFIELD, R. S. (1972) ' "Crisis" mortality', *Local Population Studies*, No. 9, pp. 10–22.

SHREWSBURY, J. F. D. (1970) *A History of Bubonic Plague in the British Isles*, Cambridge University Press.

SCHUMPETER, JOSEPH, A. (1950) *Capitalism, Socialism and Democracy*, London, Allen and Unwin.

SMITH, C. T. (1951) 'The movement of population in England and Wales in 1851 and 1861', *Geographical Journal*, Vol. 117, pp 200–10.

SMITH, J.; CHALLENOR, C. (ed) (1903) *The Parish Register of Richmond, Surrey*, Surrey Parish Register Society, Vol. 1.

SOGNER, SÖLVI (1963) 'Aspects of the demographic situation in seventeen parishes in Shropshire 1711–60. An exercise based on parish registers', *Population Studies*, Vol. 17, pp 126–46.

STEEL, D. J. (compiler) (1968) *National Index of Parish Registers. Sources of Births, Marriages and Deaths before 1837. Parish Registers, Marriage Licences, Monumental Inscriptions, Newspapers, Clandestine Marriages, Divorce, Medieval Sources, Other Records, General Bibliography*. Vol. 1, London, Society of Genealogists.

STEEL, ROBERT, W. and LAWTON, RICHARD (eds) (1967) *Liverpool Essays in Geography*, London, Longmans.

STEPHENS, W. B. (1958) 'A seventeenth-century census', *Devon and Cornwall Notes and Queries*, Vol. 29.

STEPHENS, W. B. (1971) *Sources for the History of Population and their Uses*, University of Leeds, Institute of Education.

STONE, LAWRENCE (1947) 'State control in sixteenth-century England', *Economic History Review*, Vol. 17.

THERNSTROM, STEPHAN and SENNETT, RICHARD (eds) (1969) *Nineteenth-Century Cities: Essays in the New Urban History*, New Haven, Yale University Press.

THERNSTROM, S. and KNIGHTS, P. R. (1970) 'Men in motion', *Journal of Interdisciplinary History*, Vol. 1, No. 1, pp 7–35.

THIRSK, J. (1959) 'Sources of information on Population, 1500–1760', *Amateur Historian* (now called *Local Historian*) Vol. 4, Nos. 4 and 5, pp 129–33 and 182–5.

THOMAS, BRINLEY (1930) 'The migration of labour in the Glamorganshire coalfield, 1861–1911', *Economica*, Vol. 30, pp 275–94.

THOMAS, BRINLEY (1972) *Migration and Urban Development*, London, Methuen.

TILLOTT, P. M. (ed) (1961) *The Victoria History of the County of York: The City of York*, Oxford University Press.

TRANTER, N. L. (1967) 'Population and social structure in a Bedfordshire parish – the Cardington listing 1792', *Population Studies*, Vol. 21, pp 261–82.

TURNER, DEREK (1971) *Historical Demography in Schools*, London, The Historical Association.

TURNER, G. LYON (1911) *Original Records of Early Nonconformity under Persecution and Indulgence*, London, T. Fisher Unwin.

WHEATLEY, D. M. and UNWIN, A. W. (1972) *The Algorithm Writer's Guide*, London, Longmans.

WHITEMAN, A. (1973) 'The census that never was: a problem of authorship and dating' in ANNE WHITEMAN, J. S. BROMLEY and P. G. M. DICKSON (eds), *Statesmen, Scholars and Merchants*, Oxford, Clarendon Press.

WILKINSON, RICHARD, G. (1973) *Poverty and Progress: An Ecological Model of Economic Development*, London, Methuen.

WRIGLEY, E. A. (1966) 'Family limitation in pre-industrial England', *Economic History Review*, Second Series, Vol. 19. Reprinted in DRAKE (1969), pp 157–94.

WRIGLEY, E. A. (1966A) 'Family reconstitution' in WRIGLEY (ed) (1966A), pp 96–159.

WRIGLEY, E. A. (1972) 'Mortality in Pre-industrial England: The Example of Colyton, Devon, Over Three Centuries' in D. V. GLASS and ROGER REVELLE (1972) pp 243–73.

WRIGLEY, E. A. (1972A) 'Some problems of family reconstitution using English parish register material: the example of Colyton' in D. E. C. EVERSLEY (ed) (1972), pp 199–221.

WRIGLEY, E. A. (ed) (1972) *Nineteenth-Century Society: Essays in the Use of Quantitative Methods for the Study of Social Data*, Cambridge University Press.

WRIGLEY, E. A. (1973) 'Clandestine marriage in Tetbury in the late seventeenth century', *Local Population Studies*, No. 10, pp 15–21.

YOUNGSON, A. (1961) 'Alexander Webster and His Account of the Number of People in Scotland in the Year 1755', *Population Studies*, Vol. 15, pp 198–200.

Acknowledgements

Grateful acknowledgement is made to the following sources for material used in this block:

Back cover: Bucks County Record Office.

Unit 5

Appendix: Material reproduced from the United Nations *Demographic Yearbook* by permission. (Copyright, United Nations 1968 and 1969); *Table 1:* Cambridge University Press and the authors for D. V. Glass and E. Grebenick in H. J. Habakkuk and M. Postan (eds.), 'The industrial revolutions and after', *Cambridge Economic History of Europe*, 6, 1, 1965; *Figure 1:* Royal Economic Society for information from the sketch map in P. James (ed), *The Travel Diaries of T. R. Malthus*, Cambridge University Press, 1966 p 29; *Figure 2:* Cambridge University Press for M. Drake, *Population and Society in Norway 1735-1865*.

Unit 6

Appendix 3: Cambridge Group for the History of Population and Society Structure; *Table 4:* Leeds Institute of Education for W. B. Stephens (ed), *Sources for the History of Population and their Uses*, 1971; *Tables 6 and 12 and Figures 2 and 7:* The Economic History Review and the author for E. A. Wrigley, 'Family limitation in pre-industrial England' in *Economic History Review*, Second Series, XIX (1966); *Table 7:* The Economic History Review and the author for P. E. Razzell, 'Population change in eighteenth-century England: a re-appraisal' in *Economic History Review*, Second Series, XVIII, 1965; *Table 8:* The Economic History Review and Mrs A. Howard for J. D. Chambers, 'The Vale of Trent 1670-1800' in *Economic History Review*, Supplement 3; *Table 13:* Institut National d'Etudes Démographiques for Louis Henry, *Anciennes Familles Genevoises*, 1956; *Figure 9:* Population Studies and the authors for P. Laslett and K. Oosterveen, 'Long-term trends in bastardy in England' in *Population Studies*, 27, 2, 1973.

Unit 7

Table 3: The Economic History Review and the author for Andrew B. Appleby, 'Disease or famine? Mortality in Cumberland and Westmorland, 1580-1640' in *Economic History Review*, Second Series, 26, p 413, 1973; *Figure 4 and Table 6:* from Pierre Goubert, *Beauvais et le Beauvaisis*. Copyright 1960 by Ecole Pratique des Hautes Etudes, VIe Section; *Table 10:* Jysk Selskab for Historie and the author for A. Lassen, *Fald og Fremgang: Traek Af Befolkningsudviklingen i Danmark, 1645-1960*, 1965. *Figure 1a and part cover:* Illustrated London News; *Figure 16:* Mary Evans Picture Library; *Figure 2 and part cover:* Keystone Press Agency; *Figure 7:* Biblioteca Medicea-Laurenziana, Florence; *Figure 10:* Banbury Public Reference Library, Potts Collection; *Figure 12:* Birstall Parish Register.

Unit 8

Figure 3: Royal Geographical Society; Société de Démographie Historique and the authors for T. H. Hollingsworth in *Annales de Démographie Historique*, 1970, pp 87-96, and for M. Anderson in *Annales de Démographie Historique*, 1971, pp 13-26. *Part cover:* Illustrated London News.

Notes

Notes

Notes

Historical data and the social sciences

Block one   The quantitative analysis of historical data
Unit 1   Words and numbers, sources and theory
Unit 2   Sampling
Unit 3   Describing data
Unit 4   Correlation

Block two   Historical demography: problems and projects
Unit 5   Population and economy
Unit 6   Population and society
Unit 7   *La crise démographique*
Unit 8   Migration

Block three   Introduction to historical psephology
Unit 9   The political context
Unit 10 The social and economic context
Unit 11 Radical Bath
Unit 12 Electoral behaviour in Britain, 1832–68

Block four   Exercises in historical sociology
Unit 13 Social stratification
Unit 14 Social mobility
Unit 15 Family and kinship